S

CHURCH MUSIC

IN

AMERICA,

AMS PRESS
NEW YORK

CHURCH MUSIC

IN

AMERICA,

COMPRISING

ITS HISTORY AND ITS PECULIARITIES AT DIFFERENT
PERIODS, WITH CURSORY REMARKS ON ITS
LEGITIMATE USE AND ITS ABUSE;

WITH NOTICES OF THE

SCHOOLS, COMPOSERS, TEACHERS, AND SOCIETIES.

BY

NATHANIEL D. GOULD,

AUTHOR OF "SOCIAL HARMONY," "CHURCH HARMONY,"
"SACRED MINSTREL," ETC.

BOSTON:
PUBLISHED BY A. N. JOHNSON,
90 TREMONT STREET.
1853.

Library of Congress Cataloging in Publication Data

Gould, Nathaniel Duren, 1781-1864.
    Church music in America.

    Reprint of the 1853 ed.
    1. Church music--United States. I. Title.
ML2911.G69 1972   783'.0973   78-14/
ISBN 0-404-02888-8

Reprinted from the edition of 1853, Boston
First AMS edition published in 1972
Manufactured in the United States of America

AMS PRESS INC.
NEW YORK, N. Y.   10003

INTRODUCTION.

THE principal design of the following pages is to give a plain, simple and concise account of Sacred Music in America, for the last eighty years. We have waited long, with the ardent desire that some one with ample means and skilful pen might do *well* what we are sensible we have done *imperfectly*. But, having waited thus long in vain, and being admonished by age and other circumstances that what *we* do must be done quickly, and that, unless accomplished by some one soon, the history must forever remain a mere matter of hearsay, as none will be left to perform the task, or to "speak that they do know, and testify that they have seen," we have been constrained, in view of these considerations, and the solicitude of friends, to undertake so important and in many respects difficult a task. When we find elaborate and well-digested histories of almost every other important subject touching the past, others as well as ourselves may well be surprised that a narrative of this kind has not long ere this been presented to the public; as it is a subject so intimately connected with the prosperity of Zion.

The Rev. W. Burton, a friend of education and humanity, a few years since wrote a history of the "Village School as it was;" and although it purports to be the picture of a single school, we presume the description will be found to delineate well the history of most schools in past times. So, of what we write of singing-schools,

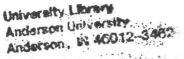

Choirs, etc., "as they were," ample testimony may be found to show that all were similar in regard to conveniences, limited time, means of instruction, and scarcity of books. We did not deem it advisable to commence our narrative abruptly at the period of 1770, lest the inquiry should come up, "What has this to do with church music?" We therefore commence back, and first take a view of music as used for sacred purposes, when patriarchs, prophets and apostles lived, and took a part in its promotion and performance. We also take a glance at the music of ancient nations since the Christian Era, not passing unnoticed on our way Martin Luther, the great reformer of religion, if not of music. We then pass hastily on to our Pilgrim Fathers, embarking for this land where no harmonious sounds had ever been heard, with some ten or twelve tunes imprinted on their hearts and fresh in their memories, and with Ainsworth's Psalms inseparably connected with their Bible.

In pursuing our history of American Music, we find W. Billings holding a prominent place as author and teacher, and in many respects a pioneer in American Church Music; and his history we have briefly noticed. Owing to the difficulty of gaining satisfactory information, we may have omitted some of those who deserve a prominent place; and may also have, notwithstanding all our scrupulous care, made some errors in statements. We have mentioned some modern authors who are not living; but of living authors, we say little or nothing.

In accomplishing our task, it seemed necessary to enter somewhat minutely into particulars in regard to the character of the music employed; the various changes through which it has passed; the different modes of teaching; the formation of societies, choirs, etc., and the manner of conducting them; the interest or lack of interest manifested by ministers and people; and the introduction of instruments in the performance of Church Music.

N. D. GOULD.

BOSTON, OCT., 1852.

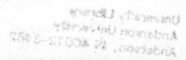

CONTENTS.

CHAPTER I.

BIBLE HISTORY OF MUSIC.

PAGE

Music when Time began. — Extract from Miss H. F. Gould's Poem, . . 13
Harmony destroyed. — Exertions to restore it, ... 14
Music and Prayer the only Acts of Worship. — The Voice of Melody the
    Gift of God, ... 15
When Music commenced. — First Music and Instruments, ... 16
The Human Voice God's Instrument. — Changes, ... 17
Holy Men of Old engaged in the Cause. — Music of the New Testament, . 18
Singing at the Last Supper, ... 19

CHAPTER II.

ANCIENT CHURCH MUSIC IN EUROPE AND AMERICA.

Music in Greece, ... 22
The Lyre. — The Flute. — The Scale. — Notation and Manner of Singing, 23
Roman National Music, etc. — Pietro Martini. — Usonian Song. — Gre-
    gorian Chant, ... 24
Musical Notation, ... 25
Popular Airs harmonized. — Pope disgusted. — Worthy Authors and
    Music, ... 26
Music in Protestant Churches, ... 27
Musical Dramas. — Sacred Subjects. — First Printed Music.— Authors, etc. 28
Sternhold and Hopkins, ... 29

1*

Confession of Puritans. — William Damon, ... 30
Directions of Westminster Divines. — Music-books destroyed, ... 31
Handel, Haydn, Mozart, &c. — Ancient Church Music in America, Ains-
   worth's Psalms, ... 32
Bay Psalm-book. — Prejudices and Scruples. — Cotton's Circular.— Objec-
   tions answered, ... 33
Walter's Description of Singing, ... 34
Singing at College and among the Indians — First Reformation of Music, . 35
First Books of Music, ... 36
Thomas Walter. — Rev. Mr. Barnard. —Williams and Tansur, ... 37
James Lyon. — Josiah Flagg. — Thomas Bayleys, ... 38

CHAPTER III.

AMERICAN PSALMODY FROM 1770.

Change of Music in America, ... 39
Prejudice against European Tunes. — State of Society, ... 41
Origin of Fugueing Music. — Billings a Pioneer, ... 42
Political Effect of Music, ... 43
Billings' Concerts and Exhibitions, ... 44
Billings' Voice; Personal Appearance and Habits. — Of Lining the Hymn, 46
Billings' Musical Publications, ... 48
American Authors. — Musical Notes and Characters, ... 52
Of English Methods of Teaching. — Miss Glover and Others, ... 55

CHAPTER IV.

PROGRESS OF MUSIC IN AMERICA.

Hubbard's Opinion of Fugueing Music, ... 57
Dark Age, ... 58
Negligence of Churches. — Character of Music and Performers changed, . 59
Authors. — Andrew Law, ... 60
Oliver Holden, ... 61
Samuel Holyoke, ... 62
Jacob Kimball, ... 63
Read. — French. — Swan. — J. Hubbard, ... 64
Dutton. — Oliver Shaw, ... 66
E. L. White, ... 68

Salem and Middlesex Societies, ... 69
Published Music. — Clashing of Old and New Schools, and Books, ... 70
Contention in Choirs. — Difference of Taste. — Ignorance of the Science of
    Music, ... 71
New Era in Musical Publications, ... 72
Advance of the Science. — Teachers. — J. Bailey and Others, ... 73

CHAPTER V.

ESTABLISHMENT OF SCHOOLS.

Description of Schools before Billings. — Limited Means, ... 76
Effect of Billings' Music and Schools. — Rudiments of Music, ... 77
Schools from 1770 to 1800. — Object of Schools, ... 78
Formation of Schools. — Subscribers for Schools, ... 79
Location of Schools. — Instruction, ... 81
Inconveniences and Want of Accommodations, ... 82
The First Movements in Teaching. — Result of Subscriptions, ... 83

CHAPTER VI.

TEACHERS AND TEACHING.

Teaching the Theory of Music, ... 85
Trying the Voice, ... 86
Difference in Voices. — Unmanageable. — Limited Compass, ... 87
Correct Ears, but Rebellious Voices. — Natural Singers have not always
    Correct Voices, ... 88
Suggestions, ... 89
Correct Voices and Ears. — Rejection of some. — Learning the Rules, . . 91
How and what Taught, ... 92
Change in the Names of Notes, ... 93
Distributing the several Parts or Voices, ... 94
Beating Time. — Different Modes of Time. — Beating is not Keeping
    Time, ... 95
Beginning to sing Tunes, ... 96
Deficiency of Books. — Music did not allow Expression, ... 97
Old Singers in New Schools, ... 98
Ready for Church, ... 99

CHAPTER VII.

MUSIC IN CHURCHES.

Exhibition of Schools, and Clergyman's Address, ... 101
Refreshments at Recess, ... 102
Organization of the Choir. — Choice of Officers, ... 103
Highest Seats. — Remedy for those who contend for Seats, ... 104
Caste among Singers, ... 105
Choir dispersed. — What the Resort, ... 106
Foibles and Virtues of Singers. — Changes in Choirs, ... 107
Favorite Leaders. — Case of Extreme Obstinacy, ... 108
Location in the Church, ... 109
One Leader ; his Responsibility ; his Place in the Seats, ... 111
Method of finding and establishing the Pitch of a Tune, ... 112
Tunes committed to Memory. — Its Advantages, ... 113
Multitude of Books at the present Day. — Inconveniences, ... 114
Same Tunes will not suit all, ... 115
Demeanor of Singers in Church, ... 116
Fault sometimes in the Leader. — Irreverence of Choirs, ... 117

CHAPTER VIII.

PROGRESS OF MUSICAL INSTRUCTION.

Change of Music. — Discussions. — Old Hundred Seceders, ... 119
Old School prevailed. — Struggle for Possession of Seats. — Reformation
    in Teaching and Music, ... 120
Attempt to Harmonize correctly. — The Public interested. — Change of
    Books, ... 121
Tenor Voices put in Place, ... 122
Example in a School. — Lectures introduced, ... 123
Children taught. — Objections of Parents, ... 124
First Juvenile Schools. — Saying of Horace Walpole, ... 125
New Methods of Teaching, and New Music for Children, ... 126
Defects in Instruction. — Exhibitions of Children's Singing, ... 127
Excitement abated. — Means for Instruction still limited, ... 128
Step towards Congregational Singing, ... 129

CHAPTER IX.

SCHOOLS SINCE 1800.

Schools. — A Praying Teacher, ... 130
Effects of Revivals of Religion on Singing, ... 131
Progress of Instruction. — Pestalozzian System. — Boston Academy of
    Music. — Old Teachers, ... 132
Consequence of Want of Time for thorough Teaching, ... 133
The Black-board in Adult Schools. — Good Results of the Academy. — De-
    clension, and Causes, ... 134
Instruments with Singing. — What was urged in Lectures, ... 135
Leaders preceding Singers. — Schools without Instruments, ... 136

CHAPTER X.

MUSIC AND TEACHING IN THE WEST.

Influence of Emigrants from New England, ... 138
State of Music in Cincinnati. — Cry of Dr. Beecher, ... 139
Kind of Notes used. — Change of Notes effected by T. B. Mason, ... 140
Juvenile and Adult Schools. — Professor of Eclectic Academy. — William
    Colburn, ... 141
Locke, Nourse and Aikin, and Others, ... 142
Teachers all from New Hampshire and Massachusetts, ... 143

CHAPTER XI.

IMPROPRIETIES IN EXECUTION.

Singing of Solos and Duets, ... 145
Inattention to Accent, Words, etc., ... 146
Unsuitable Words. — Irregular Poetry, ... 147
Words with Improper Accent. — False Accent from Location of Notes, . . 148
Force of Accent. — Governed by Words. — Enunciation, ... 149
Taking Breath improperly. — Careless Manner of Finishing Words. —
    Leading Notes, ... 150
Embellishments. — Application of Slurs, ... 151
Repeated Accent in Singing, ... 152

Inappropriate Graces in Singing. — Abuse of the letter *R*, ... 153
Gesticulation, ... 154
Bad Habits not perceived by Ourselves. — Saying of Tosi, ... 155
Saying of Battishill, and a German Violoncello-player, ... 156

CHAPTER XII.

EXPRESSION AND ADAPTATION.

Dr. Beattie's Saying. — Importance of Expression, ... 157
Hooker. — First Directions to Words, ... 158
Characters to indicate Expression. — Words must be anticipated and felt, . 159
Old Style of Singing. — Want of Adaptation, ... 160
Difficulty of adapting Tunes to Hymns. — Words for Particular Occasions, 161
Perceptible Improprieties. — A Traveller's Representation of a Perform-
    ance, ... 162
Voices inadequate to Music selected. — Pauses in Singing. — Observance
    of Punctuation, ... 164
Uniformity necessary. — Conduct badly adapted, ... 165
Feelings adapted to the Subject, ... 166

CHAPTER XIII.

INSTRUMENTS OF MUSIC.

Puritan Fathers rejected Instruments. — Bass-viol introduced, ... 168
Human Voice uncertain in giving the Pitch of a Tune. — Pitch-pipe the
    First Instrument used, ... 169
Tuning Fork, and Brass Reed. — Opposition to the Bass-viol or Violon-
    cello, ... 170
Extreme Case of Opposition cured, ... 171
Different Instruments introduced, ... 172
Flute, Hautboy, Clarinet and Bassoon, ... 173
Perplexities attending them. — Instrumental Accompaniments, ... 174
Confusion of Instruments. — Playing of Interludes, etc., ... 175
Privilege of Players on Instruments, ... 176
History of the Organ. — First Organ built in America. — The First Organ
    introduced in America, ... 177
Its History. — Organs astonish all, ... 178

Former Objections to Organs. — Change in playing it, ... 179
Difficulty of procuring Good Organists. — Organs and Singers not moving
together, ... 180
Advantage of having the Organ move in advance, ... 181
Interludes and Voluntaries, ... 182
Instruments attempt to imitate the Organ, ... 183

CHAPTER XIV.

SOCIETIES, ACADEMIES, CONVENTIONS AND CONCERTS.

Our Fathers' Meetings for Singing. — Billings' Concerts, by Schools and
Societies, ... 185
Other Teachers followed his Example, ... 186
Choirs formed into Societies. — Small Societies Tributary to Large Ones. —
Sacred Concerts, ... 187
Pecuniary Concerns. — Want of Patronage. — Deception, ... 188
Particulars of N. H. Musical Society. — Instruments in those Days, . . . 189
Billings and Holden Society. — Competition, ... 190
Conventions. —Object of Conventions, ... 191
Effect of Secular Music with. Sacred. — Concerts of Sacred and Secular
Music, ... 192
Advertisements for Concerts. — Dialogue, ... 193
Good accomplished, ... 194

CHAPTER XV.

CHURCHES, MINISTERS AND CONGREGATIONS.

Music in Churches improved. — Inattention of Congregations to Sing-
ing, ... 195
Quakers less Guilty. — Worshipping God by Proxy. — Foreigner's Visit
to American Churches, ... 196
Reasons for hiring Theatrical Singers. — Reasons for the Young under-
valuing Singing in Churches. — Errors of Clergymen, ... 197
Complaints and Perplexities, ... 198
Minister's Connection with Singers, ... 199
Attitude in Singing, ... 200
Dr. Romaine, ... 201
Churches and Congregations connected. — Likes and Dislikes of Hearers.
— Complaints of the Manner of Singing, ... 202

Complaints of Tunes sung, ... **203**
Opinions of Chants and Anthems. — Of Expression in Words and Music,   . 204
Of Organ-playing. — Promiscuous Singing in the Congregation, ... 205

CHAPTER XVI.

EFFECTS OF MUSIC.

Music God's Gift to Man for a Sacred Purpose. — Extract, ... 208
Different Effects of Music. — Effects in Scripture Times, ... 209
Sayings of Martin Luther, ... 210
Dr. Pomeroy's Description of Music in Constantinople. — Effect of the Per-
    formance of Handel's Messiah. — Of a Band of Music on Savages, . . 211
Barbarous Conquerors subdued. — Singing at the Siege of York, ... 212
Music at the Battle of Quebec. — Among the Ancients.— Peruvian Indians,213
Law-suits settled in Greenland. — Of National Music, ... 214
Cases of Insanity Cured. — Secular Music in the Days of our Fathers. . . 215
Want of Knowledge in Music. — A Sultan in Constantinople, ... 216
Ostinelli's Performance. — False Notions of Music, ... 217
Effects lost mixed with Talking. — Effects of Different Instruments, . . . 218
Vocal Music of Different Character produces Different Effects. — In the
    Theatre, — Church Music outlives all other Kinds, ... 219
Effects of Bad Congregational Singing, ... 220
Good Congregational Singing. — Convention of Singers, ... 221
Convention of Churches, ... 222
On an Individual, ... 223
Singing of Children. — The Clergyman's Family, ... 224
On Preachers of the Gospel. — Of a Single Voice, ... 225
The Nobleman's Daughter, ... 226
On the Bed of Death, and at a Funeral, ... 227
Importance of Music in the World, ... 228

CHAPTER I.

BIBLE HISTORY OF MUSIC.

Music when Time began. — Extract from H. F. Gould's Poem. — Harmony destroyed. — Exertions to restore it. — Music and Prayer the only Acts of Worship. — The Voice of Melody the Gift of God.—When Practical Music commenced. — First Music with Instruments. — The Human Voice God's Instrument. — Holy Men of Old engaged in it. — Singing in the New Testament — by Angels — Children, Paul and Silas. — Christ and his Disciples.

WHEN we reflect on the subject of music or harmony, our minds are instantly carried back more than five thousand years, when all was harmony. God, in his infinite goodness, created man with music in his soul, and melody in his voice; so that, when he had finished the work of creation, men and angels might unite in one glorious song of praise. But, alas! that song was short. A discordant note was soon heard.

The introduction of music, at the commencement of time, is well portrayed in the following extract from a poem on music, by Miss H. F. Gould:

> "Music! a blessed angel she was born,
>   Within the palace of the King of kings, —
> A favorite near his throne. In that glad child
> Of love and joy, he made their spirits one,
> And her the heir of everlasting life.
> When his bright hosts would give him highest praise,
> They send her forward with her dulcet voice,
> To pour her holy rapture in their ear.
> When the young earth to being started forth,
> Music lay sleeping in a bower of heaven;
>   When, suddenly,
> A shout of joy from all the sons of God
> Rang through his courts; and then the thrilling call:

2

Wake ! Sister Music, wake ! and hail with us
A new-created sphere !
She woke ; she rose ;
She moved among the morning stars, and gave
The birth-song of a world.
Since that blessed hour,
Whilst heaven is still her home, Music has ne'er
This darkened world forsaken. She delights,
Though man may lose or keep the paths of Peace,
To soothe, to cheer, to light and warm his heart,
And lends her wings to waft him to the skies."

HARMONY DESTROYED.

While for a moment we confine our thoughts to that first scene
and song, we are filled with admiration ; for, while our first parents
were innocent, their every breath was praise. In the midst of
this enraptured scene, subsequent history presses in upon our
minds, and we are instantly hurried forward but a step or two in
the history of man, when all is confusion and discord. Man
deigned to take the instrument, which came from God's own hand
in perfect tune, seeming to doubt its perfection, and by one fatal
act destroyed both melody and harmony throughout the new-created
world.

EXERTIONS TO RESTORE IT.

From that time to the present, good men of every age have
been attempting to restore a faint resemblance of that harmony
which was lost by man's transgression, and to harmonize the discordant feelings of mankind. No expedient, save that of the
gospel of Jesus Christ, has done so much to soften the ferocious
propensities of human nature as the employment of sacred music ;
while the arch enemy of man, who tempted our first parents to that
dreadful act, has ever since been busily engaged in frustrating the
designs of good men of every age, and nowhere else so untiring as
with the lovers and performers of sacred music. The music of
the church ever has been, and ever will be, an invincible enemy.

MUSIC AND PRAYER THE ONLY ACTS OF WORSHIP.

It would probably be interesting to some, and profitable to many, should we trace music, from its origin, all along through Bible history, and mark minutely its grand and solemn exhibitions as an act of worship. We should find, all along, equally prominent and equally solemn, prayer and praise; always coupled together as acts, and the only direct acts, by which God was worshipped, they always have gone, and always will go, hand in hand. If religion languishes, so will sacred music. The same sentiments and language are used for both; but singing seems to have been considered the higher order, and the very climax of expression and devotion; and, when the power of speech has failed to give utterance to the feelings of the heart, the addition of melodious sounds, both of voices and instruments, has been called in to give full vent to holy affections.

Neither our object or our limits will permit us to give but a mere sketch of music as alluded to in the Bible. Numerous lectures and sermons have been written to describe those grand and solemn performances, and bring them down through the history of after centuries to the present time; and, although the links may often seem defective and irregular, if not broken, still God's praises have always been sung among his saints, and he has ordained that they always shall be, — that it has been so from the beginning, and he will never suffer it to be otherwise.

THE VOICE OF MELODY THE GIFT OF GOD.

Music, though a complex and difficult art, is, in truth, evidently the gift of the Author of nature to the whole human race. Its existence, in some form, is to be traced in the records of every people, from the earliest ages to the present time, in every quarter of the globe.

The infinite variety of sounds we hear, produced by waters, birds, animals, and the human voice, affect us with more or less pleasure.

The only exceptions are those that warn us of something to be feared, such as the hissing of serpents, or the howling of wild beasts;

but the melodious sounds of the human voice affect us most when united with speech or words. It then delights the ear, touches the heart, as language alone cannot. This pleasure derived from music must have been implanted in our nature, capable, however, of great improvement.

WHEN MUSIC COMMENCED.

The history of music, as we have seen, begins with the history of man. Scanty, indeed, are the materials; and, after all, conjecture must do much in describing its pathway from age to age. Although volumes have been written to describe it, still there are few facts contained in them all which are satisfactory.

In the Bible history of the art, as used for sacred purposes, we soon find man using his voice, and inventing instruments to assist it in sounding praise to God.

FIRST MUSIC AND INSTRUMENTS.

The first mention of music is, that Jubal, the sixth from Cain, is said to be the father of all such as "handle the harp or organ." The French translate it, "violin and organ." Not knowing, however, anything of their form or sound, we can only infer that one was a stringed and the other a wind instrument. We may also infer that the voice of music had been cultivated long before the instruments of Jubal; for how could instruments be tuned, until the voice and ear dictated the tone?

What progress was made in the art of music by the antediluvians is unknown; for their improvements are buried with them in oblivion.

The next mention made of music is in Genesis, thirtieth chapter, when the language of Laban to Jacob was, "Wherefore didst thou flee away secretly, and steal away from me, and didst not tell me, that I might have sent thee away with mirth and with songs, with tabret and with harp?" Next, Exodus fifteenth chapter. Here we find that Moses and the children of Israel shouted forth these words: "Sing ye unto the Lord, for he

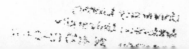

hath triumphed gloriously. The horse and his rider hath he thrown into the sea," &c.; closing with, "The Lord shall reign for ever and ever." Then comes the response from the women, when Miriam the prophetess took a timbrel in her hand, and all the women went out after her, with timbrels and with dances, repeating the same words, — "Sing ye to the Lord, for he hath triumphed gloriously." These words, sung by Miriam, contain the first specimen of lyric poetry on record.

In after time, the harp, lyre, trumpet, organ, &c., had been contrived, and used by man for the purpose of assisting the voice.

THE HUMAN VOICE GOD'S INSTRUMENT.

All unassisted instruments, however, sink into insignificance when compared with the instrument that God has given man to praise him, which is the human voice. The ingenuity of man may invent instruments to make a pleasant noise; this noise can be modulated into soft and loud, pathetic and solemn tones, to please and astonish; but, after all, it is but an accompaniment, — it is nothing but *sound*. They cannot be made to articulate these words: "Hear my prayer, O Lord!" or, "Praise the Lord, O my soul!" The human voice and tongue alone can do it. Hence the royal Psalmist, when he calls upon "everything that hath breath to praise the Lord," understands the distinction when he says, "The singers went before, and the players on instruments went behind;" an important example, not always observed at the present day, in practice, if in location.

CHANGES.

The changes that have taken place, since the days of Jubal, in the manner of using the voice, the different tones produced, the extent and division of the scale, the combination of sounds, and the manner of applying singing in the worship of God, cannot be definitely described. It is sufficient for us to know that, with all nations of the earth where God has been worshipped, prayer and praise have constituted that worship; and that those who learn to

2*

sing with the spirit and understanding on earth will be permitted to sing the song of Moses and the Lamb forever in a better world.

We can also learn that the power of uniting voices belongs only to man. The birds can sing, each its own tune; but thousands and millions of men, women and children, can unite their voices; and every additional well-trained voice adds to the effect.

HOLY MEN OF OLD ENGAGED IN THE CAUSE.

All holy men, like David and Hezekiah, are found rejoicing in the privilege and honor of leading the multitude of worshippers around them in sacred song. At one time, we find four thousand Levites in the Tabernacle, divided into twenty-four courses, with two hundred and eighty-eight teachers, or leaders; and, in all instances, they *rose up* and sung. Unlike this is the practice of the present day; when not many of the great, the rich, or the noble, are found among those who engage in singing in the sanctuary; and in many instances both singers and hearers treat the subject with so much indifference, that they cannot take the trouble to rise up in this grand act of devotion.

Solomon says, "I gat me men singers, and women singers, and instruments, the delight of men, of all sorts." It is said his songs were one thousand and five.

At the dedication of the Temple, it is supposed there were more than fifty thousand employed as singers.

The eighth psalm is addressed to Benaiah, the chief of the band of young women who sang in the service of religion.

Women were thus early associated in acts of worship, and were instructed in music; for at that joyous and glorious day for God's children, women took a part.

MUSIC OF THE NEW TESTAMENT.

Music in the first ages of the Christian church, at the time of the Saviour's birth, was used in all the religions of the nations about Judea; but what that music was, is a matter of uncertainty.

The following are some of the examples of singing when our Saviour was on earth:

The first strain of the music of the church, — "Glory to God in the highest, and on earth peace, good will towards men," — was sung by an angelic choir, telling of the birth of the Saviour.

Children sang, "Hosanna, — blessed is he that cometh in the name of the Lord, Hosanna in the highest."

"And at midnight Paul and Silas prayed and sang praises," &c.

SINGING AT THE LAST SUPPER.

When we trace this part of the worship of holy men, before we come to the close of God's word, a scene is described more interesting than any one before it, not for its grandeur and display, but the occasion. It is when the Saviour of the world and his disciples met for the last time, and closed the solemn exercises by singing a hymn. The words of that hymn are not recorded; and perhaps it is well that they were not; for, if they had been written, we have reason to suppose that in every age they would have been profaned by a wicked world, like all others in the Bible. We are obliged, however, to conclude that poetry, as well as music, was in some manner cultivated at that time; for what psalm would be appropriate for that solemn and momentous occasion? And when they had sung an hymn, they went out into the Mount of Olives. This was sung by those whose hearts were pure. How many would be glad to sing those words! Although lost, it would be well if we could imitate the pure, meek, and loving spirit that breathed forth the song.

But we must confine ourselves more strictly to narrative; for the subject of praising God, as recorded in his word, both on earth and in heaven, is too sublime for us to present in its true light. It is a subject worthy the mightiest intellect of man, — yea, great enough for an angel; and probably they alone can fully understand its import. The employment of praise or singing is, for aught we know, the only talent or acquisition on earth, transferred to heaven.

CHAPTER II.

ANCIENT EUROPEAN MUSIC AND INSTRUMENTS.

Uncertainty of History. — Instances in the Bible understood. — Inferences from what we do know. — Clashing of Authors. — Secular Music. — Noblest Strains in the Church. — Inferences. — Different Methods of Singing the Psalms. — Changes. — The Lyre. — The Scale. — Notation, and Manner of Singing. — Roman National Music. — Pietro Martini. — Eusebius. — The Lute. — Usonian Song. — Gregorian Chants. — Popular Airs harmonized. — Pope disgusted. — Worthy Authors and Music. — First Printed Music. — Authors. — Martin Luther. — Sternhold and Hopkins. — Confession of Puritans. — Ravenscroft's Music, and Reasons why all ought to sing. — Directions of Westminster Divines. — Music-books destroyed. — Handel, Haydn, Mozart, &c. — Ancient Church Music in America. — Ainsworth's Psalms. — Bay Psalm-book. — Cotton's Circular. — Walter's Description of Singing. — Singing at College and among the Indians. — First Reformation in Music. — First Books of Music. — Thomas Walter. — Rev. Mr. Barnard. —Williams and Tansur. — James Lyon. — Josiah Flagg. — Thomas Bayley.

WE are obliged now to leave the volume of inspiration, and launch forth into a wider sea of uncertainty and chaos.

We shall take a cursory view of ancient music ; but, in tracing its origin and progress, it is well and truly said by another, that "a writer in the attempt finds himself upon the margin of a boundless and unknown ocean, on which he fears to launch, because he has for his guide neither compass, chart, or polar-star. He is on a voyage of discovery in the regions of imagination and of inferences, and perhaps out of the track of truth and reality." When we leave the history of the Bible, for hundreds of years all is dark on the subject ; and even the Bible history gives nothing definite in regard to the kind of music, or the particular form or sound of instruments. But when we read passages that describe Moses and Miriam with the men and women of

Israel — singing and praising God, when they had passed the Red Sea; the song of Deborah and Barak; the singing at the dedication of Solomon's Temple; of Paul and Silas, in prison; children, when they sang, "Hosanna! blessed is he that cometh in the name of the Lord!" and of Christ and his disciples, at their last meeting on earth, the picture is vivid before our eye, and imagination has its perfect work; and here we have to pause and admire. Not so when the Bible is closed. Volumes on volumes have been written, and some of them very plausibly, on the changes and progress of music, among different nations; but when we read different authors, we find a continual clashing, each claiming for their favorite nation improvements that others claim. To reconcile these differences would be not only unprofitable, but impossible. The thousands and millions of pages of music that have been covered with black heads and cloven feet, fitted for expert fingers and flexible arms, we have nothing to do with; and we rejoice that it is conceded by all that the noblest strains ever penned by man are to be found in the archives of the Christian church, — have outlived their authors, while the former have mostly perished with the hands that executed them.

From what we *do* know, we may confidently infer that in the early ages of Christianity, when psalmody was considered an important and indispensable part of public worship, different churches used the psalms in different ways.

1. They were sung sometimes by the whole congregation,— men, women, and children.

2. In Egyptian monasteries, one person recited all the verses except the last, when all joined in chorus.

3. Sometimes one person chanted the former part of the verse, and the congregation the remainder.

4. Congregations were divided into two parts, and sung, or rather chanted, alternately, each verse.

According to Theodoret, the first singing in public assemblies was instituted in Antioch, where the disciples were first called Christians.

IN GREECE.

The Greeks are the people of antiquity whose music has attracted the greatest share of attention among the moderns. They considered music as an art of great dignity, and its practice formed an essential part of their education. Still, but little is known what the character of their music really was; for all that remains is two or three small fragments, expressed by a notation which is but partially understood. We only learn from history the extent to which its practice was carried, and its influence on society.

We read that Bruce, the traveller, brought a pillar to Rome, supposed to be erected by Sesostris, centuries before the Trojan war, which has on it a representation of a musical instrument, of two strings, with a neck similar to a lute.

Another piece of antiquity, discovered by the same man, is the drawing of a musical instrument, in an ancient sepulchre adjoining the ruins of Thebes, which represents a man playing on a harp similar in appearance to those of the present day. His left hand seems employed on the upper part of the instrument, among the notes in alto, and, stooping forward, his right hand is employed with the lowest strings, which makes it evident that harmony was understood and practised in those days. Another was observed at Ptolemais, with fifteen strings, which he thinks must have been Egyptian.

It is well known that the splendor of Egyptian arts and sciences decayed before any Grecian author now extant had acquired any knowledge of the country; although the Greeks acknowledge that in earlier periods they borrowed largely of the Egyptians, and that even in that remote period the decay of Egypt had begun, and that there no longer existed any instruments which it had formerly possessed, till, at last, under the dominion of Alexander the Great, arts and sciences, and even its language, were evidently Grecian.

Ancient Greek music was evidently composed for the voice only; and all poems, in the days of Pindar, were set to music composed

by the author, and publicly sung by the poet, before publication;
and when we have attempted to apply irregular poetry to music
of the present day, we have often wished that it was the custom
still. If so, we think very many authors would stumble, in
attempting to accommodate their irregular words and lines of
poetry to music.

THE LYRE.

Before the days of Pythagoras, there were but seven notes in
use, and but seven strings to the Greek lyre. He added the eighth
note, which completed the octave; and Euclid speaks of the Lyre
as having the strings increased to eleven. The Spartan Senate
ordered these additional strings to be cut off, and their inventors
to be banished from the city, as having corrupted the ears of youth
from the simplicity of the seven-string lyre.

THE FLUTE.

Meantime, the flute, or lute, was the popular instrument used,
both with men and women. A singular custom was observed in the
religious ceremony at Athens. An officer, who was chosen in the
same manner as, and whose name was enrolled with, the officers
of state, played upon the flute, close to the ear of the priest, during
sacrifice. This officer was called Auletes. The flute-player was
probably more interested in the prospect of a good dinner, from the
victims of the sacrifice, than in the immediate services.

THE SCALE.

The musical scale of the Greeks never reached above two octaves;
their modes, scales, &c., were somewhat similar to those of the
present day. It is generally supposed that they had no musical
rhythm, but the length of notes and musical feet, in their airs,
were regulated by the quantity of syllables.

NOTATION, AND MANNER OF SINGING.

Their systems of notation were very complicated, and, of course,
imperfectly understood by the many. The letters of the alphabet

formed the basis, at one time, and were so multiplied by marks and mutilating their forms, as to produce above one thousand six hundred signs, or characters; to learn which cost the labor of years. A few fragments are said to be preserved, in three different manuscripts; but the melodies are as barbarous as those of the rudest savages. We can, perhaps, form no just idea of them; for there may have been conventional rules, and methods of performance not expressed by notation, of which we cannot have any knowledge.

Greek authors tell us that most of their music was written in the diatonic scale, because this species could be understood and enjoyed by all classes of people. The same is partially true in modern days, because it is formed out of those elements furnished by nature.

ROMAN NATIONAL MUSIC, ETC.

The Romans had a national music, but borrowed from the Greeks. At one time, its authors carried the subject to excess, and Nero, like many modern amateurs, was actuated more by vanity than a real taste or love for music itself. His voice and performance were bad; still he is said to have kept up an establishment of five thousand singers and players on instruments; and when about to put himself to death, he cried, "What a pity it is to kill so good a musician!"

PIETRO MARTINI.

Pietro Martini was of opinion that the chants of the primitive Christian church were as old as the time of King David, as it was evident that in his reign music had a regular establishment in the worship of the sanctuary, and that they regulated their tones or modes according to the various affections, marking the path which was afterwards followed by the restorers of ecclesiastical song, who made intervals serve as fundamentals in the change of tones; and that the diatonic scale was then used.

USONIAN SONG. — GREGORIAN CHANT.

Also that Usonian song was in use in the church in the second, third, fourth, and fifth centuries, introduced and ordained by the apostles, and came originally from David, and that the Jewish chants were adopted by them. About the end of the sixth century, Pope Gregory improved and extended the ecclesiastical chant, and made the performance wonderfully grave and noble, arising from the simplicity of the strain, and totally unlike the music used on lighter occasions. The character of the Gregorian chant is still used to give the greatest effect to sacred music.

About the middle of the fourth century regular choirs were introduced into some churches, divided into two parts, who sung responsively. This was called antiphonal singing, out of which the modern fugue has arisen.

NOTATION.

The progress of Musical Notation, from the time of Gregory the Great, may be explained in a few words. Gregory's method was the very simple one of writing the words, and then placing above each syllable the letter indicating the note to which it was to be sung. Some other expedients were adopted, of writing the words on parallel lines, placing each word on a higher or lower line, to indicate the comparative height of the sound. About the ninth century, seven parallel lines were used, expressing the notes by points placed on these lines. They were afterwards reduced to four, and points placed both on lines and spaces. It has since been convenient to use five, instead of four; and, until this time, notes were used merely to express the simple sounds of the chant, the length being regulated by syllables; but, when harmony was discovered, it became necessary to mark the relative length of notes, to keep performers of the different parts together.

Marks for the length of notes appear to have been invented by Guido, and were first reduced to a regular and systematic form by Franco, of Cologne.

Eusebius, speaking of the consecration of churches, in the Roman empire, in the time of Constantine, the first Christian

3

emperor, says there was one common consent in chanting forth the praises of God. The performance was exact, the rites of the church decent and majestic, and there was a place appointed for those who sung psalms, — youths, virgins, old men and young.

POPULAR AIRS HARMONIZED. — POPE DISGUSTED.

About the middle of the 16th century, the popular airs of different countries began to attract the attention of musicians everywhere; and, like those of the present day, were harmonized for church purposes; and Dr. Burney says, " these tunes were in fashion all over Europe, and that, although the names of some of the composers of the day are retained, their music has sunk into oblivion."

Many fine compositions, however, for the church, written by Palestrini about this time, have survived, and he stands at the head of ecclesiastical composers. He was born in 1529; died in 1594. Previous to this time, the music had become so trifling that the Pope decreed that it should be banished from the churches. Palestrini entreated him to suspend his decree till he could have time to give an example of true church music, which, being done, so pleased his Holiness that he revoked his decree. Morengo, of the same century, brought forth a species of composition called Madrigal to a degree of perfection which has never been surpassed.

Bird, in his Gleanings of Music, says, in an old Greek play is the following description of a singing school:— "They went together to the house of the teacher, where they learned to sing hymns, set to a simple melody used by their ancestors. If any one of them pretended to sing in a ridiculous manner, or to make such flourishes as were allowed in the airs of Phrynis, he was severely punished."

WORTHY AUTHORS AND MUSIC.

During the sixteenth century, music made rapid strides in England. The names of Tye, Tallis, Bird and Gibbons, are among those of the fathers of ecclesiastical harmony. One of the greatest curiosities extant is Tallis' celebrated song of forty parts. It was sung June 21, 1836, by the Madrigal Society, in Free Masons' Hall, London, by about one hundred and twenty singers without instruments, and was doubtless the only performance of this grand song within the memory of any living musician.

MUSIC IN PROTESTANT CHURCHES.

In the course of this sixteenth century, the psalmody of the Protestant church was brought nearly to the state or character in which it is now found, and in which it is desirable it should continue. For this style of psalmody we are indebted to the reformers of Germany, especially Luther, who was himself an enthusiastic lover of music. Dr. Sears says, in his history of Luther, that he was early known as a melodious singer; and it was in this capacity that he had won the kind regards of Madame Cotta, his first patroness. His last evening before entering the cloister was devoted to musical and social pleasure. When the work of the Reformation was progressing, he called in the aid of sacred music. At that period there were many hymns, but no psalms; but Luther versified a few psalms, which he appended to a collection of hymns he published in 1524; all of which were set to music, as he says, " in four parts, for no other reason than because of my desire that the young, who ought to be educated in music, as well as in other good arts, might have something to take the place of worldly and amorous songs, and so learning something useful, and practise something virtuous, as becometh the young. I would be glad to see all arts, and especially music, employed in the service of Him who created them." This book, which is so great a curiosity, was reprinted in 1840, and was used in families, social circles and schools, as well as in churches; and the hymns of Luther, which the people sung with delight, had a powerful effect.

Luther himself composed music for many of his hymns, which was not only good in itself, but agreed beautifully with the sentiment expressed by the words. *Walther*, a celebrated musician of that day, lent his assistance, and says, " I have spent many an happy hour in singing with him, and have often seen the dear man so happy and joyful in spirit while singing, that he could neither tire nor be satisfied. He conversed splendidly upon music. He also composed music or tunes for the epistles and gospels, particularly for the words of Christ at the institution of the Supper, and sung them to me and asked my opinion of them. Kept me three weeks writing the notes for a few gospels and epistles, till the first German mass was sung in the parish church, and was obliged to stay and hear it, and take a copy of it to Torgua." He is believed to have composed some of the noblest tunes, such as the One Hundredth Psalm, Last Judgment, &c., admirably adapted to be sung by great congregations, making an impression produced by few, if any, of modern compositions.

MUSICAL DRAMAS — SACRED SUBJECTS.

The beginning of the seventeenth century was the era and origin of musical drama in Italy. Poetry and music were united for the purpose of dramatic representation, including sacred dramas and oratorios.

These representations of incidents, many of them taken from scripture, were introduced at religious festivals, to impress on the minds of the rude and ignorant the principal characters and events of that sacred volume of history : such as the " Messiah," " Samson," and " Israel in Egypt," by Handel; the " Creation," by Haydn; " Mount of Olives," by Beethoven, and the " Last Judgment," by Sphor, were first used as sacred dramas for the theatre.

There were sacred dramas represented in Italy at a much earlier period, on the subject of Abraham and Isaac.

FIRST PRINTED MUSIC, AUTHORS, ETC.

The first printed music was in 1503, when music was first introduced, in four parts, in the fourth century. The lowest was called

Tenor ; second, *Contra Tenor ;* third, *Motetus ;* fourth and highest, *Triplum.*

At one period, six parts are found, namely, Bass, Baritone, Tenor, Contralto, Mezzo and Soprano.

STERNHOLD AND HOPKINS.

In 1562 Sternhold and Hopkins published the hymns that were then extant, with notes to sing them, but with only one part, — the air. The only tune now in use which they published is " Old Hundred," with little variation, as will be seen by the following example ; and the last note was probably a misprint, as in subsequent editions the air is written as we now sing it.

Afterwards we find, in 1606, the following : " That the whole book of Psalms, with English metre, with apt notes to sing them, withal, were published by them. Set forth and allowed to be sung in all churches, of all the people together, before and after morning and evening praier, as also before and after sermons ; and, moreover, in private houses for their godly solace and comfort, laying apart all ungodly songs and ballads, which tende only to the nourishing of vice and corrupting of youth."

The names of Sternhold and Hopkins will be read and known in all future time. It appears, until the rupture between Henry and the Pope, the only music in the English churches consisted of the Latin masses and services of the Romish ritual. After this event, they were translated and modified, and still used, in some instances, in the Episcopal churches. Sternhold was a zealous Reformer, and was scandalized in observing songs used in court, for being so foolish as to turn into English metre fifty-one psalms of David, and causing musical notes to be placed thereto. These were published in 1582, either separate or bound with the psalm-book; some in the end of the Bible.

To the reader he says, " I have caused a new print of notes to be made, with letters, to be joyned to every note, whereby thou maiest know to call every note by its right name," &c.   The following is an example.

*V,   R,   M,   F,   S,   . L,   L,   S,   F,   M,   R,   V,

Vt,   Re,   My,   Fa,   Sol,   La,   La,   Sol,   Fa,   My,   Re,   Vt.

WILLIAM DAMON.

William Damon set the psalms to four parts.   No more than forty tunes had been published in any one book before 1594.

CONFESSION OF PURITANS.

In the Confession of the Puritans, 1571, we find the following concerning the singing of psalms, — " We allow the people to join in one voice in a psalm-tune, but not in tossing the psalm from one side to the other, with intermingling of organs."

No music in parts, and no instruments, were used in Geneva in their religious services, for more than a century after the Reformation.

In the reign of Henry VIII., the common prayer and singing psalms, as they are found in the Bible, was used as a test for all to sing who loved the Reformation.

RAVENSCROFT'S MUSIC, AND REASONS WHY ALL OUGHT TO SING.

Ravenscroft published a choice collection of tunes, better than any published, — better than any that succeeded for a hundred and fifty years, and many of our best tunes now in use were taken from this book, written by English, Scotch, Welsh &c.   Bird, from 1563 to 1610, wrote music of every description, much of it sacred and of the best character, equal, it is said, to Palestrini's.

* V used for U.

This first work was dedicated to the Lord Chancellor of England, in which he gives his reasons why every one ought to learn to sing, the substance of which we give below, spelled in the manner of the day.

1. It is a knowledge easilie taught, and quicklie learned.

2. An exercise delightfulle to nature.

3. It dothe strengthene all partes of ye breaste, and dothe open ye pipes.

4. Good remedie for stutteringe.

5. Best means to make a good orator.

6. It is the onlie waye to knowe where nature hath bestowed the benefytte of a good voyce.

7. There is not anie musicke of instruments, comparable to yt whiche is made by the voyce.

8. The better ye voyce is, the meeter it is to honor and serve God therewith.

> Since singynge is soe goode a thinge,
> I wish alle men woulde learne to singe.

DIRECTIONS OF WESTMINSTER DIVINES.

The Westminster Assembly of Divines, besides making the catechism, presented rules concerning singing, saying, "It is the duty of Christians to praise God publicly, by singing psalms together in congregations and in families. That it ought to be the chief care to sing with the understanding and grace in the heart, and that the whole congregation join, and as many cannot read, advise the minister to appoint some fit person to read the psalm line by line, before the singing thereof."

MUSIC-BOOKS DESTROYED.

Soon after this rule for congregational singing was put in force, all the choral books were taken from the churches and destroyed; churches defaced, organs taken down, and most of them, as well as the books, were burnt; so that when things were returned to their former state, it was almost impossible to procure notes, organs, organists or singers.

HANDEL, HAYDN, MOZART, ETC.

We have spoken of a period of time when a few ˙ .dividuals of different nations, that seemed to have been raised up by God with talents natural and acquired, to show the world the design and power of sacred music, such as Handel, Haydn, Mozart, Beethoven, and others. These men have supplied the world with an inexhaustible fountain of musical manna; many have feasted on it. But, alas! some are content only to hear about it, if not to loathe it; while others are too ignorant of its sweets to taste it. In 1712, Dr. William Crofts published a book, called Divine Harmony; and in 1724, by subscription, a splendid edition of music, in two volumes, called Musica Sacra, the notes stamped on pewter plates. This book of music was republished in this country about 1809.

ANCIENT CHURCH MUSIC IN AMERICA.

We are necessarily compelled to leave foreign lands, and confine our observations to our own country, where it will be found that but little attention was paid to the subject for more than a hundred years after the landing of our Pilgrim Fathers. Here let us pause for a moment, and imagine ourselves spectators of the scene when our forefathers mounted the Plymouth Rock, and listening to the first song of praise to Almighty God proceeding from strong lungs and pure hearts. There they stood, and, with the women and children, burst forth, and with united voices rehearsed some tune and words, that they perhaps had before prepared and had been anxiously waiting and longing for an appropriate time to sing; — that time had come; and think you there would not have been a difference between the effect of their singing and that which we so often hear, " where not the heart is found " ?

AINSWORTH'S PSALMS.

It appears that Ainsworth's version of the Psalms was brought by them to this country, and used exclusively till 1640, and many of the psalms and tunes were so associated with their worship that they were unwilling to relinquish either; so that, when the " Bay

Psalm-book," so called, was introduced in New England, it met with violent opposition; and the churches in Salem and vicinity did not relinquish Ainsworth till 1667, nor the church in Plymouth, where it was first used, until 1692.

BAY PSALM-BOOK. — PREJUDICES AND SCRUPLES.

The " Bay Psalm-book," which was compiled by an association of New England ministers, and approved by the churches, being something new, was considered an innovation, and naturally awakened strong feelings of doubt and opposition, and much inquiry, producing the same prejudices and religious scruples as innovations in later days. Among other scruples of *conscience*, as they are generally called, to which a different word would better apply, was this: whether the singing of the psalms of David with a lively voice was proper in these New Testament days. This and other quibbles set the churches into a turmoil, which did not subside until the Rev. John Cotton wrote a tract, or circular, in answer to the objections, which was sent to all the churches.

COTTON'S CIRCULAR. — OBJECTIONS ANSWERED.

When this was read and feelings reconciled, other objections and queries arose, namely, Whether it was proper for one to sing, and all the rest to join only in spirit, and saying Amen, or for the whole congregation to sing. Whether *women* as well as men, or men alone, should sing. Whether pagans (the unconverted) be permitted to sing with us, or church-members alone. Also, whether it be lawful to sing psalms in metre devised by man, and whether it be lawful to read the psalm to be sung, and whether proper to learn new tunes which were uninspired; for it appears that they had so long been accustomed to hear and sing the same few tunes, that they had imbibed the idea that the tunes were inspired, and that man's melody was only a vain show of art.

Some of the objections were not without reason; for instance, as, for several years after the introduction of the new psalm-book, many neglected or refused to purchase it, and others were unable to read, they were obliged to revive the practice of Luther, of reading or lining the hymn. This many objected to, as hindering the melody, understanding and affection, in singing. All these objections were considered, and wisely answered, by the learned divines of the day, and the disturbed feelings gradually calmed.

Previous to the year 1690, music or the psalm tunes, some eight or ten in number, taken mostly from Ravenscroft's collection, were in some form usually written in the psalm-books or Bible, and were in that way used for nearly one hundred years, the collection having been published two years before they left England. These few tunes were repeated, some of them once or twice every Sabbath; and in pious families two were sung every day in the week, so that it seems singing at family worship was practised by our fathers. The psalms were sung in rotation, without any regard to the subject of the preacher.

Notwithstanding the apparent neglect of this important part of public worship, it is evident that the well-informed appreciated the subject, and actually made provision for the cultivation of music in the first college at Cambridge. But soon troubles came upon the country, like the plagues of Egypt; and, whether real or imaginary, it was all the same; for, where the feelings are in commotion, music has no place. About this time, Williams the Baptist, Ann Hutchinson, the Quakers and Antinomians, ran athwart their religious views; besides numerous Indian wars and witchcraft perplexed them on every side.

WALTER'S DESCRIPTION OF SINGING.

About the commencement of the eighteenth century, music had been so much neglected that few congregations could sing more than four or five tunes, and these few the learned divine, Rev. Mr. Walter, of Roxbury says, "had become so mutilated, tortured and twisted, that the psalm-singing had become a mere disorderly noise, left to the mercy of every unskilful throat to chop and alter, twist and change, according to their odd fancy, — sounding like five hundred different tunes roared out at the same time, and so little in time that they were often one or two words apart; so hideous as to be bad beyond expression, and so drawling that he sometimes had to pause twice on one word, to take breath; and the decline had been so gradual that the very confusion and discord seemed to have become grateful to their ears, while melody, sung in time and tune, was offensive; and when it was heard that tunes were sung by note, they argued that the new way, as it was called, was an unknown tongue, not melodious as the old, made disturbance in churches, was needless, a contrivance of the designing to get money, required too much time, and made the young disorderly; old way good enough." All these objections, and many more, were answered by a pamphlet, signed by Rev. Peter Thatcher, John Danforth, and Samuel Danforth, which quelled the subject, but not before many members of churches were suspended for persisting in singing by rule, but were afterwards restored. Many congregations were ordered to sing by rote and by rule, alternately, on the Sabbath, to satisfy both parties.

SINGING AT COLLEGE AND AMONG THE INDIANS.

Rev. Mr. Symms says that " music was known and approved of in our college, from the foundation of it; and though in later time it has been unhappily neglected, yet, blessed be God, it is again reviving, and I hope it may ever be continued in that school of the prophets."

However irregular and uncultivated the singing was in congregations generally, it is evident that the Indian apostle, Eliot, taught the natives to sing psalms regularly; for Dr. Mather says their singing was most ravishing.

FIRST REFORMATION OF MUSIC.

The reform began in the churches, according to Hood, at Cambridge, Taunton, Bridgewater, Charlestown, Ipswich, Newbury, Andover, and Bradford. These churches, having godly and efficient ministers, did much to advocate and advance the cause generally, and to encourage the revival of music at Cambridge College.

Previous to this time, when it was made known that some had acquired the art of learning a tune by note, without having before heard it, all were amazed, and still more astonished that all could finish a tune together.

A writer in the New England Chronicle observes, in 1723: "Truly I have a great jealousy that, if we once begin to sing by note, the next thing will be to pray by *rule*, and preach by rule; and then comes popery."

The tunes, before 1690, were such as Oxford, Litchfield, York, Windsor, St. David's, and Martyrs, — more of common metre than all others; therefore, to accommodate churches who could not sing any long-metre tunes, some two words, in the second and fourth line of a verse, were printed in different type, to indicate that they might be omitted, and the sense retained, so as to sing the hymn in a common-metre tune, thus:

> "To God our voices let us raise,
> And [*loudly*] chant the joyful strain."

Directions were given, with these tunes, in regard to pitching them. Some were directed to have a high pitch given them, as the compass of the notes was but five or six above, such as York. Others, where the compass was eight or nine notes, were to have a low pitch.

FIRST BOOKS OF MUSIC.

About 1712 or 1714, Rev. John Tufts, of Newbury, published a book of tunes, twenty-eight in number, with rules, as he said, so that the tunes might be learned with the greatest ease and speed imaginable; price six pence, or five shillings per dozen. Small as it was, it must have been at the time a great convenience and curiosity, being the first of the kind in New England, if not in America. As late as 1770, there were not more than four or five books known. The number of tunes in this book was considered enormous, which were in three parts, reprinted from Ravenscroft,

— purely choral. This publication was considered by many as a daring innovation on the old time-honored custom of the country. " Teaching by note," says a writer, " was strenuously opposed by a large class of persons, everywhere to be found, who believe that an old error is better than a new truth." They imagined that *fa sol la* was real popery in disguise. The pages were neatly engraved, and in size to bind with the Bay Psalm-book. His easy method was placing letters on five lines, as follows :

the letter indicating the name of the note, namely, F for *fa*, S for *sol*, &c.

Where a letter had two dots after it (F :), it was equal to a breve; with one (F .), to a semibreve; (F), plain, to a minim, or half-note.

THOMAS WALTER.

Rev. Thomas Walter, of Roxbury, Mass., in 1721 edited the first book of music, except the few tunes attached to the Bay Psalm-book, with the art of singing by note, with bars to divide the notes or measures, for the first time. Printed by Benjamin Macom, and recommended by fourteen divines. Until this time, the singing of the psalms was used only as a devotional act; never for amusement.

REV. MR. BARNARD.

The Rev. Mr. Barnard, of Marblehead, published the psalms and hymns, in verse, with fifty tunes at the end of the book; the music beautifully engraved; containing such tunes as Mear, Windsor, &c., in three parts, with one page of instructions. But Hood says we cannot find any account of its being used out of his own church.

WILLIAMS AND TANSUR.

A collection of music, called the " Royal Harmony," or the " New Harmony of Zion," first published in England, containing

4

hymns, anthems, and canons, by the greatest masters, with from two to seven parts, by William Tansur, in 1754, was re-published at Newburyport, Mass., in 1756.

Another collection, similar to Tansur's, by T. Williams, of London, was republished by Bailey, in Newburyport, 1769.

The books of Williams and Tansur (for they were calculated to be bound together) were designed to bring singers together, and did create an interest never before felt in this country; and many of the books may be found bound in this way, and kept by some careful fathers to the present day. Williams' book contained the first fugueing tunes seen in this country, such as thirty-fourth psalm, &c., which were the parents and forerunners of all subsequent music of that character.

JAMES LYON.

James Lyon, of Philadelphia, in 1761, published a choice collection of psalm-tunes, hymns, and anthems, in two, three, and four parts, called "Urania." One-half the tunes plain choral music, the remainder of a light and fugueing character.

JOSIAH FLAGG.

Josiah Flagg, of Boston, in 1764 published a collection of church music, engraved by Paul Revere, containing a hundred and sixteen tunes, generally of rather a light character. In his introduction, he apologizes to the public for introducing a *new book*, there having been two or three within the last fifty years. Very unlike the present day, when not less than twenty are published every year. The author exults in the one fact, that they were not beholden to England for the paper of his book, if they were for the music, this paper being the first made in this country for such a purpose.

THOMAS BAYLEYS.

Thomas Bayleys, of Newburyport, in 1764 published two books, one containing the grounds of music, taken from Thomas Walter's collection; the other, tunes, &c., from the most approved authors, containing thirty-four tunes, neatly engraved.

CHAPTER II.

AMERICAN PSALMODY FROM 1770.

Change of Music. — Its Effects. — Prejudices against English Tunes. — State of Society. — Origin of Fugueing Music. — Billings a Pioneer. — Political Effect of Music. — Billings' Concert and Exhibitions. — Billings' Voice, Personal Appearance, and Habits. — Of Lining the Hymn. — Billings' Musical Publications. — American Authors. — Musical Notes and Characters. — Of English Methods of Teaching. — Miss Glover. — Pierre Galen. — Day and Beals.

CHANGE OF MUSIC IN AMERICA.

WE now leave the traditional history of church music, and enter a field where, for the last fifty years or more, we are enabled, from experience, observation and information, to vouch for the facts we relate. For a period of twenty or thirty years previous to that, we have reliable accounts from the lips of those who, during that time, took an active part in singing. For this epoch, we design to give a more particular history of church music in America.

Hood and Bird have each written and published valuable volumes relating to the rise and progress of music, both in this and foreign countries, to the period when this chapter commences, and have there suspended their investigations; so that, unless the circumstances relating to church music, for this latter period, are soon recorded by some one now living, it is evident that all must soon become hearsay. Among all American histories of men and things, there has never been any connected account given of church music for the last half-century.

A year or two previous to this date, music had begun to assume a different aspect, both as to its character and performance, in and out of the church; and the way seemed at hand for a still greater change; and as the style of music and the teaching of it have generally emanated, in this country, from New England, we venture to say that a picture of psalm-singing, with all its attendant customs, as practised in Boston and vicinity, at that time, will, as almanac-makers say, be fitted for any meridian of New England, without any material alteration, and will apply to about every church and congregation, at some period since. In some of them, indeed, even at the present time, the same customs, music, and manner of singing, are in use, that generally prevailed fifty years ago.

We have said that religion and sacred music ever go hand in hand. The pure spirit of active piety prompts to a desire to sing God's praise. Who has not seen those who had never before attempted to sing a tune constrained to give vent to their feelings, after conversion, by attempting to sing, and sometimes to the annoyance of those around them, by their discordant notes? Consequently, when the public mind is agitated by worldly subjects, — for instance, in the excitement of a political campaign, — a different kind of music is made use of, to add to the power of oratory. Political songs and instrumental music are the aids, and claim a full share among the instrumentalities for keeping alive political frenzy.

There are times and situations in which music cannot find a lodging-place. The children of Israel, when carried into captivity, hung their harps on the willows, and even refused to sing the Lord's song in a strange land. And when we consider the perplexities which we have mentioned, that rushed upon our Puritan fathers, in swift succession, year after year, it is not strange that sacred music should have been neglected. There were no circumstances, even in the lives of many generations, calculated to enkindle a spirit for any kind of music, either sacred or secular; — they were truly in a strange land; but at their places of worship they sang the choral tunes they brought with them, heart and soul.

For nearly a hundred and fifty years from the landing of the Pilgrims at Plymouth, much the same tunes, with very few additions, were evidently used; and the additions did not keep pace with the number that were mutilated, murdered, frittered away, and lost.

PREJUDICE AGAINST ENGLISH TUNES.

A few years previous to this time, three or four tunes had been written and introduced, from England. The air and movement of the tunes were exactly suited to the excited feelings of the people. Americans began to think and act for themselves; and the more the British government attempted to oppress, so much the more were they determined to free themselves from the yoke of bondage, that was *felt*, whether true or imaginary; and their feelings became so bitter against everything manufactured in the mother country, that even the tunes they had formerly sung began to sound tyrannical, and, consequently, with the *Tea*, were thrown overboard. The few tunes that were brought from England, and for more than a hundred years known as foreign manufacture, owing to their slow movement, but more especially for the drawling and dragging manner of singing them, became truly obnoxious.

Until about the year 1770, no native American had attempted to compose and publish a single tune, that we can ascertain. This distinction was reserved for William Billings, a poor boy, by occupation a tanner; born in Boston, October 7, 1747; died September 26, 1800.

The tunes afore-mentioned were lively and spirited airs, calculated to excite the feelings, whether for good or evil, and gave Billings a cue to his style of music. Previous to this time, church *music*, if it could be called music, was learned by rote, and performed as a sacred employment, or from duty; but from this time onward, for thirty or forty years, we have reason to fear that much of the spirit of amusement was mixed with it, and its former solemnity lost.

STATE OF SOCIETY.

Therefore it is not strange, when we consider the state of public feeling, that they should gladly accept and embrace the change of music. The first few tunes that were selected — such as third and thirty-fourth psalm, Milford, &c. — electrified the whole community ; — their noise and jingle exactly fitted their excitement.

ORIGIN OF FUGUEING MUSIC.

Foreigners have always been ready to palm fugueing tunes on America, and it has always had the appellation of "Yankee music;" but this species of music originated and spread through England, and was adopted in many of the Protestant churches, long before it was seen or heard of in this country. Billings — an American, it is true — was the first and foremost in introducing this new style of music into the churches in this country, and added to the number of such like tunes. The style and construction of the tunes may, and probably did, degenerate among the untaught American manufactures.

This new species of music was of course eagerly sought and introduced, and the first American author looked upon as a prodigy ; while others, in every part of New England, in true Yankee spirit, tried to imitate him.

BILLINGS A PIONEER.

As Billings is the father and pioneer of American compositions, so was he of choirs, public singing-schools, and concerts. We therefore feel in duty bound, as a sort of necessary introduction to the following pages, and future history of music in this country, to give a brief account of his musical movements, before we commence a history of schools, choirs, and church music generally.

However uncultivated he might have been in his manners, mind, or appearance, still we are constrained to acknowledge him as the first writer of American music who, by his teachings and publications, roused up a musical spirit that moved all New England. If the spirit was not pure, it produced combustibles that afterwards burst into a flame of systematic harmony. Like every new movement, perfection is always far ahead, and after generations secure most of the praise and profit.

Billings was born in Boston, is said to have been of humble origin, and in early life his *occupation was that of a tanner*. The building in which he labored was located in Eliot-street, in Boston. His opportunities for even common education were very limited. His means to acquire a knowledge of the science of music must have been still less, as there was nothing but Tansur's Musical Grammar to be found in this country, which he probably never read; and if he had, it was an imperfect guide.

We have been informed, by those that knew his history, that he wrote his first tunes with chalk, on the walls of the building, while tending the mill to grind bark. It will be found that he was not void of the *spirit* of poetry, — at least, he had a vivid imagination; and though, through his ignorance of language, his poetry, which he occasionally wrote and set to music, will be found sometimes ludicrous or amusing, yet now and then he approached the solemn or sublime.

There were many circumstances combined, as we have said, about this period, which tended to introduce his music, beside that of the bewitching nature of its movement. He was a zealous patriot, much attached to the *great* patriot, Gov. Samuel Adams, who was also an ardent lover of music. Adams and the late Dr. Pierce, of Brookline, used to stand side by side with Billings to perform in the church choir and concert.

POLITICAL EFFECT OF MUSIC.

The effect that music had on the people was perceived by all. In those days, patriotic songs were unknown; so Billings, from his ardent spirit, composed or procured words, of a mixed character, combining religion and patriotism, which, when set to music, answered every purpose; and the one single tune of Chester, with the following words attached, was a powerful instrument, for the time, in exciting the spirit of liberty.

" Let tyrants shake their iron rod,
    And slavery clank her galling chains ;

We 'll fear them not, we 'll trust in God ;
New England's God forever reigns.

" The foe comes on with haughty stride,
    Our troops advance with martial noise;
Their veterans flee before our arms,
    And generals yield to beardless boys."

These words, and the tune attached to them, were learned by
every choir, and in every family, and by every child, and sung in
the house and by the way, like popular songs at the present day,
and perhaps did more to inspire a spirit of freedom than any one
thing that occurred at this critical moment. Not only this tune
and these words, but many others of like character, were used,
that breathed the spirit of the day, some of which S. Adams probably had, to say the least, *seen* before they were published.

Besides, previous to this time, the old tunes sung used to be
" set," or " struck up," without any certainty of the right pitch,
and performed without any correct time or tune; but now the
singers were in some measure instructed, and the music, in
and about Boston and New England, performed by *choirs*, so that
it was a new era in the manner and spirit of singing ; and Billings
may, in some sense, be called a reformer; and although, after
many years, his music declined in the estimation of the public,
still his zeal, perseverance, originality, and native talent, were so
manifest, that his name, and many of his melodies, and some of his
tunes, in almost their original form, will outlive thousands of
more modern date. There was so much merit in some of his airs or
melodies, that some of the greatest masters of Europe have been
heard to say that if they could write an air like some of his they
should consider their names immortalized.

BILLINGS' CONCERTS AND EXHIBITIONS.

We have said Billings was the father of concerts or musical
exhibitions in this country. These, too, with the music and words
attached, tended to help on the political fever. The character

and object, however, of these concerts, and many of the customs introduced at their exhibitions, would perhaps appear rather ludicrous at the present day. For instance, when the words " clap your hands " occurred in their music, they used to make the action correspond with the words, and all clap their hands in time. We cannot, perhaps, better express the evident intent and object of these concerts, than to use Billings' own words, which were affixed to one of his introductory anthems, and sung at one of these exhibitions. He says, in regard to the manner of introducing it, "After the audience are seated, and the performers taken their pitch *slyly* from the leader, the concert begins ; " and here we find the words which we suppose express their object :

> " We 've met for a concert of modern invention;
> To *tickle the ear* is our present intention.
> The audience seated, expecting to be treated
> With a piece of the best."

And, to give our readers an idea of the character of the words generally made use of, we will add a few more of those affixed to the same piece of music :

> " And since we all agree
> To set the key on E,
> The author's darling key
> He prefers to the rest."

Then a fugue, the bass commencing, —

> " The Bass take the lead,
> And firmly proceed ;
> Let the Tenor succeed," &c.

We may reasonably infer, from the character of the words and music used at this time, and for many years afterwards, that to " tickle the ear " was the main object; and may we not also fear that, at the present day, there are many performers and hearers striving rather to tickle, and have their ears tickled, than their hearts improved ?

BILLINGS' VOICE, PERSONAL APPEARANCE AND HABITS.

We have heard the late Rev. Dr. Pierce, of Brookline, relate many incidents in regard to the life and character of Billings, he being personally acquainted with him, and having so frequently sung with him. He said Billings had a stentorian voice, and when he stood by him to sing, he could not hear his own voice; and every one that ever heard Dr. Pierce sing, especially at Commencement dinners, at Cambridge, knows that his voice was not wanting in power.

Billings was somewhat deformed in person, blind with one eye, one leg shorter than the other, one arm somewhat withered, with a mind as eccentric as his person was deformed. To say nothing of the deformity of his habits, suffice it to say, he had a propensity for taking snuff that may seem almost incredible, when in these days those that use it are not very much inclined to expose the article. He used to carry it in his coat-pocket, which was made of leather; and every few minutes, instead of taking it in the usual manner, with thumb and finger, would take out a handful and snuff it from between his thumb and clenched hand. We might infer, from this circumstance, that his voice could not have been very pleasant and delicate.

He for many years kept a music-store in Boston, and was once in a while annoyed by the tricks of boys. Having a sign projecting from his door over the sidewalk, with the words " Billings' Music " on each side, one evening a couple of cats, with their hind legs tied together, were thrown unceremoniously across the sign; and when their faces came together below, their music was not of the sweetest kind, and rather grating to the tenant's ear. A multitude of hearers soon assembled, and had an opportunity of reading the sign, and hearing their music, such as it was, a long time before they could be released.

OF LINING THE HYMN.

The reading or lining the hymn sung had been practised in some churches for nearly a century. The first innovation was the reading two lines in succession, instead of one. The reading was usually done in a monotonous, sing-song manner; still, with the singers there was a choice in the readers. One who could continue to read on the key or pitch of the tune was a great convenience, as it required some skill for singers to retain their pitch through the interlude of reading, if read on a different key; therefore, one who could sustain the pitch was a very desirable acquisition, and this often had much influence in the choice of deacons. Multitudes of anecdotes are told of ludicrous occurrences that took place while this practice was in vogue, such as may be observed at the present day, when necessity drives to this resort, where books are not at hand; such as, by stopping at the end of each line, the sense is perverted or destroyed; for instance,

> " The tidings strike a doleful sound ——
>   On my poor heart-strings deep he lies ——"

We will relate what occurred on one occasion, that we heard related by one who was present, which will give some idea of others that might happen. It will be understood, in the first place, that poetry was not just like the poetry of the present day, although there is still room for improvement. For instance, some words that we *now* pronounce as one syllable, *then* had two, and sometimes clashed with the accent of the tune; words ending in *tion*, such as salvation, the last syllable was divided and pronounced *si-on*, or *shi-on*; and two syllables of such words as *hea-ven*, *sev-en*, the latter occurring in one of Tate and Brady's hymns, where it commences, " Seven times a day I raise my voice," and the deacon read " *Sev-en* times a day," &c. The singers commenced with the tune of " Wells;" but, using two syllables to the first word, soon found themselves " out." The deacon read again. Singers had no better success. All was consternation, till a brother deacon by his side kindly suggested to the reader to try *six*, which he did, and the singing went off triumphantly.

This custom, however, of reading, or lining, or, as it was frequently called, " deaconing," the hymn or psalm in the churches, was brought about partly from necessity, first in our fathers' day for want of books ; second, as the tunes Billings had manufactured had no stopping-place, especially the two last lines of a verse, therefore the necessity of the first innovation, which was to read two lines at a time. To do away the custom wholly, Billings writes, " As all now have books, and all can read, 't is insulting to have the lines read in this way, for it is practically saying, We men of letters, and you ignorant creatures."

BILLINGS' MUSICAL PUBLICATIONS.

He paraphrased the beautiful piece of ancient music, 137th Psalm, " By the rivers of Babylon we sat down and wept," at the time the British forces occupied the then town of Boston, and the American army, such as it was, was stationed at Watertown. His language, which was substituted, may not seem to our readers very sublime, when it is compared with the original, and set to music as follows : " By the rivers of *Watertown* we sat down and wept, when we remember thee, O Boston ; " continuing the subject onward, instead of the words, " If I forget thee, O Jerusalem," &c., he says, " If I forget thee, O Boston ; " and then breaks forth in a powerful strain or chorus, with the following words :

> " Then let my numbers cease to flow,
> Then be my muse unkind;
> Then let my tongue forget to move,
> And ever be confined.
> Let horrid jargon split the air,
> And rive my nerves asunder;
> Let hateful discord grate my ear,
> As terrible as thunder."

The first book of music he published he named the " New England Psalm-singer," containing one hundred and eight pages ; this was in the year 1770. A proof that the spirit of rebellion against the mother country was not yet fully developed, are the following words on the title page :

> " O praise the Lord with one consent,
> And in this grand design

> Let Britain and the colonies
> Unanimously join."

In this book the parts were arranged for the tenor voices to sing the melody. He had no regard for the laws of harmony; and when the parts moved forward, they soon became entangled so as to cause admiration and astonishment to a hearer to find the parts all brought out in safety at the last word of the tune. Billings, in describing the effects of the music, says, " It has more than twenty times the power of the old slow tunes; each part straining for mastery and victory, the audience entertained and delighted, their minds surpassingly agitated and extremely fluctuated, sometimes declaring for one part, and sometimes another. Now the solemn bass demands their attention, — next, the manly tenor; now, the lofty counter, — now, the volatile treble. Now here, — now there, — now here again. O, ecstatic ! Rush on, ye sons of harmony " !

His second publication, called "Singing-master's Assistant," was published in 1778, one hundred and two pages, an abridgment as well as improvement of his former work ; and had the tunes been timed and harmonized scientifically, they would have done honor to any country. But he was satisfied, as he says, with nature for his guide, — probably because he knew nothing better. He says, concerning the rules of composition, " Nature is the best dictator ; for all the hard-studied rules ever prescribed will not enable any one to form an air, any more than knowing the twenty-four letters will enable a scholar to write poetry." There is some truth mixed with his extravagance. The question may well be asked, whether an air beautiful in itself, imperfect though not discordant in harmony, is not more satisfactory, than tunes or notes, piled up according to the rules of harmony, that have no air or soul to them. Apply the principle to John Bunyan, and his "Pilgrim's Progress," which, on the score of mere literary merit, would long ago have been thrown aside. We would by no means condemn good or countenance bad harmony ; but as in the case of Bunyan's works, all attempts to give literary finish are always found to destroy

5

their power; would it not be as well either to let Billings' tunes alone, or to publish them without such material alteration as to offend the ears and feelings of those who heard or sung them in their younger days, — tunes recalling early associations, which a few changed notes will instantly dissipate? He goes on and says, " Nature must do the work ; so, in fact, I think it is best for every *composer* to be his own carver. Therefore, for me to dictate or pretend to prescribe rules for others, would be a very great piece of vanity." This book was called " Billings' *Best.*" He was satisfied that he had erred in his first book, though at the time he thought it near perfection. " But now," says he, " I am satisfied that many of the tunes were worthless, although at the time I called them ' my Reuben.' Now," says he, " I find that it is Reuben in the sequel, and Reuben all over." The latter book was popular with the multitude, and spread over the land. It was carried by the soldiers from camp to camp, amusing both performers and listeners; and many at the present day, who used to listen to his and other similar music sung in church in their early life, and even some at the present day who have no such early associations, are pleased and fascinated to hear it, and its bewitching jingle, which in a great measure covers the errors of the harmony. His other publications were " Music in Miniature," — sixty-three pages original, and eleven old standard tunes. " Psalm-singers' Amusement," one hundred and three pages, in 1781. " Suffolk Harmony," fifty-six pages, 1786. " Continental Harmony," one hundred and ninety-nine pages, 1794. These, with occasional anthems, include all his published compositions.

His last book is the only one of his printed in type. In this volume he again asserts the superiority of his new music over the old tunes, and says, " It is an old maxim that ' variety is pleasing;' and it is well known that there is more variety in one piece of fugueing music than twenty of plain song. For, while the tones do most sweetly coincide and agree, the words are seemingly engaged in a musical warfare; and excuse the paradox, if I further add, that each part seems determined, by dint of harmony and strength of accent, to drown his competitor in an ocean of harmony."

AMERICAN AUTHORS.

In addition to the afore-mentioned publications of Billings, others commenced writing and publishing music of the same character, but most of it was inferior to his in merit. We can only mention the names of some of many publishers and authors, that we may give a connected sketch of the progress of music : —

Gentlemen and Ladies' Musical Companion, by John Stickney, 1774.

Williams and Tansur; printed and sold by D. Baily, Newburyport, 1774 and 1778.

Northampton Collection, by Elias Mann, 1779.

Collection of Hymns and Tunes, by Andrew Law, 1782.

Select Tunes and Anthems. Author, Oliver Brownson, 1783.

Massachusetts Harmony, by a Lover of Harmony, 1784.

Introductory Lessons, practised by the Uranian Society, Philadelphia, 1785.

Original Music, by Andrew Law; published in Baltimore, 1786.

Worcester Collection, for the use of singing-schools; printed by Isaiah Thomas, of Worcester, in 1786, one hundred and ninety-eight pages, — the first type music in America. Several editions were published; the sixth, in 1797, was edited by Oliver Holden.

Chorister's Companion, by Simeon Jocelin, 1788. Psalm and Hymn tunes.

Federal Harmony, in three parts. Psalm tunes and three anthems.

Original Music, by Abraham Wood, of Northboro', Mass., 1789.

Harmonia Americana, — Samuel Holyoke.

Musical Magazine, — A. Law, 1792, 1793, 1794.

American Harmony, — Oliver Holden, thirty-two pages, original; Charlestown.

Chorister's Companion, Supplement, — Simeon Jocelin, sixteen pages, original, 1792.

Rural Harmony, — Jacob Kimball, Topsfield ; original.

Union Harmony, — Oliver Holden, 1793.

Columbian Harmony, — Joseph Stone, 1793.

Tunes and Anthems, — Hans Gram, 1793.

Columbian Harmony, No. 1, — Daniel Reid, 1793.

Psalmodist's Companion, — Jacob French, 1793.

Massachusetts Compiler, — Holden, Hans Gram and Holyoke, 1794.

Harmony of Maine, — Samuel Belcher, of Farmington, 1794.

The Repository, — Amos Bull, Hartford, 1794.

Middlesex Harmony, — ———— ————, 1795.

Vocal Instructor, — Benjamin Dearborn.

Columbian Repository, — Samuel Holyoke, 1812.

Harmonist's Companion, — Daniel Belknap, of Framingham, 1797.

United States Sacred Harmony ; popular in South Carolina for a time, — Charlestown, S. C., by Amos Pillsbury.

Harmonia Cœlestis, — Jonathan Benjamin; church music; mostly European ; figured for the organ, 1799.

MUSICAL NOTES AND CHARACTERS.

We will now present to our readers some of the characters for notation that have been made use of to direct the voice and instrument to make melodious sounds, in ancient and modern times. Some ancient characters are unintelligible, and almost indescribable ; therefore, we have not thought it worth while to attempt to picture the unmeaning scrolls to the eye. Examples of some of them are given in " Bird's Gleanings of Music." We merely present those that are within the reach of our imagination, if not comprehension, directing to tones higher and lower in pitch.

The first specimen we shall mention, page 53, is found in the library of Cambridge College, which is a sheet about two feet square, which must have been painted, or engraved, as far back as 1300. The notes or characters are about three-fourths of an inch square, and the words under them in large black letter, as in the annexed example.

The first book in notes of similar characters, but small in size, was printed in 1453.

Je - ho - vah   God   glory.

Gregorian Notes and Rests.

In the first music written, a BAR was used to divide the note, or notes, that belonged to a word. Second, to show the end of a line in poetry. Next, to divide the notes into equal measures, as at the present day.

Specimen of Ravenscroft's Music and Words.

Ye Rulers vvhich are put in trust   To iudge of vvrong and right, Be

Different kinds of Clefs, used from time to time.

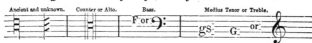

Martin Luther, in Gregorian chants, used six notes, called *ut re mi, fa sol la.* Different nations at different ages have made use of different syllables and different numbers.

5*

First letters of the syllables fa, sol, la, me, *placed on the staff instead of notes.*

While shepherds watched their flocks by night, All seated, &c.

The foregoing is after the manner of the tunes put in the Bay Psalm-book.

The round-headed notes are now used by almost all nations.

These round notes are so established and read throughout all civilized nations, that it would be about as difficult to change them for any other, as to change the letters of the alphabet.

Andrew Law's new method of Writing Music.

TUNE WELLS.

The forms of these notes indicate the name; the dots under the notes show that they are the second series of *fa, sol, la,* from the key. This plan not succeeding without lines, he next published a pamphlet with partial or broken lines, — which succeeded but very little better, — as follows:

TUNE WHITFIELD.

The diamond he called *mi*, the triangle *la*, the square *fa*, and the circle *sol*.

The plan of indicating the names of the notes by their form was, to all who were ignorant of reading music, enticing, and, as they supposed, labor-saving; and had Law consulted his pecuniary interest, and placed them on full lines at first, he would have made it profitable. After making two attempts without success, he desisted; and others profited by the form of the characters, which were afterwards, by way of reproach, called, by some, buckwheat notes. A book was published by Little & Brown, of New Haven, with notes of similar form placed on regular lines; and an immense sale of them was effected, particularly in the west, where they had little opportunity of learning music systematically. He, however, modified the system, to evade the law, by calling the diamond *la*, instead of *mi*, and the triangle *mi*, *la*. Such was the ignorance of any other kind of notes, west of the Alleghanies, that when the Messrs. Mason published their first book of church music, in Cincinnati, 1834, they were obliged, against their convictions of right, to suffer the publisher to make use of such notes, to accommodate the wants of that region, — of which they sold from fifty to one hundred thousand copies. But they soon convinced the public of their error, by teaching; and the books, if used at all, have been crowded to the far west, mostly out of sight and hearing

OF ENGLISH METHODS OF TEACHING. — MISS GLOVER.

We find in English publications that many plans and experiments have been tried, for the purpose of facilitating instruction, particularly to the poor and laboring classes, in order to teach a multitude at the same time; such as the following, by Miss Glover, written on a horizontal line, which was received with much enthusiasm, and very considerable success for a time, for the purpose it was designed; as follows: —

—:—d—:—r—:—m—:—f—:—s—:—la—:—t—:—d—

Thus, letters, instead of the forms of notes, indicate the name; or, like the "Bay Psalm-book," only having seven different notes, instead of four. The names of the seven she called, *do*, *re*, *mi*, *fa*, *sol*, *la*, *te*, the latter instead of *si*, to avoid the repetition of the letter *s*. These letters stand as representatives of sound. She gives the following as some of the rules for imparting instruction: — Where there are half-tones, the letters are red. When intended to be sung an octave above, they are marked thus, *d' r'*, were placed around the principal letters for different purposes, to direct the singers. This plan was introduced at first for the purpose of teaching Sabbath-schools and laboring classes to sing together; having, instead of a gamut or scale, a modulator or pointing-board, on which these letters were written, tunes were taught by pointing to the modulator, to save the expense of books.

In 1817, Pierre Galen, professor of mathematics in the lyceum of Bordeaux, taught music by what he called the Meloplast method. This was a board with ruled lines, without notes. Upon these lines a clef is placed; then, pointing to a line or space, the pupils take the sound as though an actual note was there. He taught his pupils that the open hand was an indicator, or staff, which was only a revival of the old Guidonian plan of the eleventh century.

The last plan introduced in this country for learning music with greater facility is of Day & Beals, in 1849; where, instead of letters to indicate the note, numerals are used for the same purpose, with the additional advantage of indicating the distance of one note from another, as follows : —

TUNE OF ARLINGTON.

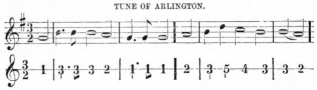

Books printed and published on the plan of the latter, through the energy and perseverance of the author, have had quite an extensive circulation, and learners somewhat numerous. There is no doubt that many of the variations from the round notes, which have been from time to time adopted, are conveniences, to say the least, so far as the *names* of notes are concerned. So it would be for the learner of English grammar to have some kind of mark over each word, indicating the parts of speech. But whether the former assists the learner in giving correct *sounds*, or the latter a *knowledge of the principles of language*, admits of a doubt.

CHAPTER IV.

PROGRESS OF MUSIC IN AMERICA.

Hubbard's Opinion of Fugueing Music. — Dark Age. — Negligence of Churches.
— Character of Music and Performers changed. — Authors. — Law. — Hol-
den. — Holyoke. — Kimball. — Read. — Swan. — Hubbard. — Dutton. —
J. Bailey. — O. Shaw. — E. L. White. — Salem and Middlesex Society. —
Published Music. — Clashing of Old and New Schools and Books. — Conten-
tion in Choirs. — Difference in Taste. — Ignorance of the Science of Music. —
New Era in Musical Publications. — Advance of the Science. — Modern
American Authors mostly living. — Teachers.

WE have now given a list of the books of music to the nineteenth century, mostly written in the Billings style. With a few
exceptions, the whole mass was destitute of correct harmony.

Professor Hubbard, in an essay which will be mentioned hereafter, speaking of the music of Billings and others of his day, is
rather severe; but, being in the day of reformation, allowance must
be made. He says, " Almost every pedant, after learning his
eight notes, has commenced author; with geniuses generally as
sterile as the deserts of Arabia, has attempted to rival the great
masters of music. On the leaden wings of dulness he has
attempted to soar into the regions of science never penetrated but
by real genius. The unhappy authors, after torturing every note
of the octave, have fallen into oblivion, and have generally outlived
their insignificant works. To the great injury of true religion, this
kind of music has been introduced into our places of public worship. Devotion, appalled by its destructive presence, has fled from
the unhallowed sound. He mentions, for example, a passage in

the tune of " Montague," where the words move together as
follows : —

Your   songs in - vite, Those

Let   the high heavens your

Those   spa-cious fields of

Of   brill-iant light where

He says, " To catch an idea
from such a chaos of words, uttered
at the same instant of time, a hearer
must be furnished with ears as
numerous as the eyes of Argus.
Such music can never be of more
consequence than an oration in an
unknown tongue."

Another author says, " The
tunes were admired in proportion
to the popular taking character of
the melodies, or to the wonderment with which the different parts
were introduced, entangled, bewildered, evolved, and at length
brought out in safety; amusement took the place of edification
and worship. Congregational singing was, of course, hushed, —
their harps were hanged upon the willows. Devotion fled, and
admiration occupied her place." After all these defects, they
gratify the ear of the multitude. Most of them have had their
day, and are laid aside. Here and there one appears in modern
publications, either in its original or a patched form. Some will
probably continue to hold their place before the public for ages,
as specimens of the art in by-gone days.

DARK AGE.

So far as real devotional music was concerned, the thirty
years referred to was a dark age. Many a sincere worshipper had
the same feelings of a certain Pope, when he was disposed to
banish music from the churches entirely, because the tunes were so
inappropriate. Although there was no Palestrini to write suitable
music, yet there were always very many who appreciated good music,
and were anxiously waiting for a change in public sentiment, that
they might introduce it, and were ready to lend a helping hand and
voice to bring about so desirable a reformation.

NEGLIGENCE OF CHURCHES.

During the aforementioned period, and for many years afterwards, ministers and churches who ought to have had a voice, if not the direction, in this part of public worship, suffered it to be wrested from them, and to be managed and executed generally by those who apparently had no higher object in view than to please, astonish and amuse. The music sung was so constructed that none but the choir could take part in its performance. Ministers, Christians, and all good men, and men of correct taste in regard to music, looked on, sometimes grieved and sometimes vexed. But they had let go their hold, and the multitude had the whole management of it, and sung *what* and *when* they pleased ; until finally hearers had well-nigh given up all interest in the subject, and settled into indifference.

CHARACTER OF MUSIC AND PERFORMERS CHANGED.

During this time, very few of those engaged in singing had ever heard any but American tunes, except, perhaps, now and then one, such as Bangor, St. Martin's, or Old Hundred, sung by their fathers and mothers, which they listened to as being something out of fashion, and unfit for modern use. Old Hundred by some means acquired extraordinary credit in the community, and retained its place in the memory and approbation of singers through all generations, and was occasionally sung. Well do we remember when the most said about it was that " it had *grand chords*." It stood in the midst of spurious music, like some few professors of religion, whose conduct is so consistent that all are constrained to say, " I think that man is a Christian." After the commencement of the present century, many, from curiosity or judgment, were led to try other tunes of the same character, by way of experiment, and were soon convinced that there were some sweets in them that they had never heard of or tasted. Lovers of pure church music watched and hoped, and were ready and willing to join heart and voice in the cause, and encourage every appearance of change to genuine devotional music, till by and by rays of light seemed to penetrate the dense and protracted gloom. But, before we enter minutely on this subject, we feel it proper to mention some of the agencies exerted to disseminate a more correct taste, and a better style of music.

AUTHORS.

The account we have given of books and authors is not without exceptions; nor can we, in justice to the subject, refrain from taking notice of some who lived and labored in those days, who never fully yielded to the popular tide, either as it regarded the prevailing music or manner of conducting it. Although, during the thirty or forty years, no apparent material improvement took place, still, all the while, there was a gradual advance in public taste. Those who, as teachers, choristers or hearers, undertook the work of reform, were far from being the most popular. We shall speak of those whose talents were known to us and others, and whose labors speak for themselves. The first whom we shall mention is Andrew Law.

ANDREW LAW will be found to have published a collection of music a short time after Billings' second book, in 1776. He was a well-educated man, of good character and talents. His first book contained many excellent tunes. He never partook fully of the spirit of the times in which he lived, either in feeling or action; but had stood aloof from the swelling current that swallowed up and carried off all regular church tunes written by masters in England and Germany. His taste and judgment were in advance of the age in which he lived, and he was probably better informed in the science of music than any other teacher of his day.

He was the author of the tune of Archdale, made familiar to every lover of music, by being published in almost every book of music for the last forty years. This tune is characteristic of the man, and no one written at that time has suffered fewer alterations by those who have re-published it. He afterwards compiled and published a valuable collection of anthems and psalm-tunes, taken mostly from European authors, such as " O Lord God of Israel," "Arise, shine, O Zion," &c. The work was expensive, being neatly engraved.

About thirty years ago, he published a small collection of tunes, principally his own composition, written upon a new plan; the characters placed on the page without lines, having the appearance of being written on lines, and then the lines erased. (See p. 54.) In the course of his life he taught more or less in most of the New England States, particularly in colleges, where the officers and students could better appreciate his talents, they being accustomed to investigate every subject connected with education. They could readily perceive the difference between his instruction and those superficial teachers commonly found at the head of schools in his day; and if his peculiarities sometimes rendered him tiresome, his evident devotion to the benefit of his pupils caused them to excuse every seeming inconvenience. Connecticut was his native state, and there he died, in the city of New Haven, at a good old age, some ten or fifteen years ago. Although he was probably the most thorough teacher in the country, still, as is often the case, his thorough method of training made him unpopular with the multitude. He was very particular in forming, or what he called tuning, the voice, not only of individual voices, but the voices of each part in connection, so as to make the whole to harmonize together; not allowing any one voice to be prominent above all others. He was also the first in this country to insist on the propriety and adopt the practice, which has since been generally adopted, of giving to female voices the air, or soprano, of the tunes; but this was then a new, unpopular doctrine. Nothing, however, could divert him from his opinions and purposes of right and wrong; and although his views often clashed with those of the multitude, he persevered, and those now living who knew him best admire his talents the most.

OLIVER HOLDEN, of Charlestown, Mass., who but a few years since left this world of imperfect harmony for that where discord is not known. Early in life, he was a true and enthusiastic lover of music. His compositions were much admired, and extensively used in New England. Few of his tunes were of a fugueing character. There was something pleasing and devotional in his style. The truly animating tune of Coronation, written by him, has been universally sung, if not admired, and will carry with it his name to all future generations. There were many tunes that gave evidence of much native genius and correct taste. We have heard a select piece of his, called " Dedicatory Poem," performed with good effect for the occasion. There were one or two solos and duets in it, truly beautiful. If he had continued to devote his time and talents to the subject, after the means of acquiring a knowledge of the science became more accessible in this country, he would probably have stood among the first of American authors.

Thirty years ago, or more, he retired from public schools and choirs, still retaining, however, his taste and love for music of every description, and occasionally, when he found words suited to his taste, set them to music. A short time before his death he probably wrote the following words, and adapted music to them:

> " God of my life, nigh draws the time
>   When thou wilt summon me away,
>   To dwell with those who dwell on high, —
>   To sin no more, no more to die.
>
> " My youthful days and riper years,
>   My joyful hours and hours of tears,
>   Passing away like fleeting wind,
>   Leave but a remnant yet behind."

This was published by the family, on a sheet, after his death, for the use of friends exclusively. His death was lamented by all who knew him, not only for his musical talent, but for his private character, and valuable public services as a citizen. He died at a good old age, at peace with God and man.

SAMUEL HOLYOKE, son of the Rev. Elizur Holyoke, of Boxford, Mass., was an indefatigable laborer in the field of music. His first book, called " Harmonia Americana," published in 1791, was of his own composition. He, as well as Law, stood aloof, more than any others of that day, from jingling, fugueing music. We have seen many of his musical compositions in manuscript, written in the latter part of his life, that discovered much taste, skill and originality, which will probably be lost to the public. His first book, not being exactly fitted for schools in the day in which he lived and taught, was not very extensively used, except by himself. He taught both instrumental and vocal music. His voice was never melodious. In the latter part of his life, he made use of a clarinet in his schools, while teaching singing, and the tone of his *instrument* was as harsh as his *voice*. But his talent for teaching was rather popular. The most prominent of his labors, as an author, was a work called " Columbian Repository," published about 1810, in which he not only selected and adapted a different tune for every psalm and hymn of Watts, but had the whole of the words printed in connection with the tunes. It was mammoth in size, and astonishingly mammoth the labor must have been to prepare it for publication.

It was published by subscription, at three dollars a copy; but the expense of the book was such that its circulation was very limited, beyond the subscription list. It was published on the presumption that choirs were, or would be, so well versed in reading music, that they could, when any psalm or hymn was given out, sing the tune on the same page; but the public were not prepared for it; still, for his labor, perseverance, and extensive collection of tunes, he deserves much praise. He died at Concord, N. H., about fifteen years since; but while the tunes of Arnheim, Mentz, and many others of like character, which he composed, are known, his name will also live.

He, in connection with Hans Gram and Holden, published a book called the " Massachusetts Compiler." The music was collected from European publications, except one tune from each of the compilers.

JACOB KIMBALL was a native of Topsfield, Mass.; a man of superior talents, when young; a lawyer by profession, but being ardently fond of music, he neglected law, and for many years made music his profession. He published a book of original music, called " Rural Harmony," in 1793. He taught and introduced his music in different places in New England, with great acceptance ; had a splendid voice, enthusiastic in his performance, was a popular teacher ; and when we are told that he died in the alms-house, the reasons for this change need not be mentioned.

READ, whose name is associated with Windham, Lisbon, Victory, and others, is said to have been a native of New Haven, Conn. ; was a popular teacher and a worthy man, and his tunes speak for his musical talent.

FRENCH, was a respectable teacher ; resided in Stoughton, Mass. ; composed a quantity of music, some very pleasing. Among other anthems, was one called " Farewell Anthem," — words, " My friends, I am going a long and tedious journey," and which were admired by many, at that day ; but few, if any, of his tunes, however, have survived, and had a place in modern collections.

SWAN, the author of " Poland " and " China," that have ever since had a place before the public, was a native of Northfield, Mass. ; spent part of his life in Vermont; published a book of original music in 1802. His tunes were remarkable for originality, as well as singularity ; — unlike any other melodies. The two tunes mentioned — the former of which had the words, " God of my life, look gently down," and the latter, " Why do we mourn," &c. — obtained considerable favor through the country. These tunes, having been tortured and altered by some editors, so that an old acquaintance would hardly recognize them, have, however, within a few years, been published nearly in their original dress. Nature had evidently done much to fit him for an eminent musician. He died respected by all.

JOHN HUBBARD. — We are now about to speak of one who was known only in a limited circle as a musical character ; but it frequently happens that the most profound knowledge is found among those who have neither opportunity nor inclination to make a noise in the world.

We take the liberty of mentioning his name, not as a voluminous author, but as a man of superior talent, knowledge and taste, in the science of music; and at the time he lived, about the close of the last century, had in his possession more means for acquiring a musical education than any other man in America, having more English publications and treatises on the science of music than any other individual, many of which are now to be found in the library of the "Handel Society" of Dartmouth College. Of some of them the like cannot be found elsewhere. His avocations were such as to prevent him from taking an active part in the musical world. In early active life, after acquiring a liberal education, he was preceptor of an academy at New Ipswich, N. H., and afterwards judge of probate, Cheshire county, N. H.; then appointed professor of mathematics, in Dartmouth College. He made a selection of anthems and select music, from European authors, for the purpose of publishing them; but God saw fit to take him to himself, in the prime of life, to sing anthems on high. His death was a grief and disappointment to lovers of music. A short time before his death, he delivered an address before the Middlesex Musical Society, at Dunstable, N. H., in 1807, — which society we shall have occasion to notice hereafter, — which was published, and called "Hubbard's Essay on Music," and was at the time considered a masterly production, making plain, through the whole, his superior taste and knowledge of sacred music. It would be read with interest and profit at the present day, were it republished.

The collection of anthems which he had prepared in manuscript was published by the Middlesex Society, after his death, for the benefit of his family, and called "Hubbard's Anthems." This collection was at the time considered the best in the country, and was extensively used, for many years, by singing societies in New England. In this collection there was one anthem of his own composition, the words of which were, "Thy mercy, O Lord, is in the heavens." The music and words speak the man, breathing the spirit of devotion. Although this anthem is the only music of his that has been printed, to our knowledge, we know it was not all he wrote; but his was not of a character to be received at that time, even if it had been presented to the public, differing from the popular music of the day. We well remember when, about the commencement of the present century, he used to ask two boys, with soprano voices, who had acquired the art of reading notes, to meet him in his study, and request us to sing music in manuscript. We wondered, at the time, why he should write *such* tunes, being unlike the music we had been accustomed to sing; but, notwithstanding, it gave a peculiar sensation, which will never be forgotten; and the more so, as it seemed to delight and gratify him so much; for, as he used to lead us with his voice and violoncello, singing one part, and we, two others, when we mounted the high notes, well do we remember how he shook his sides with laughter, so as, many times, to prevent his singing. Some passages and tunes sound in memory's ears still, distant, but sweetly. How gladly would we sing the same tunes again, with our grum voice of age, had we an opportunity!

DUTTON, who was preparing for the ministry, in connection with Mr. Ives, published a book of church music, in Hartford, called the "Hartford Collection," in which were many tunes of his own composition. His skill and taste were of the most promising order, and the tune of Woodstock, with the words "I love to steal a while away," will be associated with his name, and handed down to future ages, and be sung by many on earth, while he is singing the song of Moses and the Lamb in heaven.

OLIVER SHAW. — The name of Oliver Shaw is a household word in every family where music is heard. A minute account of his life would be read with thrilling interest, did our limits permit; but we forbear, as we have reason to believe that a biography of his life will be soon published in a volume.

We cannot, however, refrain from giving a sketch of the man, in connection with others who have taken an active part among American teachers and authors.

He was a native of Middleboro', Mass., born 1779, lost one eye when quite young, spent several years with his father at sea, and, in taking nautical observations, injured and lost the sight of his other eye, and total blindness followed.

In this pitiful situation, " What shall I do, in this doubly dark world ? " was the all-absorbing question. Music was the prominent answer. He was first placed under the instruction of an eminent teacher, in Newport, R. I., Dr. Brinkerhead, where he spent two years. As day and night were both the same to him, consequently he had nothing to divert his mind by the sight of the eye, which, added to an intense love of music, combined to strengthen and brighten his imagination, so that, as might be expected, he made rapid strides both in the theory and practice of music. He afterwards spent two years with Professor Graupner, of Boston, to perfect himself on the piano and organ, and Mr. Granger, to learn the use of wind instruments. He commenced teaching in Dedham, Mass.; then in Providence, R. I., where he spent the remainder of his life. He was a faithful and successful teacher, had pupils from many other towns and states, besides going from house to house, led by some friendly hand. By his amiable deportment, he was always received as a friend and teacher with cordiality.

In some of the last years of his life, we have seen him, with feeble health and tottering frame, hurrying from house to house, to teach what had become a part of his life; till, at the close of the year 1848, he closed his labors, on earth.

In connection with a Mr. Noyes, he taught many singing-schools, with good success; presided over several singing societies; was the first to import the works of Haydn. His musical compositions were truly original. His song, " There 's nothing true but Heaven," to use the language of another, " broke upon the musical world like strains from another world, the copy-right of which he sold for fifteen hundred dollars. It was repeated night after night at the Boston Handel and Haydn Society. Other songs, duets, — such as "Mary's Tears," "Arrayed in Clouds," &c., together with "Christmas Ode," — and a multitude of other pieces, sacred and secular, marches and piano-music, have been commended by their use, so that they need no praise from the pen. On the last day of the year, and nearly the last hour of the day, he left the darkness of earth; and from the evidence of a long life of piety, we venture nothing in saying that the light of eternal day broke in upon him, and the words which he and others so often sang here on earth he has realized from that moment, — that "There's nothing true but heaven."

E. L. WHITE acquired considerable celebrity, both as a teacher and author. He closed his labors on earth, in Boston, in 1851.

White was a native of Newburyport, Mass.; a man of more than ordinary musical talents; commenced teaching in New Bedford; then in Boston, where his labors were incessant as a teacher, writer, and publisher of music, sacred and secular. He was cut down in the midst of life and usefulness, and the hands that used to move the keys of the organ and piano so gracefully are stilled and mouldering in the grave.

We have not the least disposition, even if we had space and talent, to discuss the relative merits of modern American authors now living. What little we have said has been of those who have finished their labors here on earth. We suppose the comparative merits and exertions of those now living, — whose works have been, and are now, before the public, — to effect the marked improvement in sacred music, will not be rightly and fully appreciated until the grave covers party feelings and prejudices. They will, however, form an important item in the history of church music.

The foregoing names we mention as being prominent members of the musical world, and many of them were all the while waiting for a favorable time to bring about a reformation of church music, loathing that which was calculated to divert rather than direct the mind to anything like the worship of God. The same kind of music, however, generally prevailed in the churches till about the year 1806, of which era we shall endeavor to treat in the next chapter. Societies and associations began to be formed soon after the present century, for the purpose of reviving ancient music, a more particular account of which will be given under the head of *Societies*.

SALEM AND MIDDLESEX SOCIETIES. — INSTRUMENTAL.

The most decided and efficient exertions by prominent singers commenced in Salem, Mass., and vicinity, led by Rev. Dr. Worcester, and in the western part of the county of Middlesex, in and about Groton, with the venerable Dr. Chaplin at their head, extending to several towns in New Hampshire. Clergymen and other professional men taking an active part, made the associations appear rather formidable; and no wonder that the whole movement was denounced as aristocratic, by those who had previously managed the public singing; and as most of the members, when they came together, were found to be of a political party called Federalists, their meetings were pronounced by many as a political combination.

The Salem and Middlesex societies were put in operation about the same time. New England books and shelves were ransacked, and every piece and parcel of old music-books was brought forward at their meetings. Psalm-tunes and anthems were selected for every subsequent meeting, that all might provide themselves with copies, either printed or in manuscript. Finding the inconvenience of accomplishing their object without a selection and publication of such music as they desired to practise and recommend, each society, about the same time, set about the work of collecting and publishing desirable music, and chose committees for that purpose.

PUBLISHED MUSIC.

The books were printed, the former under the agency of Rev. Dr. Worcester, of Salem; the latter, under that of Rev. David Palmer, of Townsend. The tunes in both publications were printed with similar tunes in a long, narrow book, with but four parts, or one brace on a page, containing only one common psalm-tune, about one hundred and twenty in number. Soon after, a similar collection was published by Amos Albee, of Medfield, Mass., called the Norfolk Collection. The books were a convenience and gratification to the lovers of devotional music, but were looked upon as subversive to the general tide of singing, and treated with contempt by many. About the year 1804, when individuals first convened for the purpose of devising the best means of effecting a change, it was at first the prevailing opinion that it would be best to retain some of the most acceptable tunes of American compositions. But when the question came to be canvassed and decided, *which* and *what* tunes should be the favored ones, opinions clashed; every one had his favorite tune or author, so that they did not adopt the measures that temperance societies in this country tried, by cutting off the stream of alcohol, and letting that of wine run on; but cut off and discarded all American compositions at once. It was a startling move, and many of those in favor of a change of music in the churches feared the consequence; but it was done, and public opinion sustained the movement. And the books with such tunes as Old Hundred, Mear, St. David's, and kindred names, stared the singer in the face from every page.

CLASHING OF OLD AND NEW SCHOOLS, OR BOOKS.

Then came the struggle between the "Old Hundred" singers, as they were called, and those who had never sung anything but modern music. And they were determined to hold on and hold out with the music which had so long and successfully conflicted with devotion and solemnity. And when schools were raised for the purpose of using the books just published, opposition schools, in many instances in the same neighborhood, would be immediately put in operation, sometimes within hearing of each other. But the weight of character and singing talent in most of the towns was enlisted on the side of the former, till one singing choir after another came into the ranks of the reformers.

Soon societies, associations and choirs, were formed in different cities and towns, with objects similar to those of Middlesex and Salem, and shortly the influence spread through New England, and since that time has been spreading through the country; although it is found that music of a light character gains the first residence in new settlements, even at the present day.

CONTENTION IN CHOIRS.

In some places, at the commencement of the change of music, singers in towns and churches were so equally divided that the struggle was long and tedious, to decide which should carry on the singing in the church; where neither party, in fact, were strong enough to sustain it acceptably; so they had to compromise, and in some instances sing alternately their favorite tunes on the Sabbath. But the effect of this was sad; each would sing from his own book with energy, while the opposers would sing with indifference, and destroy the effect. This state of things could not prevail long, for " a house divided against itself cannot stand."

DIFFERENCE OF TASTE.

But there were then, as now, itching ears, that choose the jingle of music rather than the harmony; for we find here and there, in modern publications, tunes somewhat of the character of Billings & Co. Although constructed more systematically, still the words are sometimes clashing; and whenever and wherever you go to church, and hear these tunes sung, they are apparently listened to and sung by some with admiration; and sometimes we are even saluted with the real " Simon-pure," such as Lenox, Northfield, &c., of the propriety of which we leave for others to judge.

IGNORANCE OF THE SCIENCE OF MUSIC.

At the time these books of ancient music were published, no one was considered competent to make any corrections, except where, by copying, printing and reprinting, palpable and gross errors were perceptible. Therefore tunes were taken as they were found, and so published, and this was probably the most judicious course; for the oldest and most experienced dared not expose their ignorance by attempting to correct errors. To show how little was known by the wisest, we will just mention that a committee for publishing one of the books saw fit to introduce one tune from a recent English publication, with the figures of the harmony attached; and when one of their number was asked the use of these figures, he honestly answered he "did not know," but they meant to make the public believe they knew something.

NEW ERA IN MUSICAL PUBLICATIONS.

From this time, publications that had been used in schools, such as Village Harmony, Bridgewater and Worcester Collection, and soon many others, perceiving the change of public sentiment, wisely, either from inclination or approbation or interest, began to expunge some of the trash on their pages, and substitute ancient tunes in their stead. Formerly, the pages of their books presented but few notes except with *black* faces, and *white* ones were treated with neglect and unworthy of notice, unlike the order of things at the present day in society.

As the American music had been discarded *en masse*, it seemed no more than justice that those who had pronounced it worthless should give their reasons; for it is too common for those who condemn the works of others to be still more ignorant themselves, being unable to tell a better way. All this opposition and competition had a tendency to turn the attention of many worthy men to investigate the science of music. Among the first were Mitchell, Brown, Shaw, Hastings, Mason, Holt, and others. Alterations and corrections in old tunes were found necessary; and the public were satisfied and reconciled to the inconvenience of the first corrections. But when in the editions, one after another, were found corrections corrected, and the singing community obliged to purchase a new book every year, this, to say the least, was vexatious and mysterious to some, especially when a tune was altered several times, and then published as it stood originally. It was difficult to keep the public reconciled ; and the important question, when will these authors satisfy themselves, was difficult to be answered.

ADVANCE OF THE SCIENCE.

Now these scenes have passed by, and, suffice it to say, that from the commencement of the labors of the many authors who have made themselves eminent, the theory and practice of music has been advancing with rapid strides. At first they used to criticize each other in regard to the rights and wrongs of harmony ; but that time has also passed, and books have multiplied so rapidly that authors have no time to look after each other; and if we cannot say the world cannot contain the books, we can safely say that schools and singers' galleries can scarcely convene them.

TEACHERS.

Ichabod Johnson was, we think, a native of Woburn; was a fifer in the Revolutionary army, and about the commencement of the present century, and many years after, was rather celebrated as a teacher of vocal and instrumental music. He could hardly be said to have any voice for singing, but had a wonderful faculty of enlisting young and old in his service ; and when he commenced a school, by the assistance of his violin, with his forced voice, and the voluntary services of old singers, he scarcely ever failed in advancing a school rapidly. The music he taught was not of the most inferior kind. He taught to play on instruments, both wind and stringed, in many towns in New England, very successfully, and was very celebrated as a teacher and conductor of bands of martial music.

Joseph Bailey was a graduate of Dartmouth College, and was

7

a teacher in Boston about 1820. He commenced teaching music-schools in evenings. He was justly considered one of the best teachers of sacred vocal music then known. He was thorough and faithful in teaching both the theory and practice of the art, and by his perseverance and correct example did very much to promote and establish correct time, intonation and general improvement, in schools and choirs. Removed to New York, where he died.

Many others, about the same time, taught with good success, and *deserve* and will have a place in the memory of the lovers of sacred music generally, while they will be remembered with favor and affection by thousands of their pupils. Among others, we would name Mann, Shaw, Col. Newhall and brother, Bartlett, Claggett, who taught in Salem, Portsmouth and Maine; Perry, of Worcester; Col. Warriner, of Springfield; Moore, of Concord, N. H.; Marcus Colburn, a few years later, whose fame both as a teacher and public performer is known through the country. If I proceed any further, or rather to the next generation of teachers, hundreds present themselves with equal claims, many of them hailing under the banner of "Boston Academy," — some truly worthy, — others doubtful.

Among the earliest stands the name of Elnathan Duren. The singing of the choir at the dedication of Park-street Church, in 1812, and on the Sabbath and other public occasions for many years, will be among the last things forgotten by those who were performers or hearers. Although the preaching by Dr. Griffin, pastor of the church at the time, was not exactly in accordance with the public taste and opinion of the day, still his superior oratory, and perhaps still more the excellence of the music, in comparison with that of other choirs in those days, drew there great multitudes from all denominations, besides being a resort for all strangers who visited Boston. There was an exactness of time, correctness in tone, a power and expression given to words, as well as music, such as had never been heard before. Many of those now living, who took an active part in its performance, start and awaken like an old soldier at the sound of martial music, when the singing of those days is mentioned. This choir was an important nucleus to the Handel and Haydn Society at its formation, and took a prominent part in its performances. Mr. Duren did not engage as a teacher of schools till about 1825, and his labors were principally confined to the western part of New Hampshire and the eastern part of Vermont. Delicacy would dictate silence, on our part, respecting one so nearly related, had it not been urged and insisted upon by others, to speak of him in connection with other teachers. Nothing is hazarded in saying what thousands have said, — that for native and acquired musical talent, skill in communicating to others the theory and practice of music, power and sweetness of voice, energy of expression, and the art of instilling the same into his pupils, together with the power of moving a school or choir, at his will, with precision, were talents united in him which few ever possessed, or even acquired. He was a surpassingly good reader, his conceptions of the meaning of an author were just, his enunciation perfect, and the whole was uttered in the most melodious tones, with an expression of countenance which told that his whole soul was absorbed in his performance. This talent assisted him much to instil expression, as a teacher of music.

CHAPTER V.

ESTABLISHMENT OF SCHOOLS.

Description of Schools before Billings. — Effect of Billings' Music and Schools. — Rudiments of Music. — Teachers. — Formation of Schools. — Subscription for Schools. — Location. — Inconveniences. — Results.

AFTER giving an account of the principal music-books that have made their appearance before the American public, it seems proper to notice the use that has been made of them, particularly in schools and churches. If it should seem that the description of schools and teaching was intended as ridicule or burlesque, we disclaim anything of the kind. We wish only to present and preserve this portion of the history of past times, so that the present and after generations may know and realize how great and multiplied their means and privileges are, compared with those of former generations; and inquire whether, with these additional privileges, they have made corresponding improvements.

LIMITED MEANS.

The facilities then available were very few, and it may be that, fifty years hence, if some one should continue this simple history of the progress of music, our present practices, in some instances, may appear as inconsistent and strange as the account we now give of by-gone days.

These limited means were not peculiar to instruction in singing. In schools for common education, similar scenes and inconveniences were experienced. We know it, for we have had experience in both; and a picture of common schools in past times has been beautifully delineated in a work by the Rev. Mr. Burton, called the "District School as it Was."

SCHOOLS BEFORE BILLINGS.

In regard to singing-schools previous to 1770, tradition says, that meetings of either young or old, for the purpose of learning the theory or practice of music, were scarcely known; and that even the meeting together of neighbors, for the purpose of learning to sing the tunes then in use systematically, was opposed by many as time foolishly occupied, and by others as being morally wrong, and even wicked. It is, however, evident, that, from 1720 onward, singers, few in number, did meet occasionally, in some towns, for the purpose of improvement. The principal object appears to have been to learn to sing by note, or rather by letter; for it was to them a new and mysterious art, so much so that when it was first rumored that a man had, by his superior skill and application, acquired the art of giving sounds to given notes, so as to sing a tune that he had never heard, he was looked upon with astonishment, and reckoned by some as participating in the witchcraft of the day.

EFFECT OF BILLINGS' MUSIC AND SCHOOLS.

When Billings came upon the stage, with his fascinating music, and could not only *read* old music, but had actually *made* new tunes, the musical community was in commotion, and filled with admiration and surprise. A new era commenced in the American singing world; and at the bidding, or even suggestion, of this wonderful man, schools were collected in and about Boston; and at his rehearsals his room was crowded, inside and out, with listeners, like the hearers of Jenny Lind, or the Germania Band; and he could not possibly make them desist, except by promises to sing publicly, in some church, and give them a chance to hear.

RUDIMENTS OF MUSIC.

Of the rudiments of music, as we find them in the books of that day, nothing more was taught or learned than the simple characters used in writing music, and the notes and letters, as applied to the lines and spaces of the staff. The *names* of the notes, as ap-

7*

plied to the octave, were, in order, — *fa sol la fa sol la mi*, — *mi* being called the governing note; and this note, with others stationed above and below it, were removed by flats and sharps. These subjects, added to that of "keeping or beating time," were sufficient, at the time, for all practical purposes.

Soon, others aspired to gain his popularity and exert his influence; so that, all along, till near 1800, we find teachers, particularly the authors of the books we have mentioned, scattered over New England, and some of the cities in the Southern States, laboring either to promote music by teaching the tunes to others, or to recommend and make sale of their own works.

SCHOOLS FROM 1770 TO 1800.

In the following account of schools, we have particular reference to the time we have designated as "the dark age," namely, from 1770 till about 1806; but we cannot be particular in regard to dates, for light on the subject broke out in different places and states at different periods; and we presume there are still many dark spots, in regard to the character and practice of sacred music, in this broad land.

OBJECT OF SCHOOLS.

It is not for us to define the motives which usually led to the formation of singing-schools. We are aware that classing them with amusements seems rather extravagant; but we have reason to fear, from the *kind* of music practised, and the demeanor at the schools, that they could be considered as little else.

The talent of singing, we have said, is given by God to be *improved;* and in this, as every other duty, there is a pleasure and satisfaction in performing. A singing-school, collectively, unless frequently and affectionately reminded by the teacher of its object, will be likely to seek pleasure and amusement, and forget the main object sought by the patrons of the school.

FORMATION OF SCHOOLS.

The usual method of parishes, in country towns, to resuscitate or sustain singing, has been by establishing schools for those to learn to sing who had what were called "natural voices;" and as a generation of singers does not usually continue in active life more than three or four years, it was necessary, in most instances, to raise and support a school as often, for the purpose of manufacturing new singers.

When singing began to decline, or had become insufferable in the churches, after a few preliminary remarks, by the minister, perhaps, or by members of the church or congregation interested, or, what was more likely than all, after the continued persuasion of some of the children, who were anxious for an opportunity of meeting their associates frequently, the fathers were urged to assist in providing means for hiring a teacher. As singing in schools or at churches was a sort of individual or private education, of course the raising of money by the church or town, as such, was out of the question. Individuals, more or less, would meet and choose a committee to present a subscription paper, which was the only resort for raising the money necessary for the purpose. We will, for a moment, follow the man with the paper, and listen to some of the reasons and excuses of those who were solicited to subscribe; — some of them true. Before starting on his mission, he will be careful to procure the names of some of the principal advocates, as it is well known that much of the success of such enterprises depends on a right beginning.

SUBSCRIBERS FOR A SCHOOL.

The paper is presented to some one who has means and influence, and is, of course, a lover of music. He reads, hesitates, and then says, "I desire to have good singing, and should be willing to pay for its promotion, were it not that singers, after they have learned, will not keep together in church, and money seems to be lost." He is told, perhaps, that none would be permitted to attend but such as would obligate themselves to sing in church. He subscribes. He then, perhaps, goes, with cautious steps, to the clergy-man, who as cautiously remarks, "I feel the effects of bad singing, and the importance of that part of worship being performed acceptably, to prevent the people from leaving the church ; but singers are so sensitive that I wish to avoid any interference with their doings." But, after being reminded of the importance of having *his name* to the paper, by way of example, he subscribes. The paper is then presented to the officers of the church. They, with one consent, begin to make excuses ; the most prominent one, perhaps, is, that they had been giving all their lifetime, and singing was no better, but rather worse ; and they are discouraged. But, as the minister has subscribed, they will give something. He then meets with a wealthy individual, who "cares for none of these things." He speaks *out*, what perhaps others *thought*, namely, that "if any one wishes to learn to sing, let him pay for it. What use will it be to me ? Neither I nor my family can sing. If I could sing, I would not go about begging for others to pay my tuition." Another says "he has no inclination to encourage a parcel of giddy young folks to sit in the gallery to show off their skill, which is apparently all they care for, — singing over tunes that are more like dancing than psalm tunes. I had rather they would sing as they did in good old times, when one man got up and 'raised the tune,' in a pew below, and all joined in singing as well as they could." He now commences soliciting the aid of the "old singers," and those intending to learn. One of the former says he can learn tunes without going to school, and that he has paid his share heretofore. Besides, if he has been leader of the choir, he secretly thinks he ought to be employed as teacher, of which he is not sure. Another, that he has learned already, and if he gives his time to promote singing, that is his part. Another, who understands the usual manœuvres of new-organized choirs, — to clear out the old singers from the choir, — refuses to patronize a new school. Another, that they have no need of a school, — that they sing well enough now. Those who intend to be benefited by the school subscribe more or less, but are not to be compelled to pay, unless they succeed in learning. Altogether there appears to be a sum subscribed sufficient to authorize preparations for a school. A meeting is called for the subscribers to make preparations for a school.

LOCATION OF SCHOOLS. — INSTRUCTORS.

A committee is chosen for that purpose. Some important questions then arise, by way of inquiry, in regard to a *teacher*, and where the school shall be held. The first question usually caused many serious and important remarks. As teachers of regular habits were generally engaged a year in advance, the question was not so much whether this or that man's talents were good, as who will be likely to be the most regular, especially in school-hours; and it is known by every one that lived forty years ago, that at meetings for the transaction of business of any kind a *spirit* was entertained not very favorable to that of sacred music, and that none were more exposed to its fatal effects than a teacher who could sing a good song and play the viol. Common civility forbade his refusing the common beverage of the day; and by that means he was often ruined by kindness. Let it not be understood that there were no teachers of steady habits; but it cannot be denied that most of the men of superior musical talent, and most apt to teach, were to be found among those who were in the habit of *steeping* their talents. We once knew one of a committee, whose duty it was, if need be, to carefully dispose of the teacher when he was in a situation to disgrace himself and the school. We have no knowledge that he had to exercise his authority more than once. Then the teacher came into school, and immediately requested the school, which was numerous and in their places, to sound A; they obeyed, he continuing to draw his bow back and forth on his viol, muttering, with an awful scowl, " Keep sounding on't! " That A was the first and last sounded, that evening; but he appeared again, the next evening, as clear, bold and bright, as though nothing had happened.

The next important question was, " Where shall the school be kept ? " Lecture-rooms then were scarcely known. A common school-house was too dull and lonely a place. A hall in a public house, then called a tavern, of which more or less were to be found in every village, was the only place to meet the approbation of the majority. Besides, the terms for the use of the hall were generally made easy ; for it was well understood, by all parties, that the profits arising from the sales in the bar-room, to scholars and spectators, would amply compensate for the use of the room.

INCONVENIENCES, OR ACCOMMODATIONS.

All things being thus far arranged, the reader may now imagine the school seated round the hall, one, two or three deep, as the case might be. To accommodate the scholars with a place to lay their books before them, different methods were resorted to ; barrels, boxes, old chairs, &c., placed so as to bear up a strip of board placed at a proper distance, were sometimes made use of. To save expending the money subscribed, the scholars were usually requested to provide their own lights in the evening schools. In those days schools were frequently kept three hours in the afternoon, and as many in the evening. The young reader, who has been supplied with chandeliers or gas-light, and seated on a cushion, may smile, and even ask what is meant by a *candle ;* but we speak of days before even lamps and oil were in common use, which is not going back a long time. But this strip of board placed before the scholar answered the purpose of holding the book, and a standing-place for the candle. Different means were resorted to for the purpose of saving the unpleasant task of holding it in the hand ; some would turn the candle the lighted end down, and leave a quantity of the melted tallow on the board ; then setting the other end in the tallow, when cold it would stand alone. Others would make use of an apple, turnip or potato, making two sides square or flat, and in a hole in the centre put the candle therein. Others, who possessed mechanical powers and ingenuity, made a small square block, with a hole bored in it ; this was nearly the climax of convenience, with which sometimes some generous mechanic would supply the whole school. But if, perchance, any one deigned to bring an iron, tin or brass candlestick into the hall, this was looked upon with scorn, as the height of aristocratic presumption.

THE FIRST MOVEMENTS.

Thus seated, teaching commences, all is attention and eagerness to learn. Notwithstanding, the *recess* of the school in the course of the evening is anticipated with deep interest; and when the word is announced, joy lights up every countenance, and moves every tongue. The movement is sometimes intermingled with alarm and vexation, by the upsetting of barrels, boxes afore-mentioned, and consequently candles, books, &c., scattered on the floor. In addition to the eagerness to meet each other for a chit-chat, there were attractions for some in what was called the bar-room. To this place, also, at the close of each evening school, common civility and justice required that a proper respect should be shown to the keeper of the tavern, and also that the singing-master should be present; and if he was an adept on the violin, it was not considered indecorous for the scholars to invite him to play a tune, while they used their feet, instead of their hands, to beat time to the measure of the music.

We would merely suggest to our readers not to be too severe in your criticisms in regard to the impropriety of their conduct in this kind of exercise, after the school had closed, lest it should be written, some twenty years hence, of us, that we sung, during the hours of school, sacred and secular music alternately. We hope the readers will not be too severe in their denunciations, when they are told that in the hours of school every individual was intent on learning sacred music, lest it should be written of them hereafter that in the schools at the present day, sacred and secular music are sung alternately, not only so, but published in the same book.

RESULT OF SUBSCRIPTIONS.

Having, at the commencement of the chapter, given some account of the labors of the committee in procuring subscribers, perhaps it will be proper to accompany them through their labors, to the end of the school.   The amount of the subscription, on paper, justified them in employing a teacher a given length of time, besides paying other necessary expenses; the master is employed, and promised accordingly.   But, alas! some who subscribed did not succeed in learning, left the school, and refused to pay.   Some subscribers were not to be found; some had been unfortunate, and *could* not pay; others *would* not; but the teacher *must* be paid, and the employers must pay him; so that, for the honor of being one of the honorable committee, one might consider himself highly favored if he had not more than five or ten dollars extra to pay.

CHAPTER VI.

TEACHERS AND TEACHING.

Teaching the Theory of Music. — Trying the Voice. — Different Voices. — Unmanageable Voices. — Limited Compass of Voice. — Correct Ears, but Rebellious Voices. — Natural Singers not always Correct Voices. — Suggestions. — Rejection of some. — Learning the Rules. — Change in the Names of Notes. — Distributing the several Parts. — Beating Time. — Different Modes and Characters for Time. — Beating is not Keeping Time. — Beginning to Sing Tunes. — Deficiency of Books. — Music did not allow Expression. — Old Singers in New Schools — Ready for Church.

WE shall next proceed to give some account of the manner of teaching, in those days, preparatory to assuming the important station of singers in the choir.

TEACHING THE THEORY OF MUSIC.

To communicate the simple rudiments of singing, or what is called learning to *read* music, every teacher, probably, formerly, as now, had something peculiar to himself in his manner of imparting the art, be the printed directions in the text-book few or many. After the simple elements are learned, it is by practice and hearing alone that the power of giving notes at given distances their proper and relative sounds can be acquired. We know that it is the common opinion of parents who have had no experience themselves, that if a child has been to a singing-school, and cannot, afterwards, sing tunes at sight, it is because the rudiments have been neglected. It may or may not be so. No rules or directions can be given to guide the voice to a given sound; practice alone can do it. As well might we suppose that

8

a pupil who could appreciate beautifully proportioned and well executed letters could at once form them elegantly himself, without practice. Nothing but application, in either case, can effect the object; — the theory and practice must go together; and to succeed, there must be perseverance in both cases. Perhaps you will ask, "Do you mean to say singers learn by rote?" We answer, "Yes. They learn almost everything by rote, where sound is concerned. How could any one, by committing rules to memory, learn to pronounce a foreign language, without first hearing the sound communicated by a teacher?" The same may be asked of musical tones.

TRYING THE VOICE.

The first process, after the scholars were seated, was what was called "trying the voice," which was nothing more nor less than trying the ability of each scholar to imitate a given sound. This was, indeed, a critical moment; and none but those concerned can know or imagine the trembling and heart-beating excitement of the pupil, caused by the approach of a teacher. There was no escape for any one, nor was any one even allowed to have the voice of a friend near by, to assist him at this perilous moment; each one was taken separately, and had to answer for himself. He must sound *out* audibly, so that all might hear, in response, right or wrong, to the master; there was no discharge. And it was curious to observe, that, if a scholar under immediate trial was so unfortunate, either through fright or want of talent, as not to be able to imitate the given sound, how those who had been more fortunate would exultingly smile; while those who had yet to go through the ordeal, however confident they might be of success, had nothing but a crimson flush or mortal paleness visible in their faces. It was understood that, however unsuccessful at the first trial, their fate was not to be decided by that effort; for experience had proved to teachers that fear, excitement, or other causes, would sometimes so affect the nervous system and throat, that the organs of sound would refuse to act in obedience to the knowledge and will of the person on trial. If the school was large, this operation of trying the voices occupied the first evening, and perhaps a longer time; at the close of which, the joy and confidence of some, that they were among the favored ones, and the evident anxiety and suspense of others, made the scene one of peculiar interest to a critical observer; and, by the picture presented, one would be led to suppose that the future destiny of all worth living for was depending on their admission or rejection by the teacher. In fact, he seemed to hold the destiny of all concerned at his disposal, for some two or three of the first evenings.

DIFFERENT VOICES.

Perhaps it will not be amiss to give some account of the different voices and degrees of talent which present themselves at the commencement of a school. I presume it will not be contended that all have equal power, tone or flexibility of voice, or the same nicety of ear to discriminate sounds.

UNMANAGEABLE.

Some have strong lungs and strong voices, without much sensibility; or rather have not perception enough, in regard to sound and tone, either to know or fear the wrong, when they attempt to imitate a given note; and if you desire them to sound a note higher or lower, they may happen to succeed or not, in attempting it; and if you ask them to sound higher, it will, perhaps, only be louder. There the voice is, and there it is determined to stay; and there, perhaps, it must stay.

LIMITED COMPASS.

The next class are found capable of moving the voice up and down two or three notes, or more, correctly; and then they seem to be at the top or bottom of their ladder, and nothing but patience and perseverance can coax the voice either up or down any further. These two classes are generally insensible to the wrong, having, as a teacher once said, "leather ears," so far as music is concerned, and cannot discriminate sounds.

CORRECT EARS, BUT REBELLIOUS VOICES.

The next class we shall mention are those who have correct ears, but rebellious voices, either for want of practice, or some other cause. When a sound is given them to imitate, they instantly know if they fail, — stop, and "try again" of their own accord. These, by practice, often succeed in acquiring the power of managing the voice, and sometimes make the best of singers.

NATURAL SINGERS HAVE NOT ALWAYS CORRECT VOICES.

Another class are those that are found among what are called sometimes natural singers, who, having been praised too much to learn systematically, or to believe it possible for them to err, when a sound is given or heard will imitate it *almost* right, but just enough out of the way to distress the hearer or teacher. These, of all voices, are the most to be dreaded; for their possessors, generally, have strength of voice, and still stronger confidence in themselves, and have been made to believe that they were, or would be, wonderful singers, — probably because they made a wonderful noise.

Such voices have been the cause of more discordant music than any other. Those who have correct voices and ears may possibly avoid perfect jargon, by singing in concord, and all sink or rise together. But, if there be voices inflexibly true, or instruments accompanying, the tones of which cannot yield, they make music intolerable. The instruments proceed correctly, of course, while the great and heedless voice moves on triumphantly, sinking or slipping downward, and rendering the chasm wider at every note. Mutual criminations between singers and players on instruments ensue, the latter being accused of having their instruments out of tune; and even the innocent organ, which cannot change, is accused and condemned, as being untuned or unskilfully played, the singers never dreaming that they may be in fault. In such cases it is easy to perceive that something is wrong, and nine times out of ten the hidden secret of the trouble begins and ends with one or more voices such as have been described. And what makes it the more unfortunate is, that such persons often read music with facility ; and that their voices, being prominent, not mixing with others, are heard and praised by the multitude ; and if a teacher or chorister intimates to them that all is not right, it is considered a great insult by the individual and his friends.

Teachers have found that nothing will convince such of their error but the experiment of giving them the first note of a tune with some instrument, and, after letting them sing the tune through alone, to compare the last note with the instrument. Hence, a tune may be sung through, and seem correct, when an imperceptible depression has been going on with each successive note, and consequently not one, from beginning to end, has been correctly given.

SUGGESTIONS.

We may be asked the reason and the remedy of this difficulty. These are questions more easily asked than answered ; and this leads us to leave our history, and make some few suggestions, which we believe to be correct. It is evident that deviations from the pitch, of which what is called "singing flat" is infinitely more common than "singing sharp," will arise from two causes : first, a defective training ; second, a failure in the delivery of the breath, either from physical weakness of the respiratory apparatus, or from unskilful management of it. Among those who fail from the first cause, are some who are heedless, and will not listen ; others whose ear has been vitiated by practising with treacherous voices or instruments imperfectly tuned ; and others who have never been properly exercised upon the scale.

The second class of causes includes some who fail from physical weakness of the muscular apparatus, where there is a lack of energy and tone in the respiratory muscles, in common with other parts of the body. Such persons can only find a remedy in invigorating the general system. Most persons, however, have

8*

sufficient muscular energy, but fail in the management of it. Some will partially fill the chest; and others will take in a large volume of air, but allow it to escape in singing two or three syllables. Such persons always make languid singers, and rarely sustain the pitch. A well-trained singer fills his chest and discharges it so gradually that the reservoir seems to be inexhaustible. Some begin each note with a sort of explosion, continuing it with a strongly-marked diminuendo, till it ends as if from exhaustion; such are almost sure to go inevitably down. Others fail for want of giving sufficient *impulse* to the sound, especially when they attempt to sing soft; and the voice drops like a spent arrow. They overlook the distinction between volume and force; so their amplest sounds evaporate, as it were, and penetrate to no great distance. We might compare the effectiveness of sounds, however full, emitted with deficient force, and those uttered with full force, however suppressed, to the impetus of the foot-ball compared with the rifle-ball. Every one who heard Jenny Lind must have been struck with the distinctness with which almost inaudible notes penetrated to the most distant parts of immense apartments, by means of the impetus with which she threw them from her; and still more astonishing was it to witness that wonderful training of the ear and voice by which she was enabled to turn from the piano-forte, and, after sporting in echoes of her own voice for some minutes, finally close with an almost interminable note, completely dying out in the distance, turn again to the instrument, and, by a gentle touch of the key, show that her voice had not swerved a hair's breadth.

Much may be done, by a judicious teacher, to remedy these defects; but the remedies must be adapted to the case. Early attention must be bestowed; for when a habit of "singing flat" is once formed, the voice will inevitably sink, much like the tones of a string which is rapidly stretching. It is a common thing to hear leaders of choirs command them to "keep their voices up to the pitch," with just the same effect as it would have to tell a man standing on a quagmire to keep himself from sinking, when the more he exerted himself the deeper he would be sure to sink. Few are aware how much depends on the management of the breath. By a skilful husbanding of it, a cautious commencement of each note, and a gentle increase of its force, and such a *rapidity* of the issue of the breath as to give due impulse to the sound, great accuracy may be attained where great defects originally existed.

It may be asked what is to be done, and what has been done, where such voices are in a choir, and the trouble cannot be remedied while they are present. Truly, what can be done, but to leave them to sing alone, or, in a kind manner, to request them to withdraw ? As was said in the outset, we consider such voices the greatest possible evils; and we presume that the length of our observations will convince every reader that we are sincere.

CORRECT VOICES AND EARS.

The last class includes such as have ears, organs and feelings, that will not allow them to vary from any given sound; and of them nothing need be said.

REJECTION OF SOME.

The time has now arrived when the opinion of the teacher, and of most of the scholars, has passed a fatal sentence on some, as deficient in musical talent, and the sentence must be and is passed; the separation, however painful, must take place, and, in some instances, their dearest friends are under the necessity of hearing the sentence, and of seeing them turn their backs upon the school with blasted hopes, not only as not being counted among singers, but as shut out from the amusements and comforts anticipated from the social interviews of the school.

LEARNING THE RULES.

The instant the scholar was released from the trial of his skill in using his voice, he gladly commenced the trial of scholarship in committing lessons to memory. And it was curious to observe that those who were the least hopeful as to their voices would usually be the first to commit their lessons, and so on through all the exercises or the rudiments; one part of the school seemed to be triumphing over those who could not command their voices, the other equally rejoicing because they excelled as scholars in reciting the rules.

The scholar was first shown the gamut, as it was called, and taught the location of each of the seven letters on the five lines and their spaces, which had to be committed to memory. The same letters were on different lines and spaces, for the different parts, as indicated by the Clef at the beginning of the tune; namely, Bass or *F* Clef, placing the letter *F* on the fourth line; the Counter or *C* Clef, placing it on the first line, and fourth space; Tenor and Treble, or *G* Clef, on the first space, or fifth line.

Next, he was taught the names of the successive notes on the scale, which were, as we said, *fa, sol, la, fa, sol, la, mi,* — *mi* being called the governing note, from which followed, *fa, sol, la,* &c., above, and *la, sol, fa,* &c., below. For every different key, this governing note was removed to a different line or space on the staff, and with it the whole scale, maintaining its relative situation with the governing note; and flats and sharps were used to designate each change. These changes were repeated over and over, to make them familiar to the learner, as follows: " The natural place for *mi* is on *B.* If *B* be flat, *mi* is on *E; F* be sharp, *mi* is on *F,*" &c. &c. The repetition and committal of this lesson answered all purposes, to enable the learner to call the notes by their right names. The causes and effects of these changes was considered too intricate a subject to be understood by the learner, or explained, except by degrees, as he advanced in practice.

Among the lessons, an important item for the exercise of memory, as well as observation, was the fact that the last note in the bass was the key-note of the tune; and if it ended first above *mi,* this being the governing note, is was called a *major ;* if below *mi,* a *minor.*

The scholars were then allowed to proceed *together* in what was called rising and falling the eight notes of the octave, and were taught the names and comparative length of the notes. Nothing was known or heard of *whole, half, quarter notes*, &c. ; it was, *semibreve, minim, crotchet, quaver, semiquaver, demi-semiquaver*.

CHANGE IN THE NAMES OF NOTES.

The reader will perceive that but four different syllables were used, namely, *fa, sol, la, mi ;* therefore, the syllables *fa, sol, la* were repeated, so that the scholar was taught to say, above *mi, fa sol la* twice, then comes *mi* again ; below *mi, la sol fa* twice, then comes *mi*. This method of singing by note, although inconvenient and inconsistent, was continued till about thirty years ago, when the present syllables, *do, re, mi, fa, sol, la, si*, were introduced.

This change in the names of notes created a great deal of trouble and perplexity, not in teaching beginners, but with those who had learned the "old way ;" some denouncing it as unnecessary, and no improvement. Some would meet to practise with new schools, but would not take the trouble of learning the "new way," and would either keep silent while others sung by note, or make unknown sounds, without any articulation ; while others would abandon singing entirely. It was then asked, and in some parts of the country is asked still, " What better is this new method ? " Without going into the particular merits of the case, we would adopt the true Yankee style, of answering one question by asking another, — Why would it not be just as well to repeat the four first letters of the alphabet in applying them to the staff, and, instead of *A, B, C, D, E, F, G*, use the first four in this manner, *A, B, C, A, B, C, D ?* The answer must be obvious to every one ; for, in either case, in applying the principles of music, if we ask where the letter *C*, or the note *fa*, is to be found on the staff, before it can be answered the question must be asked, which *C* or which *fa*, the first or second, above or below *mi*, is meant.

DISTRIBUTING THE SEVERAL PARTS, OR VOICES.

After these introductory lessons, the distribution of the voices to the parts best suited to individuals was attended with many difficulties, and often gave offence. The air, or leading part of the harmony, — now usually called soprano, — was sung by male voices. This part being prominent, all gentlemen who, by the greatest exertion, could reach a note that had any claim to be called high, were sure to plead the right of being placed among the privileged ones. Of these many soon found, by experience, that whatever their *desire* might be, their *voices* could not be persuaded or forced to so high a point as was necessary, and contented themselves with the humbler part of bass. The part usually sung by the ladies was written on the upper staff in the brace. The alto — or *counter*, as it was then called — had a place on the third staff, and had a clef peculiar to that part, called the *C* clef, formed thus : ⸺ This part was originally designed for boys, being written ⸺ an octave higher on the staff than it is at the present day. It was rarely sung by female voices ; and, when attempted, was usually sung at the top of their voices, just as written. It was therefore too shrill to be pleasant, and was soon abandoned. Boys could seldom be found who had skill enough to lead the part, and but few gentlemen could reach the high notes ; so the consequence was that this part was seldom sung, although an important one in the harmony.

Singers of the present day will probably be astonished at this distribution of the several parts. The idea of the gentlemen singing the air, or soprano, the ladies singing the tenor, or upper staff, inverts all harmony, as made on the organ ; but when they are told that organs were scarcely known in those days, and that the harmony of tunes was generally written in such a zig-zag manner that it mattered but little how the voices or parts were distributed, they will be satisfied that the theory and practice of music were alike uncultivated.

BEATING TIME.

In the mean time, the motions of the hand necessary to measure or mark the movements of music were practised and explained.

The *motions* of the hand for "beating time," as it was called, varied at different periods, and with different teachers. They were not so nicely defined as to be considered obligatory on either master or scholar; although uniformity was recommended, yet human nature does not like confinement; and the peculiarities of individual character might often be read in the latitude, altitude, velocity, and eccentricity of the movement of the hand in beating time.

DIFFERENT MODES OF TIME.

There were three measures of time, as at present; then called *common*, *triple* and *compound*. Common time had three modes or marks, namely, first, C, or $\mathbb{C}$; second, $\ni$; third, $\frac{2}{4}$. The first had four beats, practised as follows: first, rest the ends of the fingers; second, the whole hand; third, raise the hand on the ends of the fingers again, then raise it entirely; or, third, clenching the fingers; then opening or raising the hand for the fourth. The second and third mode required but two beats, or motions, one down and one up, the motion being made more or less extensive, according to the taste and ambition of the singer; $\frac{3}{2}$, $\frac{3}{4}$ and $\frac{3}{8}$, all alike in execution, had three beats, the two first beats like those of the first mode of common time; the third by raising the hand. $\frac{6}{4}$, $\frac{6}{8}$, compound time, formerly had but two beats used, like the second and third common time, one beat to three crotchets or quavers, the first of the three, being accented.

BEATING IS NOT KEEPING TIME.

Many suppose that, because they keep on beating through a tune, they must be correct in their time. Not so; few performers keep time so correctly as to stand the test of a regular mechanical motion; and a great many sing, and conform their beating time to their progress and success in calling notes or performing the tune.

But, to beat time exact, and make singing conform to a regular motion, is a different thing. A whole choir may beat time exactly together while singing a tune, following their singing, and yet keep no correct time. The fact is, there must be some machinery within, that vibrates regularly, and cannot be diverted, and will sacrifice notes rather than time. A singer must hear and feel. Deliver us from a plodding singer, that labors with his hand and voice, without *ears* or feeling!

Observe an audience listening to music in accurate movement; — they hear, and involuntarily make some kind of motion in sympathy with it; but, the moment the performers fail to move together, motion ceases. Before accompaniments were written, mechanical time was not observed. The performer gave length and strength to notes to suit his own taste, in giving expression to words; so that, when correct time was found necessary, on account of additional parts, it was considered a fetter to expression, and caused old singers to say that time made slaves of singers.

BEGINNING TO SING TUNES.

Thus much being learned in regard to notes, time, &c., the scholars would begin to be restless, anxious to sing or learn tunes; and if the master hesitated, it would be suggested to him that Master B. permitted his scholars to sing tunes the third evening; so, to keep up with the times, tunes must be attempted immediately; and it would be said by the teacher, "We must attend to rudiments hereafter."

As the means for supporting schools were limited, teachers, scholars, parents and patrons, were anxious to have rapid strides made in the school. The time not usually exceeding twenty-four evenings, of course, the rudiments, if learned at all, must be learned in a short time; and, the practice of singing once commenced, it became unpleasant, if not degrading, to turn from singing to the dull music of rudiments, which the teacher had promised; so that even the few lessons they had committed to memory were in part forgotten, except those necessarily applied.

DEFICIENCY OF BOOKS.

Books were rare; for it ever has been the case that there is an unwillingness to expend money to purchase books of sacred music, as well as for tuition. It was not uncommon to see some two, three, or four singers, depending on a sight at one book; some holding an ancient book, containing here and there one of the tunes given out to learn; others with manuscript copies of one part only, so that the position of the school was not always so regular as might seem desirable.

MUSIC DID NOT ALLOW EXPRESSION.

In modern times, we inculcate the idea that the object of learning music, and applying it to words, is to give additional expression to sentiment. To effect this, the manner of teaching and examples given are as various in singing as in reading; but formerly the tunes were so constructed that, instead of making use of the tune to give expression to words, the main object, from necessity was, to learn the tune; and that was done by singing it by note about twenty times; and when about committed to memory, the words were applied, instead of the syllables *fa sol la*, to sing the tune, and with just as little thought about their meaning. Besides, it mattered but little, with tunes generally used, what words were applied, or how they were spoken, since different words were spoken by different parts at the same time, so that language was as much confounded as at the tower of Babel. The two first lines of the words and music were generally found to move on peaceably together, but the anticipation of what was to follow absorbed the mind of the singer; for soon each part was to take its flight, and each knew the necessity, even if doomed to be the last to start in the race, of arriving at the last note simultaneously. Therefore there was no time for thought; — all was action.

OLD SINGERS IN NEW SCHOOLS.

It was not expected that those who had before been through the common though superficial training of a former singing-school should take part in the preliminary exercises; and, however necessary it might be, they would consider it as degrading to be seen plodding through the mazes of the rudiments; and when they came in to join in practising tunes, the new school looked at them with a jealous eye.

It was one of the greatest difficulties attending the teaching of schools, where necessity obliged old and new singers to meet together, to give satisfaction to all, or even to one's self; the former wishing only to sing tunes, and perhaps by word only, and the latter needing to proceed more slowly and surely. All have subscribed equally, and all claim attention to their particular wants; and necessity requires that both should be prepared for singing in church together. There seemed, therefore, no other way but to compromise, and attend to the theory and practice alternately; and this, many times, was done against the better judgment of the teacher and many of the singers. This difficulty ever has existed, and ever will exist, until the means for supporting schools are so enhanced that proper classes can be formed.

Although a generation of singers, as we have said, does not generally exist more than three or four years, yet there are, here and there, individuals who have stood as pillars in the singing choir, known, and perhaps revered, by all. There were usually, also, others that were never of much consequence as singers. They, too, would take their seats to practise with the school, and evidently felt themselves to be of much importance. They were, of course, watched, with eyes and ears, by the young. The master had perhaps been teaching his pupils some peculiar manner of beating time; forming sounds, or pronouncing words; or to avoid particular habits in accent, slurs, &c., and having, perhaps, ridiculed all other methods but his own. The old singers take their seats, commence in full confidence, expecting to astonish their young hearers, when, lo! the quality of sound, the habits, &c., that they have heard so often ridiculed, are brought out in full colors and power, to the great amusement of the school! The new comer wonders, is provoked to see the smile which he perceives is not that of approbation, — perhaps stops singing. The school hesitates, and between them both, every tune seems ready to perish by the way. Among old and new singers, there are always those to be found who have never learned to sing by note; but, having good ears and flexible voices, and having received a full share of flattery, pass for the best of singers. Such will look on with disdain, while a tune is being sung by note, seeming to say, "I am beyond that," and so wish to have it understood by hearers; listening, all the while, to learn the tune; and when directions are given to sing the words, then is the time for them to display their importance, and they commence with a tremendous power, that astonishes some and provokes more. One who understands singing will cheerfully conform to the doings of a school; so that you may calculate, for a general rule, that he who does not become a learner when with learners never did learn properly. And permit us, in passing, to observe, that teachers, in all departments of education, are apt to be too tenacious of their own peculiar mode of teaching, condemning all others; and, trying to make their pupils believe there is no other good way, they dwell with great emphasis on some particular point which they find has been neglected by teachers before, and which, perhaps, is of little consequence in reality, and magnify it, as if the whole destiny of a learner depended on this one thing, and that they, by their timely interposition, had saved him from fatal error.

READY FOR CHURCH.

We have now come to the close of the school, and the scholars are prepared and waiting for an opportunity to appear in public. During the meetings of the school, many parents and others interested have called to witness their progress, and perhaps listened, at recess, with delight, to the song by the teacher, to say nothing of the beverage introduced by way of interlude; — clergymen and officers of the church, who, although they perfectly understood that the school was soon to appear before them, and take part with them in public worship, never, perhaps, have been near the school. Not so with all, — there were honorable exceptions of those who felt the importance of having this part of public worship performed with decency and in order; also of forming a friendly intercourse with those who sing in church; — these have met with them, sung with them, and, by their precept and example, led young learners to attach due importance and sacredness to the employment. This was as it should be; and by this kind of influence a reformation was eventually commenced, which has been progressing from year to year.

CHAPTER VII.

MUSIC IN CHURCHES.

Exhibition of a School. — Clergyman's Address. — Refreshments at Recess. — Organization of the Choir. — Choice of Officers or Leaders. — Highest Seats. — Remedy for those who contend for the Highest Seats. — Caste among Singers. — Choirs dispersed, and what the Resort. — Foibles and Virtues of Singers. — Changes in Choirs. — Favorite Leaders, or Choristers. — Extreme Obstinacy. — Location of Choirs in the Church. — One Leader; his Responsibility; his place in the Seats. — Method of finding and establishing the Pitch of a Tune. — Tunes committed to Memory. — Advantage of committing to Memory. — Multitude of Books at the present time. — Inconveniences. — Same Tunes will not please all. — Demeanor of Singers in Church. — Fault sometimes in the Leader. — Irreverence of Choir.

EXHIBITION OF SCHOOLS, AND CLERGYMAN'S ADDRESS.

THE singing-school, which we left rather unceremoniously in the hall of a tavern, we will now conduct into the meeting-house, the place assigned for the first appearance of the scholars in public, there to give parents and patrons an opportunity of judging of their proficiency and their fitness to perform on the Sabbath. The members of the former choir, who have attended more or less, are perhaps among them. The rights and honors of neither old nor young have as yet been canvassed. We will suppose (for that was the usual course) that the minister of the parish is to address them on the subject of music, this being included in the performance, as a sort of relief or interlude to the singing. After rehearsing some of the tunes prepared as a specimen of their skill, then comes the address. Teacher and pupils expect to be particularly noticed. They listen with intense interest. If little is said to flatter their feelings, sad is the disappointment. He ventures, though trembling-

9*

ly, to say, that singing is a talent given by God to sound forth his praise on earth, and that it is the duty of those who possess it to cultivate it, and to assist in that part of worship in his house. It would then be immediately whispered around, "We will have our minister to know that we are under no obligation to him. We have paid our own tuition, and devoted our time, and shall sing if we please, and not otherwise." And the adversary, as we have before stated, ever an enemy to music in the church, is ready to magnify a kind suggestion into actual abuse, and helps and urges them to quit at once. For example : on one occasion, a clergyman expressed a hope " that those who gladdened the house of God with the harmony of their voices would be particularly careful to cultivate the much sweeter, and, to the ear of Heaven, the much more acceptable harmony, which resulted from a unison of pious hearts." This appropriate suggestion was considered an insinuation sufficiently insulting to cause the whole choir to show their indignation towards the interfering pastor by vacating their seats.

The address being ended, they rehearse more of their choice pieces of music. Then comes a recess, which seems to be necessary in order that their parents and friends may have an opportunity to meet and congratulate them on their success.

REFRESHMENTS AT RECESS.

We have heard with our ears, if not seen with our eyes, that during the recess, ardent spirit was generously handed round among the singers in the gallery of the church, to cheer them on their course ; and surely it could not be said, during the remainder of the exercises, that they sung without any *kind* of spirit. This was done publicly, the minister, elders, church-members, and the whole congregation, looking on with apparent satisfaction to see the young people enjoy themselves, congratulating each other on the prospect before them of having good music in the church, in future.

However preposterous this may seem to the young reader, and even to some of mature age, we mention it more especially to show the power of custom. But it was at a certain period, in the memory of many, when by way of beverage, or the entertainment of friends, anywhere and everywhere, a glass of liquor was looked upon to be just as proper and innocent as a cup of cold water. Those who refused to drink it were regarded as destitute of common civility; and those who declined had to excuse themselves by saying it did not agree with them.

ORGANIZATION OF THE CHOIR.

The exercises being finished, before adjourning, a general notice is given for all the singers to meet, at an appointed time and place, for the purpose of choosing a leader, or leaders, and otherwise organizing the choir. This is a startling subject. From that moment, every mind is absorbed in the great question, Who shall be leaders? Fortunate, in such cases, if there happens to be any one singer so prominent and popular as to unite the whole, for a chorister or general leader; for, in the history of choirs, one gentleman was formerly deemed sufficient to lead the whole; but in latter days, custom requires one or more on each part of the music. In this case, the excitement was often intense, for the time being; and what rendered it more interesting and animating was the fact that the ladies were permitted to take part in the choice and to vote; besides, there was not a little anxiety about disposing of the old singers. Common civility seemed to require that they should share in the honors of office; but the new school had enough among their number, as they supposed, qualified to fill all offices, and even to sing without any assistance from those more experienced.

CHOICE OF OFFICERS.

The time arrives, — they meet. They who have taken part in such scenes, and expected promotion, can best describe the emotions. The former leaders expected, and had a right to expect, that due notice would be taken of them. But the thought, if not the language, of the majority was, "We don't want these old singers among us. These old bigots will always be complaining of every smile and whisper. We can do well enough without them. Besides, they have sung long enough, and ought to step out of the way." This has been too often the language of those wishing for an office for themselves or some friend; but the more considerate think it best to compromise and divide the honors. The election being over, some are sorely disappointed, and, with a wounded spirit, they turn their backs on the whole, the next Sabbath.

HIGHEST SEATS.

In connection with the choice of leaders is that of *seating* the singers, both leaders and their assistants in each part. Every singer who has been a member of a choir knows, that among singers, as well as at feasts, there are seats that are regarded as the uppermost, which are looked upon and sought after with jealous and longing eyes, — especially by those who can make themselves prominent only by their location; while those who sing best care but little where they are placed, for with their voices they can command the attention and notice of hearers. But, after all, this placing or seating the choir disaffects some, who, the next Sabbath, are among the absent, virtually saying, "If I cannot have the seat I choose, where to sing God's praise in the church, I will not sing at all." It would be well, perhaps, for teachers to impress on the minds of scholars, beforehand, that the highest seat in a choir is where the best singer sits, no matter where it is located. As this subject has caused more altercation than almost any other, we recommend for uneasy spirits the hearing or reading of the following incident, which may, perhaps, prove a sovereign remedy. We hope to be excused for introducing the ladies as prominent actors; it is not because they are the more guilty, but because the picture presented is not easily effaced from the memory, connected with the circumstances.

REMEDY FOR THOSE WHO CONTEND FOR SEATS.

A certain choir had made choice of *three* treble leaders; but unfortunately it was a general ticket, — no first, second, or third.

Being, therefore, equals, the first one that arrived in church took what was understood to be the highest seat, of course, and no one had a legal right to say, "move down." This answered the purpose, at least, of making them punctual; and they did not wait for the tolling bell, but hastened to secure this envied seat. One of the three happening to live near the church, and where the others had to pass had only to be prepared, and, when they came in sight, to hasten forward and lead them into the meeting-house, whatever might be her talent to lead them in the choir. On a certain Sabbath, the moment arrived; and while putting on the last glove, she heard the request, or command, "bring down grandma's bonnet." She caught it instantly, placed it on the top of her own, while she adjusted everything to her mind, and hurried down stairs; her competitors gaining ground, there was no time to be lost, — grandma's bonnet was forgotten, and she hurried on, doubly crowned. It was an old-fashioned country meeting-house, with the entrance to the galleries at each end. After entering, she had some distance to walk, before arriving at the front gallery. There were a few singers present; they smiled, and their smiles soon turned to laughter. She was provoked, — turned about scornfully, — went down stairs, and took a seat in a pew in the broad aisle. In a few moments, a little sister came and whispered in her ear, — "grandma wants her bonnet." The remainder of the scene and feelings we will leave for imagination to supply.

CASTE AMONG SINGERS.

Caste is often felt in this country, especially among church choirs, although it does not show itself in the same form as in some distant lands. It would be strange to hear any individual object to meeting those of different standing in society in the church or prayer meeting; and there can be no reason given why all classes should not meet with the same cordiality to sing God's praise. But we regret to say it is not so. In country towns and parishes, all hands and faces are alike exposed to the sun and hardened by labor,

except here and there a professional man, such as a doctor, lawyer
or merchant; but they, being few in number, and desirous to
court patronage, generally mix cheerfully with the multitude.
But, unfortunately, among the females, there must necessarily be
some who, to use the softest term, are called "help;" and these
frequently have voices and skill excelling those who feel superior
to them. To have one of these noticed by the congregation or choir
would be more than human nature can conveniently submit to,
and to sit by their side insufferable; and it is not uncommon,
at the present day, to hear parents say, "if such and such individuals sit with the singers, my children shall *leave the seats.*" In
this way, and for this reason, another portion of singers leave the
choir. The old singers whom we have mixed with the young, by
the wry looks and cold treatment of the choir, added to their levity,
are grieved, disgusted, and disturbed in their devotion, and retire
to their seats below. The remaining few struggle on, perhaps,
many months, till some prominent singer takes his seat below,
casting a significant look toward the gallery, seeming to say, "Now
see how you can get along without my help!"

CHOIR DISPERSED, WHAT THE RESORT.

Those who remain in the choir lose their courage, and fail
to sing as well as usual. So one after another drops off, till
by and by the singing-seats, as they are called, are deserted.
And now, what is to be done, is the question throughout the congregation. There are two alternatives: either to do without singing, altogether, or for some of the singers of former generations,
with some few of the considerate of the last taught, to associate
and sing either in a congregational manner, or collected together in
the gallery to unite their voices; they decide on the latter, and, if
their voices are, some of them, tremulous from age, and not quite
so harmonious, they make respectable singing. The deserters
look on and sneer, perhaps; but when they find the singing is
likely to go on, some return; and in this way they worry along
till another season of evenings arrives, when another singing-school

is organized, and the same scenes are acted over again, with the same results.

We are quite sure that many of our readers will recognize, in the foregoing description of choirs, many features common to all, most of them indeed scenes that are past; if so, our hope is, that our young readers will read, consider, and avoid similar improprieties.

FOIBLES AND VIRTUES OF SINGERS.

There always have been, and, perhaps, always will be, many things in choirs to complain of, if not to condemn,— freaks of passion, whims and follies; but with them we find an unusual combination of virtues, not to be found in any other association.

We know that there is difficulty and perplexity in transacting all the numerous little affairs necessarily attendant on the charge of a choir, or even to be a humble assistant in this part of worship, and at the same time to keep the feelings in a devotional frame. Want of familiarity with the tunes to be sung, fear of failure to perform acceptably to ourselves and others, aside from the vain ambition to please and astonish, — these, and a multitude of other circumstances, all tend to dissipate the spirit of devotion, and leave us mere *performers*, rather than *worshippers ;* and how often are those who listen, and are wrought into ecstasy, and, perhaps, weeping admiration, ashamed when they come to reflect that pure devotion has had but little share in the act.

CHANGES IN CHOIRS.

Where there have been good choirs of singers, and of long standing, the death of some, and the marriage or removal of others, will sometimes break them up. A new leader is selected, necessarily; he sets about collecting forces for the ensuing Sabbath, and scenes like the following have often been witnessed. They gather about the door of the church in the morning, to consult about means and measures, until the minister commences; then all rush to the gallery, and crowd confusedly together. The hymn is read

— every heart flutters. The new-created chorister names a tune, perhaps not of the right metre. Fear disturbs his nervous system, contracts the organs of sound, confines thought, and unhinges reason. The pitch is given, but so high, perhaps, that when the first high note in the tune is met, the voices are found incapable of reaching it, all are brought to a halt, and have to commence anew ; and, perhaps, with no better success.

FAVORITE LEADERS.

In some instances, where parties in favor of this or that one for a leader were nearly equally divided, and no means of reconciliation could be devised, each party would sing alternately morning and evening ; this was a real stimulus for mastery, but the spirit with which this controversy was carried on we will leave for others to conjecture. The only benefit derived was the exertion to excel, which led them to practise, so that all were benefited as singers.

EXTREME OBSTINACY.

But, so far as the spirit manifested is concerned, what we have said will appear mild and childlike, compared with the following instance, which is, to be sure, an extreme case, but yet true. A church and congregation in a country town, which had been for some time destitute of religious service, had invited a man to preach as candidate for a pastor. The singers in the town, being more numerous and better versed in singing than is usual in parishes in the country, were called together to prepare for the coming Sabbath. But, alas ! when the question arose, who should be leader, they were nearly equally divided. Both parties were determined to rule, and so declared it, in language too strong to retract or be misunderstood. The Sabbath came ; all were present, and one-half took the right and the other the left of the railing between the seats of the front gallery. There was no time for compromise. The clergyman read a hymn, — each chorister named a tune, but not the same, — each choir commenced their own selected tune, and sung the words to the end, proving their decision of character, skill and independence in music, whatever may be said of their humility or devotional spirit. The clergyman, being amazed, wisely omitted reading again, depriving them of the privilege and pleasure of "trying titles the second time." This, perhaps, was the first and last extreme case on record ; but not very different from another that occurred in former days, when the deacon began and read the first line of words, and the singers went on through the verse regardless of his reading afterwards. The deacon, after waiting a reasonable time, commenced reading the second line, but finding it was not regarded, he refrained from further reading, till they were through the hymn, when he commenced the hymn again, saying, "The world's people have sung, — now let the Lord's people sing;" and the words were sung over again, in the old way. To say nothing of the solemn mockery in either case, it shows, in glowing colors, how the will and passions of man will make him so reckless as to exhibit them openly, in their most hideous forms, even in the house of God.

LOCATION IN THE CHURCH.

We have now taken the schools into the church, and accompanied them through some of the scenes that are incident to choirs. These scenes were not universal ; and fortunate is it, if the description will apply to no schools or choirs at the present day.

The location of choirs in the meeting-house, when they were first established, was a source of very considerable altercation. On examining old town-records, we find it was not uncommon for an article to be inserted in their warrants for town-meetings, to see if the town would grant liberty for the singers to sit together in some convenient place in church. Also, to see if they will dispense with the words of the psalms and hymns being read by the deacons. Also, to choose some person to raise the tune, &c.

Meeting-houses, in those days, usually had three or four long seats in front of the pulpit, on each side of the broad aisle, for the aged and the deaf, and for those unable to purchase pews. There were, also, the like kind of seats in the galleries, on the right and

10

left of the pulpit; in the front gallery sometimes the same, and
sometimes square pews. Which of these seats should the singers occupy, if allowed to sing as a choir, was a serious question.
As the singing had usually been performed on the first floor, some
singers chose to continue there, and to have two or four of the long
seats partitioned off, making a long pew or pews; and when they
rose to sing, those on the front seat would face about, it being considered important for singers to face each other, in order that their
voices might mingle and harmonize. This situation did not suit,
but in a short time their judgment and aspirations led them
higher. The next resort was for liberty to sit in the gallery.
The front gallery was usually made into pews owned by individuals, and so the choir was obliged to take one of the side galleries;
but this was sitting rather too much sideways from the minister;
besides, one part of the congregation could not see them; so that
there was no rest till they gained occupancy of the gallery in front
of the minister. Nor was it so easy a matter to obtain these pews.
On one occasion of this kind within our knowledge, two or three
of those who had been accustomed to occupy the seats refused to
give place to the intruders. One old man in particular, who had
occupied the middle of the front seat, was found in his usual place,
which brought him cheek by jowl with the leader. But, whether
by design or accident, the leader's fiddle-bow so frequently got
entangled in the old man's grey locks, that he was at last forced
to give up. Sometimes the pews were made use of as they stood.
In this case, every one rose in their place, and thus stood, from
necessity, in hollow squares, face to face and back to back. This
did not answer;—the pews were ere long demolished, and long
seats substituted, with one partition in the centre, to separate the
ladies from the gentlemen.

More recently, houses have been constructed, in some instances,
so as to give the singers a gallery directly behind the minister.
This position for the singers has been generally abandoned, and
the front gallery established as the singers' home in church; and
every accommodation has been provided, such as curtains, sofas,

cushions, for their ease and comfort while sitting, and places for their books, whether sitting or standing, — very unlike the accommodations of our fathers.

Curtains of different widths and dimensions, from one to six feet in height, have been placed in front of the singers, within the last thirty years. At first they were used to hide the books, and the necessary moving of the same, connected with an inclination to hide the singers, — not to mention particularly their conduct, — from the congregation. We have seen, in some cities, where professional singers were employed, curtains that reached above the heads of all, as though they were ashamed to be seen singing psalm-tunes in a church on the Sabbath, though they probably would not hesitate to be seen on the stage of the theatre through the week.

ONE LEADER. — HIS RESPONSIBILITY.

Choirs, for more than half a century, were satisfied, as we have said, with one leader, or chorister, sometimes chosen by the town, sometimes by the church, sometimes by those who joined them in singing. Others occupied the post, by a sort of common consent, on account of their skill or *courage*, the latter being frequently wanting. Before choirs were formed, it required no little experience and self-possession for a man to rise up in the midst of a sitting congregation, and lead off a tune, when a failure in the attempt would oppress his spirits for the week; and when choirs were first introduced, it was expected of a leader, or chorister, to sound the key-note, and then give the pitch successively to other parts; and all this, too, without any artificial aid of pipe or string.

HIS PLACE IN THE SEATS.

Beside this, his place in the choir was on the front seat, facing, when he commenced, both minister and congregation; and, withal, he was expected to beat time conspicuously, in some way. He sang what is now called by different names — air, treble, soprano — then called the tenor, and had next him, by his side and behind, the most experienced of the performers. The ladies, or treble,

were on his right when sitting; but, as they rose to sing, and those
in the front seat turned their backs on the congregation, the order
was reversed; and when a fugue commenced, his motions and
activity, in turning from one part to another, to give them the
catch-note, were then, and would be now, astonishing to an ignorant spectator, but only amusing to those acquainted with music.
But this activity was the proof of his musical spirit and skill.
We shall retain him in the front seat of the front gallery till
within thirty years, singing the air; and there he is found at the
present day, singing the same part, in many regions of the country.

METHOD OF FINDING AND ESTABLISHING THE PITCH OF A TUNE.

About forty years ago, to assist the chorister in finding or making the sound for the pitch of the tune, some simple artificial means
were made use of, such as a pipe, reed, or fork, which sounded
one note or letter only. If this note did not happen to be the
key of the tune about to be sung, it required no little skill to find,
from that sound, the wished-for note. After it was found and
established, by all uniting and sounding it, then came a more difficult operation, to be performed by the whole choir, which was,
to call the notes by name, thus:

This exercise was considered necessary, in order, as it was said,
to fix the key of the tune in the mind, by sounding the common
chord. This being done, when all was hushed the leader gave to
each part their introductory note, or pitch, to commence without
further ceremony. Do this method and exercise appear to the
reader a mere formality? If so, what may be said, some thirty
years hence, when it shall be told that, in order to fix, not only the
key, but the whole tune, in the mind, organs or instruments now
rehearse the whole tune before singing?

TUNES COMMITTED TO MEMORY.

This parade in commencing a tune may be accounted for, in some measure, by the fact that no singing-book or note-book was to be seen, except the one sometimes in the hands of the chorister, to assist him in selecting the tunes; and lest that should be found too cumbersome, he would usually write the tunes used on the Sabbath in a manuscript; or, what was more likely, write the *names* only of the tunes, with the addition of the letter of the key, and a flat or sharp to designate the key of each tune. Every tune, before it was sung in church, was committed to memory, either at the singing-school or by the fireside (for there were no choir rehearsals), by singing it over some twelve to twenty times by note, and then by applying the words. And a teacher or leader, who had to look at notes when teaching others, was considered incompetent. Another reason was, that the tunes sung in former days were generally so rapid that there was no time to pass the eye from the tune to the words.

When the ancient music was revived, near the commencement of the present century, those who had been habituated to sing rapid music found it difficult to commit to memory slow choral tunes, and it was common to hear the saying, " How can we learn them? there is no tune to them."

ADVANTAGE OF COMMITTING TO MEMORY.

Whether singers are capable of giving as much expression to words, when obliged to read notes and apply words at the same time, or not, is a question for others to answer. But we have seen instances where it was, to say the least, very doubtful. A certain individual, a few years since, witnessed a scene in church as follows: A book of notes being placed before two singers, one stood directly in front of it; the other, of course, had to look sideways. They commenced a tune that was not very slow in utterance; soon the attention was attracted by a head, flying from right to left, like a shuttle, at every note. First, the eye glanced at the words, then at the notes, during the hymn; and we then thought

10*

that, amid this rapid vibration of the head, there could not have been much time to think or feel. Such is the constant changing of tunes, that a choir cannot be expected to commit to memory all the tunes sung in church; still, we cannot but think that when clergymen are scarcely allowed to look at a sermon of thirty or forty pages, it would seem that individual singers might, with some propriety, be expected to commit the few notes of a tune, or make it so familiar as not to be obliged to hold a note-book and a hymn-book in their hand; some wide open, some doubled back, and the eyes of every one (if the head is kept still) glancing from one book to the other. If, as a certain writer says, much of the expression of words and sentiment depends on the expression of the countenance, all this must be lost in such a case. It is true, all these appearances and customs are trifling to the singer, if the heart is right, but to the hearer and observer not so interesting.

MULTITUDE OF BOOKS AT THE PRESENT DAY. — INCONVENIENCES.

As schools increased, books increased also; and as books increased, so the disposition to sing a multitude of tunes. At the present day, the singers' gallery is flooded with books, and there are piles on piles, on the seats and under the seats, that have had their day, and are laid aside. But let us watch the movements of a choir. In each of the *piled-up* and *cast-away* books, there are some favorite tunes; and every now and then it happens, from the fancy of the chorister or the importunity of some of the choir, that nothing will do but that some particular tune, from a particular book, should be sung to some particular words; for the prejudice of some is so strong, that a favorite tune would not be acceptable, or sung in good humor, from any other than their favorite book. Let us look at a choir on some such occasion. They have just sung a hymn to a tune in the books at hand. Another hymn is read. The chorister, organist, or some influential singer, thinks of a tune in another book; just before the reading is closed, the tune is found by the chorister; and then the pulling, hauling, turning, and slapping of books, in selecting and passing them round, put in requisition two or three of the most dexterous hands ! Nearly all have been too anxious to hear the name of the book, page and tune, to hear the minister's directions. It would seem, in such cases, that the change of books was made for no other purpose than to make it appear as if there was such an exquisite taste for adaptation, that such a tune, and no other, would give any expression to the words; but we are slow to believe that there is not a sufficient variety in any one collection to answer for one half-day. But this is not all; before the tune is found and commenced, the patience of the congregation is exhausted; the minister is in doubt whether to wait longer, or go on with the other services. The choir, having a majority in readiness, commence; some having the tune, others trying to find it, fumbling their books and grumbling along, with the tune half sung, and words half spoken; and, when all are at last prepared, they move on with great power, the delinquents, one after another, beginning with unusual energy, — when, lo ! it is found that some are singing one verse, and some another, for the minister had directed a verse to be omitted. They look and almost sing daggers at each other; but it is of no use, — all is confusion till the verse ends; then, perhaps, they are prepared to sing together. It is easy to judge whether this is a necessary or a self-made perplexity.

SAME TUNES WILL NOT SUIT ALL.

It is as much impossible for all to be pleased with the same tune, as to find all men to look alike; and it would seem that those who took part in the solemn service of singing God's praise would not be very tenacious in regard to the particular *tune* used for the purpose. But it is not always so; oftentimes, when a tune has been named, individuals will give evidence, by their countenances or motions, that they were displeased. The book will be opened with violence, and they will rise with reluctance. It so happens that singers have extremely expressive countenances, and, when anything displeases, they have no need of speaking out, — their looks speak loud enough. Some of the choir will be so conscientious (to call it by no harder name), that they will not rise to sing, not thinking that if they had the privilege of proposing a tune which all disliked, they would be left alone, if others followed their example.

Restless spirits are to be found in almost every choir, who are always teasing to have some tune sung that the choir cannot sing; but because *they* have learned it, there is no peace till the attempt is made. We had rather hear Old Hundred twice on a Sabbath, than to hear a choir stumble through and half sing a tune, be that tune ever so good when well sung.

DEMEANOR OF SINGERS IN CHURCH.

We cannot explain the reason, but we presume the fact is known and read by all men, that the conduct of choirs of singers, both in city and country, was formerly unworthy the place they occupied. Themselves being judges, it has been such, to say the least, as they would condemn in those who occupied the lowest seat in a congregation, and would be regarded as scandalous if seen among the higher class of hearers. They have ever seemed to conduct as though they considered themselves privileged above others, and not subject to common rules of propriety, but designated merely to sing the hymns, and that then their duty was done. We will make all due allowance for the necessity that sometimes happens, in communicating the tune, page, hymn, and giving and receiving other necessary directions, when about to commence singing; and, if the privilege would stop here, we could pass over and forgive it; but the tongue once at liberty, does not so easily stop. And it is often said, that the curtains were not so much wanted to conceal the person from the gaze of the congregation, as to hide unwarrantable levity during the services. We should regret that any one, a stranger to our modes of worship, should have a glance behind them, and see the billets circulated, the poetry, pictures and drawings of every description, executed on the blank leaves of the hymn and note books. Let any one examine the books of almost any choir, and he would be led to conclude that there were poets, limners, and artists of every grade and kind, among the singers.

FAULT SOMETIMES IN THE LEADER.

This manner of spending time, and amusing one another, may very often be attributed to the chorister, or leader. He, perhaps, sets the example and leads the way, by being continually engaged, during divine service, in giving directions, tumbling over the books to select tunes, and then humming, whistling, or breathing them over. He being leader, what he does all may do; and when all are busily engaged in their several time-killing occupations, no one will dispute the propriety of their being in a secluded situation.

This picture and management is fitted especially for the meridian of New England, as we have said before; but we may say, without much fear of contradiction, that it will apply, at some period, to every choir in the hemisphere.

IRREVERENCE OF CHOIRS.

"The result of my observations," says a minister of the gospel, "is, that there is a great lack of devotion (not to say of common good breeding) in the choirs of all our denominations. Especially is this manifested by smiling and whispering, and looking over tune-books, in the time of sermon. I once, in a strange church, had before me a leader, who formerly took up his tune-book as soon as I had named the text, and began poring over it. Seeing some little boys of the Sunday-school similarly engaged, I took occasion mildly to reprove them, and noticed that the offender in the gallery took the hint, and mended his manners. A thousand times would I prefer the *precentor*, as I have seen him in the Presbyterian churches in the South, in the front of the pulpit, rise and lead the congregation, to the best-trained, most exact, scientific, undevout choir in the land."

"Many years ago," says a writer in a New York paper, "I boarded, when very young, with a family in the South, the head of which was the organist in the church. Not being attached to any church or form, I sometimes attended divine service with him, and, for convenience, sat in the organ-loft. As I do not mention names or places, it is no breach of confidence to reveal the secrets with which

I became acquainted, as connected with the choir. The loft was railed in, and furnished with substantial, thick, crimson curtains, which, when drawn, were sufficient to exclude vulgar eyes from the hallowed interior.

"It was customary, when the excellent ritual of devotion was gone through, and the rector had named his text, for the singers to draw the curtain around them, and read or sleep, as it suited them best. In very warm weather they also took care to be supplied with *refreshments ;* and thus the tedious half-hour allotted to the sermon was pretty easily consumed, without much weariness. I recollect that one very warm Sabbath afternoon the singers had *water-melons* and *lemonade*, wherewith to console themselves ; and it happened that one of the gentlemen, in handing a slice to a lady singer, overset the pitcher of lemonade. This might not have been of much consequence, had the *floor* of the organ-loft been liquor tight. But there were many chinks in it, and the lemonade trickled through pretty freely down into the broad aisle, to the discomfiture of the rector, and such of his congregation as were wakeful enough to notice passing events."

In conclusion, we will venture to mention one or two extreme cases of impropriety, where most of the singers in a choir were hired servants, of course not numerous. The gentlemen, after the second singing, were known to retire stealthily from the gallery at the commencement of the sermon, for the purpose of spending their time more at ease in a neighboring refectory, and return in season to perform the last tune with additional spirit, but sometimes too late. We once knew an organist so out of tune and balance as to fall from his seat backward among the singers ; the consequence may be easily conceived, but would not look very becoming on paper.

These strange scenes and inconsistencies we hope, and have reason to believe, have passed away, and are among the things that were.

CHAPTER VIII.

PROGRESS OF MUSICAL INSTRUCTION.

Change of Music, and Discussions. — Predominance of Old School. — Struggle for Possession of the Seats. — Reformation in Teaching and Music. — Attempt to Harmonize correctly. — The Public Interested. — Change of Books. — Tenor Voices put in Place. — Example in a School. — Lectures. — Children taught. — Objections of Parents. — First Juvenile Schools. — Saying of Horace Walpole. — New Methods of Teaching, and New Music for Children. — Probable Defects in Instruction. — Exhibitions of Children's Singing. — Excitement abated. — Means for Instruction still limited. — Step towards Congregational Singing.

CHANGE OF MUSIC, AND DISCUSSIONS.

Soon after the commencement of the present century, when more just ideas of sacred music began to be entertained, and a few publications containing ancient music had been introduced to the public, the subject was canvassed at social meetings; animosities as bitter as in any political combat arose between the fugueing and Old Hundred singers, as they were called.

OLD HUNDRED SECEDERS.

The latter, who had seceded from the music that had prevailed for forty years, moved on calmly but decidedly; formed societies; sung in public; had addresses from some of the worthiest of men in the community, setting forth the propriety and necessity of a change in the character of music in the churches. Although every attempt was made by their opponents to thwart the doings of the reformers, still they persevered, and the effect and influence of their doings spread from town to town, till all New England was more or less affected. It was, emphatically, "Old School" and "New School." And, in numerous towns, schools of each denomination were raised and put in operation, side by side. All this excitement, however unpleasant, tended to awaken an interest, and produce examination and practice in music; so that whatever the cause might have been that moved to action, the public were advancing in the art, and the cause was promoted.

OLD SCHOOL PREVAILED.

The result was, that in proportion to the amount of experience the more were there accessions to the ranks of the old school; so that in three or four years from the commencement of the reform, we could seldom hear of a congregation where the former popular music prevailed.

STRUGGLE FOR POSSESSION OF SEATS.

When schools of different character had been taught in the same town or parish, and had closed, then came the struggle for a place in the church. Sometimes the right was determined by numbers; sometimes neither party had strength and talent enough to proceed separately; then a compromise would, perhaps, take place; but they could no more mix than water and oil, and one or the other party must by and by prevail and control. The consequence was, that in most instances the music-books of the dark age were laid on the shelf, and the dust on them was seldom afterwards disturbed.

REFORMATION IN TEACHING AND MUSIC.

The method of teaching continued much the same for many years, except that a natural progress resulted from experience in communicating instruction more fully in the theory of music; and every new publication attempted to improve their introductory lessons. About the year 1822, was the first appearance of " Templi Carmina," with the rudiments of music in the form of questions and answers, which was substantially what we had before published, in a pamphlet, for our own convenience in schools.

ATTEMPT TO HARMONIZE CORRECTLY.

The harmony of the tunes, where gross errors appeared, was cautiously corrected ; but still, those who did not know the difference, doubted the expediency of it, and even the competency of those who ventured to make any change.

The common saying that had prevailed, that "Americans did not, and could not, know anything of the science of music," had been so long sounded in the ear, that all were slow to believe that others knew better than themselves, and, therefore, could know little or nothing.

PUBLIC INTERESTED.

Singing-schools now assumed somewhat of a different character. The object and solemnity of church music began to be seriously contemplated. Ministers and officers of the church began to express their views and feelings on the subject. And the public generally began to be interested in the cause. As evidence of this, we could occasionally hear that an article was inserted in the warrant for town-meeting, to see if the *town* would raise money, some fifty to seventy-five dollars, for the encouragement and support of the music in the church. This was something new, and caused much altercation in towns and parishes, when first proposed. As might be expected, it was sometimes granted and sometimes refused.

CHANGE OF BOOKS.

It was a long time, however, before the habits and customs of schools could be materially changed. In addition to the books that we have mentioned, as being collected and published under the patronage of societies, there were many others, containing a variety of music designed to suit the tastes of all, with a sufficient number of tunes of different character for all practical purposes, such as "Bridgewater Collection," "Worcester Collection," "Village Harmony," with the arrangements of the parts much improved.

11

TENOR VOICES PUT IN PLACE.

One of the first steps that agitated the singing community, was that of giving the air or leading part of the tune, usually called *Treble*, or rather ihe *tune*, to the females; this was an interference with the rights of man, not readily acceded to, especially by those who had tenor voices and had always sung the air. They, of course, claimed it by possession. And, as in all other innovations, the question was asked with petulance, " What better is it? We have always sung the part, and the singing has been pronounced good by all." And the general want of information in regard to harmony rendered it difficult for any one to give reasons, so as to be understood, even if an explanation was desired; and if made to be understood, it was still more difficult to reconcile persons to the practice. No teacher had previously enforced the rule and practice in schools but Andrew Law. This change commenced, practically, about a quarter of a century ago. For several years previously it had been agitated, and partially put in operation, but it was several years after, before it was fully adopted; and is not yet practised in many places in the country. Some individuals who had always sung the air, either could not or would not sing any other part. They did not, perhaps, go so far as some of our forefathers, who would debar females from singing in public altogether, regarding it as one manner of speaking; still, they were but little less consistent, for many claimed the part as their right, being men, to lead; and wrong for women to sing the governing part. But it is futile to take this ground; for the voice of woman is so constituted, that whatever part she sings will be heard, call it leading or what you please. In this one respect, if in no other, men must be led by women. At the time, there was much written on the subject; and we have seen a long and labored treatise to prove it to be wrong, on many accounts, to suffer the part to be sung by females, on the ground that it was contrary to Scripture, and of course a sin, for females to take the lead in singing, or any other religious service.

EXAMPLE IN A SCHOOL.

About this time, we were teaching in the vicinity of Boston; had a numerous school, and many good singers; but nothing could induce some of the gentlemen to relinquish the air or soprano. Some of the ladies chose to sing the tenor, as they had heretofore done. At length, a public exhibition came off. The editor of a musical publication was present. In his next number he praised the performance generally, but gave a severe and well-deserved censure for this single but obvious impropriety. We not only bore it patiently, but gladly; for it proved, as we hoped, a timely help to accomplish, by *publicly* exposing the error, what we and others had been trying to accomplish, for months and years, in private schools. This was a decisive blow. Singers, afterwards, generally kept their voices to their appropriate parts, in this region, but not through the country. We would not say that it is unnecessary for gentlemen to learn the air; for, in the absence of females, that part must be sustained by them, in order to make singing acceptable; for a tune is as unmeaning without the air as a sentence without a verb.

LECTURES INTRODUCED.

Among other means of influencing public sentiment, lectures on sacred music were given, in New York and Boston, by men well qualified to present the subject in all its bearings, both as it regarded the manner of performance, the duty of learning to sing, and the obligation of congregations, churches, and ministers to encourage and sustain this part of public worship. It would seem as if church music were as proper a subject for the minister to present in the pulpit as that of prayer; but no; — heretofore he could not, without giving offence, even approach the subject, especially if he spoke of it as a duty, and at the risk of being accused of selfish motives. But laymen — of whom we will mention Mason and Hastings, known through the country — could enforce the duty and obligation of all who had the talent to improve, and, although accused of selfishness, could recommend proper music for the church, and prescribe the manner of performing it. Organs were recommended, as a substitute for the multitude of stringed and wind instruments which had found their way into the church.

CHILDREN TAUGHT.

Reason had long taught those interested in sacred music the necessity of cultivating the voices of children, as a part of education, before music could approach the position it deserved in communities and churches. The work of persuasion was soon commenced — hesitatingly heard, indeed, by parents who had children that could readily learn; consequently schools at first were not numerously attended. We had supposed that we had the pleasure of teaching, in the year 1824, the first regular class ever collected, for that purpose, in this country; but we have since learned that a number of families from Germany, who located in Pennsylvania, some fifty years ago, brought with them teachers to instruct their children; and, as was customary in their native country, had their children taught music systematically, as a part of juvenile education.

OBJECTIONS OF PARENTS.

It was with the greatest difficulty that parents could be persuaded that it was expedient and possible for their children to learn to sing. It was a new idea, and no one wished to commence the experiment. The general impression and language was, that for children to sing while young would injure their voices, their health, and take their attention from other studies; and although to learn to sing was well enough, still it was of secondary consequence. It might be done if perfectly convenient; if not, just as well to omit it. Although it could be made evident that the employment was a pleasant one, useful through life, and a source of comfort when many other branches of education would cease to be useful, or even noticed; yet, after all the persuasion in our power, we could not succeed in obtaining a class until we resorted to the expedient of teaching the art of writing in connection with music; writing and singing alternately half an hour, for two hours.

FIRST JUVENILE SCHOOLS.

In this way, for the sake of the writing, we collected schools of about twenty-five each, in Boston, Charlestown, and Cambridge; and our patrons were so well satisfied with the experiment, that after one term there was no difficulty in collecting scholars to attend to singing alone. Of juvenile singing-schools generally, we shall have occasion to speak hereafter. It was a well-known fact, in all places, notwithstanding the fears expressed by parents that it would injure voice and health, that the best voices and the best singers were those who belonged to musical families, who were accustomed to sing from childhood upward; and those who feared injuring the lungs did not or do not consider how any part of the system is strengthened by constant use; and we presume the same parents never troubled themselves about the crying and screaming of their children, through fear of injury to their lungs. Much less should they fear the gentle exercise of the voice to make melodious sounds. Besides, the child that loves to sing will be singing something, in some way, whether taught or not. How necessary, then, that they learn to sing understandingly! As to its diverting the mind from other studies, experience has proved the contrary. Teachers of common schools where singing is made a part of the exercises have universally acknowledged that the best singers were usually the best scholars in other studies.

SAYING OF HORACE WALPOLE.

Horace Walpole says, "*Teach your children music.* You will stare at a strange notion of mine; if it appears even a mad one, do not wonder. Had I children, my utmost endeavors would be to breed them musicians. As I have no ear, nor ever thought of music, the preference seems odd; and yet it is embraced on mature reflection. It is the most probable method to make them happy. It is a resource that will last them through life. It is capable of fame, without the danger of criticism; is susceptible of enthusiasm, without being priest-ridden; and, unlike other mortal passions, is sure of being gratified in heaven."

11*

NEW METHODS OF TEACHING, AND NEW MUSIC FOR CHILDREN.

After the schools for teaching children had become numerous, it was found absolutely necessary that some more simple and inductive system of teaching should be devised, and a different kind of music made use of for juvenile minds and voices. In our first attempt to teach juvenile schools, our attention was directed to devise some means of facilitating and simplifying the mode of teaching musical notes and characters. Our first experiment was, for all those who could use a pencil to have a slate with the five lines drawn upon it, and from the black-board each copied given lessons. This method was found of great utility, not only in teaching the lessons, but at the same time taught them to write music. In a few years after, by the persevering energy of some one or two, engaged in the cause, the Pestalozzian system of instruction, applied to music, was procured and introduced. Juvenile music was obtained from Germany, and words were translated, and taught by competent teachers. A new impulse was thus given to the teaching of music generally, and everything that pertains to music has since been rapidly advancing. This new system, notwithstanding its simplicity, needed skill, judgment and experience, to administer it. A teacher of any art or science must be so familiar with the subject as not to be confined to any written rules ; and must have ingenuity to state principles in a new form, when not clearly understood as written. This being introduced, the black-board became a necessary appendage to schools. Soon the experiment was tried in the public schools of Boston, with much success, and has been continued till this time. Other cities and towns followed the example. Much of the teaching may have been superficial, if not imperfect ; for such was the anxiety to follow the example of those who commenced the work, that many began teaching others before they were properly taught themselves. Notwithstanding this, voices have been exercised, and prepared the more readily to improve, when an opportunity presented for more thorough training.

DEFECTS IN INSTRUCTION.

The universal excitement for learning to sing, like all other new movements in this country, had undoubtedly some evils and mistakes attending it; we conceive, however, that less evil has arisen from superficial instruction in the rudiments than from want of care in forming the voice, and more especially from the false intonation given by untutored teachers for imitation. As has been already remarked, it is not every one that *sings tunes* who sings *in tune*. Almost everything we learn is by imitation; and when children at the infant school are taught to sing tunes by one who sings incorrectly, or out of tune, they will be sure to imitate all the wrong, and it is with great difficulty that their voices or ears are corrected; for, as in everything else, so it is emphatically with the voice, — much easier to learn than unlearn; yes, easier to learn a whole tune than to unlearn one note of a tune. And we cannot see why it is not just as necessary that those who undertake to teach children, be the scholars ever so young, should not be examined and approbated by those competent to judge, as that teachers in any other branch of education should be examined; for those who have treacherous voices are never conscious of it themselves.

EXHIBITIONS OF CHILDREN'S SINGING.

With the teaching of children came exhibitions and juvenile concerts in abundance. The effect of these on the public mind was favorable, satisfying every one of the possibility and utility of children learning to sing. It was then to children an amusement; all were interested; all mixed together, rich and poor, without distinction; but, as in all other schools, some children excelled, and were praised, whose parents were not, perhaps, reckoned among the rich in gold; this was annoying to some who stood high in the scale of society in their own opinion, and they soon became indifferent, if not envious; and their indifference and observations led others to sympathize.

EXCITEMENT ABATED.

For this and other causes, it is to be feared children, as well as the community generally, at this time, have far less interest in the subject than was manifest twelve years ago; and this may be accounted for more particularly from the fact, that young as well as old are so constituted, that on any subject or employment, be it ever so important, if a sense of duty or interest does not govern, they soon seek for change — grow restless. In fact, *change* is the order of the day. New scenes are continually presenting themselves, and parents, being willing to gratify the wishes of children, have allowed their attention to be directed to other subjects; and if their eyes and ears are enchanted by the sound of the viol, or anything of that character, no wonder if the love for the simple sounds and strains made by the voice should seem to them insipid. But the same spirit that prevailed at the commencement of juvenile schools has been spreading far and wide, till it has pervaded a great portion of the country. One thing is certain, that the labor of teaching and learning singing will not be lost, for the day will soon come when all will realize the importance of singing God's praise. One thing, rather mysterious, and to be lamented, is, that, notwithstanding all the expense and labor of teaching in common schools, the singing generally in Sabbath-schools has depreciated.

MEANS FOR INSTRUCTION STILL LIMITED.

After all the exertions, public and private, for the promotion of schools and teaching, in this country, means for instructing adults are very limited. One quarter, or twenty-four evenings, in a country town or parish, is as much as can usually be maintained. This short space must seem very trifling to those in cities, where they meet for practice once or twice every week through the year, and year after year. But where families live separated in the country, and have not the advantage (if it can be so called) of *hearing* others sing, or learning by rote, scholars, after their limited instruction, if they learn to read music, are obliged to sit down and study out the names, and by experiment learn the sounds and distances of notes, and in this way learn to read music independently ; so that it is not strange to find some of the best readers of music among those who are principally self-taught.

STEP TOWARDS CONGREGATIONAL SINGING.

We are thankful that we have lived to see the principle of teaching the young carried forward in some good measure, and a conviction of its importance spreading till it has pervaded a great portion of our country, and led to the general introduction of music in public and private schools.   Indeed, the old notion, that children could not be taught to sing, has been so completely reversed, that, on the introduction of infant schools, singing was made the leading exercise.

CHAPTER IX.

SCHOOLS SINCE 1800.

Schools. — A Praying Teacher. — Effects of Revivals of Religion on Singing. —
  Progress of Instruction. — Boston Academy of Music. — Old Teachers. —
  Consequence of Want of Time for thorough Teaching. — The Black-board in
  Adult Schools. — Good Results of the Academy. — Declension, and Causes. —
  Instruments with Singing. — What was urged in Lectures on Music. — Lead-
  ers preceding Singers. — Schools without Instruments.

SCHOOLS.

BEFORE the commencement of the present century, and several years afterwards, we have said that one who might happen to witness the management and conduct of teachers and schools would never suspect that the object of learning to sing was to perform a prominent part of worship in the house of God. It would have been almost as unexpected to have heard the voice of prayer in a school for learning sacred music as in the ball-room.

A PRAYING TEACHER.

We well remember, when a boy, about 1795, that a singing-school was talked of, to be kept by a young man, who, although belonging in town, had been several years absent, learning a trade, and, having become pious, was now preparing for the ministry. A report ran through the town that in the pious family where he boarded he sometimes prayed. This was a startling fact, at that time, and rather disrelished by those who thought of attending the proposed singing-school. We ventured, however, to attend this, the first and last we ever attended as a pupil ; and to this day we revere the man,* who still lives, and preaches occasionally; and his long-continued ministry in one place is an evidence of his worth. Perhaps it will be said we must have lived in a dark and benighted spot. Dark enough, to be sure, but among the most highly favored of the day, in regard to religious privileges.

EFFECTS OF REVIVALS OF RELIGION ON SINGING.

Nor can any close observer have failed to notice a direct relation, both in the individual and the general mind, between the standard of piety and the interest in sacred music. The awakening of the public mind to the subject of music, twenty-five years ago, was nearly coincident with extensive revivals of religion.

We have before observed that the language of the awakened sinner is, *Pray* for us; and when brought to rejoice in pardoning mercy, he spontaneously *sings*, and calls on his friends to *sing* with him; and when there has been more than an usual attention to religion, singing has been observed to assume a corresponding import in the minds of a community. It is also true that those who have been accustomed to sing in the choir, however thoughtlessly they may have applied sacred words to music, are usually among the first fruits of a revival. We have taken much pains to ascertain the proportion who become pious of those who have taken a part in the performance of music in the church; and although it cannot be ascertained precisely, yet, from what we have learned, we venture to say, unhesitatingly, that there are three of the singers, to one of the rest of the people attending public worship with them, who are hopefully converted. Were there no other inducement than this, it would seem to be a sufficient reason for parents to spare no pains to have their children learn to sing sacred music. We do not pretend to say that there is any religion in singing a tune, neither is there in the words of a prayer; but both are enjoined duties, and direct acts of homage to God, and both have a like tendency to prepare the heart for the reception of truth.

* Reuben Emerson, of Reading, Mass.

PROGRESS OF INSTRUCTION. — PESTALOZZIAN SYSTEM.

We have spoken of the black-board as an indispensable accompaniment to carry on the inductive mode of instruction. This new system, with its attendant benefits to teacher and scholar, kept alive the interest that was awakened. Those who wished to qualify themselves for teaching found new and important facilities presented, and necessary to be understood, in order to keep pace with the times.

BOSTON ACADEMY OF MUSIC.

To give an opportunity for all that desired to prepare themselves for the work, the great school of schools was established in Boston, called the " Boston Academy of Music." Here were professors and teachers well qualified to give all necessary instruction, both in the theory and practice of music, on this new system. A good degree of interest was manifested, and a respectable number attended its first meeting in 1833.

OLD TEACHERS.

Old teachers, many of them, came forward, much like old singers into a new school, rather doubting whether there was anything for them to learn; but they had a curiosity to hear this new doctrine and mode of teaching, and therefore they edged in, rather in the attitude of hearers than laborers or learners. Every one knows, who has had much experience as a teacher in any branch of education, what a long stride downward it is from the teacher to the pupil; and many have too much pride to take such a step, and therefore live and die unimproved. But, with a few exceptions, after it was found that public opinion was in favor of the Academy, but more especially to secure employment as teachers, persons attended the annual meetings year after year, that they might know, or, at least, pretend to know, something of the system of these professors.

CONSEQUENCE OF WANT OF TIME FOR THOROUGH TEACHING.

Although the time assigned by this institution for instruction was of too short a duration to acquire anything like a thorough knowledge of the principles and practice of music, and was so represented by the professors, and but few pursued their investigations any further than while in a body or class together; and as instruction, where there is such a multitude together, must be general, many, who came with bad habits in regard to the voice or manner of singing, not only went away with those habits still clinging to them, but, what was worse than all, they were, in their own opinion, soon out of the reach of admonition or correction, not having learned enough to know that they did *not* know. A reference to the authority of the Boston Academy, where, in their own opinion, they had been educated, silenced all opposition. Their practical application and teaching bore no resemblance to the instruction they had received; and every new idea they had heard suggested, when put in practice by them, would either be tortured or over-done. For instance, when the professors inculcated the importance of correct articulation, and would give exaggerated examples, in order to present their meaning in strong colors, the scholars would catch the idea, as represented, and, without skill or judgment to give proper examples to others, ran into still greater extremes, and made their own performance and that of their schools or choirs, in many instances, perfectly ridiculous. *Their* instruction at the Academy was to speak the words distinctly, by sounding the vowels, and closing the note short and distinct on the consonant; but, with a pretence of following the instructions of the Academy, the result was, that their manner of singing was such that, if written as sung, the notes would have to be written thus:

DUKE STREET.

Lord, when thou didst as-cend on high

12

THE BLACK-BOARD IN ADULT SCHOOLS.

With the inductive system went the black-board, as a necessary and indispensable appendage. It was truly a great acquisition and convenience in teaching the rudiments of music; but, simple as its use might seem to be, still, in the hands of a teacher half taught, and with little experience, and less judgment, it was made a time-destroyer. The whole attention was directed to the board, as though there was some hidden virtue in the board and chalk, to the neglect of directing the eye, at the same time, to the same lessons, on a smaller scale, in the book; so that when the book was used, pupils hardly knew the same characters there, neither could they calculate the distances of notes. However useful and indispensable written, or printed, or painted rules, may be, no man can be called a good teacher who is confined to them. He must have made himself so familiar with the subject that he can instantly see and communicate, so as to meet the peculiar difficulties and inquiries of every scholar. A mechanical teacher will be sure to make a lifeless school.

GOOD RESULTS OF THE ACADEMY.

The Boston Academy has been the means of doing much good, not only as it regards the progress of music generally, but in giving character to schools, church music, and teachers. Ministers and people have been led, by its efforts, to turn their attention to this important part of public worship; and the whole community, from the infant school to the college, has moved onward in this important work.

DECLENSION AND CAUSES.

It is evident, however, that within a few years there has been a reäction. Existing causes, although not exactly of the same nature, have had the same effects as those we have mentioned about the time of the American Revolution. Nothing is more obvious than that sacred music cannot prosper in company with any unusual worldly excitement. The Mexican War, political strife, worldly prosperity, California gold, ask for no sacred music to aid them. Tunes to create political excitement, like those of Billings, which were once used for that purpose, would not now answer the wants and feelings of a political campaign. In these days, music and words " light as air " can be used successfully for the same purpose.

Singing-schools, either juvenile or adult, it is true, do not prevail to that extent and with that interest they have in former years. Still the cause is generally advancing. Teachers of music have made themselves more thoroughly acquainted with the best methods of instructing. The inability of many who have formerly attempted to instruct has been discovered and discarded. Most of the modern books, in addition to original music, contain introductory lessons, for exercising the voice, to supersede the necessity of the incessant use and labor of the black-board; and by that means scholars are made familiar with the *form*, *size* and *place*, of notes on the staff, such as they have to use in singing afterwards.

INSTRUMENTS WITH SINGING.

We are aware that we are handling a delicate subject when we speak of instruments, and we hardly dare to introduce them in connection with church music, and should certainly avoid it, did not necessity compel us, by their coming in contact with each other, to take a passing notice. Of instruments and performance on them we plead incompetency of judging, before being accused. Let it be distinctly understood, however, that we do not disapprove of instruments in schools or elsewhere; — we speak only of their use when voices and instruments do not move exactly together.

WHAT WAS URGED IN LECTURES.

In the lectures on church music which we have heretofore noticed, it was urged, very properly, as was supposed, that in schools and choirs it was indispensable that voices should be prominent, and instruments be subservient to them, — accompanying, not leading, them. Let any one, who has not been initiated by degrees to hear singers with the piano, organ, and other instruments, following them with the voice, listen impartially, and ascertain whether these things are not so. We speak with the more confidence, because we have been frequently asked by strangers, of acknowledged musical cultivation, what it meant when they have heard the words or voices following in the track of the instruments. We are aware that the answer of singers, if asked why it was so, would be that the players on the instruments would not suffer them to keep with them.

LEADERS PRECEDING SINGERS.

In former days, teachers of schools that could play the violin,— sometimes they used it to *assist* the voice, and sometimes in the *place* of one. Even this simple instrument, as a constant accompaniment, was objected to by many, as detrimental to that self-reliance necessary to make a good singer. Then, again, some, who used no instrument, had the habit, in school and church, — which, we believe, is not wholly extinct at the present day, — of rushing on in advance of the body of the singers, as if they must literally precede in time and space; seeming to say, as they commenced every word, and more emphatically the first word to every line, " Come on ; overtake me, if you can ! "

The appropriate duty of a leader, in any capacity, does not consist in accomplishing more, physically, than many of his subordinates; but he is to be leader in the sense of deciding how and when to act, on his own responsibility.

SCHOOLS WITHOUT INSTRUMENTS.

From observation, we are led to believe the fact, that schools and choirs, who have usually, from choice or necessity, practised singing without the aid of any prominent instrument, are more prompt and simultaneous in their performance, and their accent is less mechanical, than is found in those who have been constantly led by some powerful instrument. We have sometimes been led to believe that the doctrine of instruments being designed to sustain voices had become extinct. It is certainly convenient for learners of anything to have some leading string, to save them the trouble of exertion, or close application. It seems, however, that some individuals or associations have become so dependent that they may be compared to the child who can walk by touching another's finger ever so lightly; but, take the finger away, and it falls. So with these singers; — take away instruments, and they fall. We do not pretend to say that what we have been describing is universal, or even general, in schools or associations; only that what we have said is even so in some, if not many instances.

12*

CHAPTER X.

MUSIC AND TEACHING IN THE WEST.

Influence of Emigrants from New England. — Pestalozzian System introduced by T. B. Mason, in 1834, in Cincinnati. — State of Music in that city. — Kind of Notes used. — Change of Notes effected by Mr. Mason. — Mr. Mason's Juvenile and Adult Schools, and first Instruments introduced in Church. — Mr. M. Professor of Eclectic Academy. — William Colburn and Juvenile Schools. — Mr. Lincoln at Pittsburg. — Mr. Bingham at Cleveland and Pittsburg. — Locke, Nourse and Aikin, at Cincinnati. — Teachers all from Massachusetts or New Hampshire. — Music in Churches.

From our silence hitherto of the "Far West," as it is sometimes called, our readers may be led to suppose that music had never found its way across mountains and lakes, to that region of our country. Not so; we have crossed both, and our eyes and ears testify to the contrary.

Cincinnati, sometimes called the Queen City, seems to stand in the same musical relation to the western country as Boston does to the eastern, — that is, the musical and other educational institutions of the respective regions centre in those cities.

INFLUENCE OF PEOPLE FROM NEW ENGLAND.

The multitude of eastern people, particularly New Englanders, that have established themselves in the Western States, especially in Cincinnati, enables them to introduce the customs and institutions of their eastern homes. The spirit of enterprise and imitation that pervades all the Western States, especially the State of Ohio, and the concentration of the men in active life in the "Queen City," give visiters an opportunity to become acquainted with every step of improvement, and carry everything of importance to their homes, to investigate it and carry it into execution as soon as may be. It cannot be expected, however, in sparse settlements, and even villages and cities where, in some instances, the inhabitants are composed of different nations and languages, that accomplishments of any sort will prevail immediately. They have to struggle hard, as the first settlers of New England did, to give their children an opportunity even to learn to read and write. In the principal towns and cities, however, the seeds of music have been sown by skilful hands, in a good soil, — well rooted and grounded, — and have sprung up, and the branches spread far and wide.

We have said that Mr. L. Mason introduced the Pestalozzian System of teaching music in Boston. We will now introduce his brother, T. B. Mason, located in Cincinnati in 1833 or 1834.

STATE OF MUSIC IN THAT CITY.

The reader can form some opinion of the state of music in that city at that time, when he is told that no instrument, unless it were the "tuning-fork," had been suffered to sound within a church, and that had to be used *slyly*, as Billings said concerning giving the pitch at his concerts. Imagine, then, what must have been the feelings of the elder Dr. Beecher, who had recently been transferred to the second Presbyterian church in that city, from Bowdoin-street church in Boston, where L. Mason presided at one of the best organs in the country, assisted by the best-trained, and, perhaps, the most effective choir in America at that time. In addition to this, the doctor was a great lover of music, besides considering it an essential aid in the promotion of religion.

CRY OF DR. BEECHER.

He could not endure that this part of worship should be thus neglected and marred. He soon sent to his friends in Boston, saying, "Come over the mountains and help us ;" or (to use the language of Billings) our "nerves will be rent asunder" with discordant, unmeaning singing in church.

The voice was heard and heeded ; and Mr. T. B. Mason, brother of the professor, was selected as the man to supply the place. He was received with joy by those who knew how to appreciate good music ; and he soon commenced his labors, assisted by the influence and action of many of the principal characters of the city.

KIND OF NOTES USED.

There were no books in common use in the city, and probably nowhere west of the mountains, but those printed with buckwheat notes. A collection of church music had been prepared for publication by the Messrs. Mason. But what was to be done ? To force the whole community at once to adopt new notes, was injudicious, if not impracticable. The publisher refused to use the round notes, knowing the sale would then be limited. Therefore, for the time being, the editors had to submit to the mortification of having their music published in a style to accommodate the mass, with the expectation and determination of soon convincing the singing community of their error, by showing them a better way. The book was called the "Sacred Harp." Mr. Mason had other books enough to commence teaching, and his introductory lessons soon convinced every one who attempted to learn of the impropriety of using such characters.

CHANGE OF NOTES EFFECTED BY MR. MASON.

The book of diamond notes *was* published; and such was the interest excited by Mr. Mason's introductory lessons and lectures on the subject of music, in the city and the country around, that *seventy-five thousand* copies were sold the first year. But, to show the change effected in public opinion, we will state that the *cornered* notes were soon rounded, and within two years eighty-five thousand copies were sold in that type, and the former edition, or manner of printing it, abandoned. Still, however, we have reason to believe that *buckwheat* notes are not all eaten up, but are to this time preserved and used in many places in the great west.

HIS JUVENILE AND ADULT SCHOOLS.

Mr. Mason continued his labors for many years, having as many schools, juvenile and adult, as he could attend to. Having the charge of the singing at the second Presbyterian church, he soon introduced, by degrees, instruments of various kinds; but, as it used to be in New England, some of the good people pretended to be grieved; the sounds were new, and disturbed their devotion, as they thought; and when the double bass made its majestic appearance, and some of the strings happened to sound out, while snapping to tune them, it was too much. Some of the good old worshippers turned their backs on the preacher, and left for home; but, being sensible men, they were soon convinced, by reasoning, that the instrument was not to blame for the noise, and that there was not, in reality, anything wicked in it.

MR. MASON PROFESSOR OF ECLECTIC ACADEMY.

A musical association, somewhat similar to the Boston Academy, called the "Eclectic Academy," was established in Cincinnati, by the most influential men in the city, with Judge Burnett for president. Mr. T. B. Mason was chosen professor. Many, both old and young, were taught under the patronage of this society; and its influence has been spreading like leaven through the western country, and many teachers and choristers received their instruction at this institution.

WILLIAM COLBURN.

After Mr. Mason had retired, in a great measure, from the labors of teaching, William Colburn, one of the earliest juvenile singers in Boston, who had previously been teaching in Louisville, Kentucky, established himself as a teacher of music in Cincinnati. Mr. Colburn soon suggested to the school committee the propriety of singing being taught in the public schools; but none could be found to favor his plan, especially if it was to be attended with any expense to the public. He then, for the purpose of testing the fact of the proficiency that might be made by children, offered to teach the scholars in two schools, gratis, for one year. His services were gladly accepted, and two more were urged upon him at the same time, all of which he attended; and in the course of the year, and more especially at the close, he had public exhibitions of his pupils; and their performance was such as to astonish and delight all who heard. The evidence was so strong in favor of the utility and practicability of juvenile instruction, that he was employed the next year to teach many of the schools, and a salary paid him. He also taught in the principal seminaries in the city. In a few years he engaged in other business, and others were employed in his stead.

LOCKE, NOURSE AND AIKIN, AT CINCINNATI.

Mr. Locke and Mr. Nourse were first engaged, and soon after Mr. Aikin, so that every public school in the city was supplied with a teacher of music twice a week, and has so continued to the present time. Perhaps some one will ask, — and with what success? We can answer, or rather *give* an *opinion*, from personal hearing, — for their schools there, and comparatively with schools in other cities, — having been familiar with the singing in the schools of Boston and Providence. We have never anywhere heard scholars sing in schools, where there was greater evidence of thorough training in the first principles of music, of attention, and ambition on the part of the scholars, than in Cincinnati, having visited the schools several winters, and taken them unawares, when there was no chance for display. But their greatest excellence consisted in their exactness and promptness in the time. There were no instruments for them to catch the sound from, or to lean upon; but the moment the pitch and time of a tune were given, it was carried through by the scholars, without the aid of even the voice of the teacher.

Mr. LINCOLN, about 1840, commenced teaching children in the city of Pittsburg. He found music in a low state, and prejudice, indifference and ignorance, in regard to the subject of music, hard to contend with at first; but the people, being active and ambitious, soon came forward and patronized the teaching of schools, and juvenile schools were introduced among them, that will be favorably remembered by all concerned, and good and great results to the cause will be known and felt hereafter.

Mr. BINGHAM has now taken the place of Mr. Lincoln, a gentleman who had been teaching for several years with good success in Cleveland, Ohio.

TEACHERS ALL FROM MASS. AND N. HAMPSHIRE.

The foregoing teachers, mentioned as having introduced and carried on the work of reformation in the West, were all natives either of Massachusetts or New Hampshire.

MUSIC IN THE CHURCHES.

As to the music in the churches, we cannot say so much. In some we may hear and see a man under the pulpit who "strikes up the tune," generally with a noble voice, and all follow on, the best way they can; not every voice would be considered quite in tune or in time to a critical ear. Some use the real Scotch versions of psalms, as they were printed and sanctioned centuries ago. In others, a man rises in his pew and sings on, and all join him; and, in some instances, it was really devotional. Some churches have very good choirs; others have merely quartet choirs, and seem to consider four individuals amply sufficient to sing for the whole congregation. In some instances, a great proportion of the congregation seem to join their voices in some familiar tune. But if any one visits Cincinnati, and wishes to hear heart and soul stirring singing, let him go to some German Lutheran church, where, after the tune and some introductory words and exercises are performed by the organ and choir, the whole congregation joins and sings heartily, and understandingly, all on one part; if it does not rouse the hearer from his seat, it will be because he can withstand more than the writer.

In regard to instruments, we have mentioned their introduction into Mr. Mason's choir. But, as is always the case, different kinds, of instruments brought together, with the breaking of strings and squeaking of reeds, soon become tiresome.   Organ is the word, and the instrument, which alone can satisfy in the church.   The first organ that sounded west of the Alleghany Mountains was placed in the second Presbyterian church in Cincinnati, in 1837. This instrument was procured principally by the influence and labor of Dr. Beecher and Professor Mason.   There is now an organ, or some similar instrument of inferior construction, in almost every church; and other instruments driven out.

CHAPTER XI.

IMPROPRIETIES, IN EXECUTION.

Singing of Solos and Duets. — Inattention to Accent, Words, &c. — Unsuitable Words. — Irregular Poetry. — Words with Improper Accent. — False Accent from Location of Notes. — Repeated Accent in Singing. — Force of Accent. — Inappropriate Graces in Singing. — Enunciation. — Taking Breath improperly. — Careless Manner of Finishing Words. — Leading Notes. — Habits and Customs of Singers. — Application of Slurs. — Repeated Accent in Singing. — Abuse of the Letter *R*. — Gesticulation. — Bad Habits not perceived by Ourselves. — Saying of Tosi. — Battishill and a German Violoncello-player.

SINGING OF SOLOS AND DUETS.

In former times, all the voices attached to each part kept on, wherever they found notes. If there was a tenor or bass solo or duo, all the tenor or bass voices sung, while those on the other parts kept silence; and such passages were marked *pia*, or *soft*. Each part was expected to execute what was written for it, asking no questions. The words, characters or letters, for indicating soft or loud, or other modes of expression, were considered part and parcel of the tune; and, no matter what might be the words to be sung, the tune must be sung as directed. In anthems and select pieces of music, passages were found, in different parts, evidently intended to be sung by single voices; but to accomplish it was the question. In many choirs, however, it was accomplished; and when the Handel and Haydn Society was instituted, conformity to the directions of European authors was attempted, and successfully achieved. This was an example for imitation to choirs and other minor societies. Before this time, and in most of the choirs in the country for a long time afterward, a male or female

13

singer could scarcely be found to make the attempt; or, if they did, their voices were suppressed to an inefficient, unmeaning tone, so that, however correct and melodious the performance might be, much of the effect was lost. If some, however, had ability and courage to display the voice, they were sneered at, as being immodest, bold and brazen-faced. In cases where no one could be found to make the attempt to sing alone, then two or three or more united, who, together, would not produce so much volume of voice as an individual at the present day. As soon as they heard their own voices, they were frightened, as though it was something they never heard before; so that help had to be near, to assist when they began to falter.

And here we may adopt the language of a good old divine, who said Christians were seldom in the path to heaven, except when crossing it; so, when singers of later years are taught to develop their voices, they are apt to step to the other side, and sing as much too boisterous as formerly too tame.

Moreover, it has since been the case, that, instead of importunity being required, many are ready, willing and waiting, for an invitation to sing alone; and unkind feelings are often manifested towards a leader or chorister, because he does not give individuals an opportunity to exhibit their voice and skill.

INATTENTION TO ACCENT, WORDS, ETC.

In the days of our forefathers, as we have said, very little attention was paid to time, tone, accent, emphasis, style, or even words, each one making use of the words on his own account, and pronouncing them in his own way. Of course, the same word would be treated very differently by different singers. In singing poetry, the *accent* in music would naturally follow the rhythm of the verse. But poetry is very irregular as regards rhythm, and poets seem to deem it a mark of their skill to vary as far as possible from regular rhythm, without actually doing gross violence. If the measure of verse were strictly observed, the subject of adaptation of words to music would be more easily disposed of. But

- this not being the case, while the accent of tunes is stationary, it must be obvious that care and skill are necessary, to give sense and expression to sentiment, where rhythm is irregular.

UNSUITABLE WORDS.

The Italian says, " Read well, sing well ; " but the saying will not always apply to the English language. Although it is not true that all who read well sing well, — for we have heard many good readers whose enunciation, when they applied words to music, was lost in sound, — still it is obvious that one who cannot read well cannot be expected to give the best effect to words in singing. When our poets weave into their measure such words as *pleasurable, perpetuity, incomprehensible*, and the ' like, the idea of expression is out of the question ; and when we consider the limited practice of singers generally, the imperfect education of many, and the irregular construction of poetry, it is not strange that many practices and performances should not bear scrutiny.

IRREGULAR POETRY.

Lines of poetry with an even number of feet have, or ought to have, an unaccented word or syllable at the commencement of the line. Tunes are generally so constructed as to meet this rule ; but poets are lawless, and often vary from the rule, and you find a line read thus :

> " Nature with all her powers shall sing
> God the Creator and the King.''

Here the accent of the tune will occur on the unaccented syllable of *nature* in the first line, and on the word *the* in the second.

To apply such lines to music written for regular verse requires care and judgment ; and it has not been uncommon to hear choirs sing them regardless of the change of accent, thereby making nonsense. To remedy this evil, some authors introduced small choice notes at the commencement of particular lines ; but this experiment did not have its desired effect, otherwise than to direct attention to the subject; for it was found that if singers did not know enough to vary the accent so as to accommodate the words, these additional notes tended only to create embarrassment.

WORDS WITH IMPROPER ACCENT.

We often find words of three syllables with a full accent on the first syllable only, the third syllable, of course, falling on the accented part of a measure; and when the accent is mechanically applied, it makes amusing language. Take the words Majesty, Prodigal, Paradise, &c., which, when applied to music, and sung on carelessly, will meet the ear as follows:

A - dorned with ma - - jes - te - e - e and grace
or To see a pro - - di - gal re - turn

The unavoidable result is to make an apparently distinct word of the last syllable, as the example will show; while in words of three syllables, accented on the second, as Hosanna, Salvation, Redeemer, &c., all is right. The line of poetry in the hymn " Rise, my soul, and stretch thy wings," familiar to all, " Rise from transitory things," in the days of the American Revolution, might have had some meaning, sung, as we have frequently heard it, " Rise from transi-tory things;" but when sung in these days, and applied strictly to the accent of the tune, it is less significant.

Slurred notes very greatly interfere with distinct articulation.

FALSE ACCENT FROM LOCATION OF NOTES.

In cases where the note that follows an accented one stands many degrees higher on the staff, singers are driven to make a false accent, unless particular care is taken. The following is an example, where the intervals are not great : —

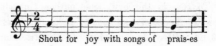

Shout for joy with songs of prais-es

FORCE OF ACCENT.

The rudiments of music indicate the particular parts of a measure to be accented; but the degree of accent is left undefined, of necessity. Some individuals and choirs sing smoothly on, with a full, natural tone, on the accented note, giving the unaccented ones with less strength of voice, as they properly should do. But when we have heard the unaccented note sung with the full strength of voice, and a painful effort made to sing the accented part of the measure still louder and stronger, we have been constrained to pronounce it labor without effect, or noise without music.

GOVERNED BY WORDS.

We have often listened to choirs in church, where they seemed to be governed by individual words, rather than by the sense of a whole phrase; for instance, where the line of the poetry read thus,

" No *peace* I find, no *joy* I see,"

the four first words would be sung very soft, then the sight of the word joy seemed to animate them to pour out a volume of sound on the last four.

ENUNCIATION.

We suppose every singer imagines that, as for himself, he articulates every word distinctly. He sees the word, and, with the sound of the note, begins to speak it; but, his attention being directed onward to the next note, he perhaps neglects to notice how he finishes it, or whether at all; but, should he listen to the conclusion, himself being judge, he would often find it to be unintelligible even to his own ear, and still more so to that of the hearer.

To murder such a word as Incomprehensible, which, in common or short metre, supplies a whole line, and where, in a slow tune, the beginning of the word is forgotten before the end is reached, is quite excusable. But we have heard choirs sing lines of well-written poetry in such a drawling, inarticulate manner, that, if written as heard, would strike the ear like some long, unmeaning word.

TAKING BREATH IMPROPERLY.

It is not uncommon for individual singers, and sometimes for whole choirs, to take breath, when singing, at measured intervals through the tune, regardless of the necessity of keeping the syllables of each word properly connected.

Sal - va - - tion, glo - - - ry, joy   re - main

As sung, Sal - va,   tion glo,   ry joy,   remain

CARELESS MANNER OF FINISHING WORDS.

The great secret of distinct enunciation is, to sing the vowels and speak the consonants. If the latter, after sounding the principal length of the note on the vowel, are not articulated carefully, distinctly, and finished almost instantly, the word is lost. It is not uncommon to hear the consonants, such as m, n, d, st, t, &c., at the close of a word, reserved, and applied to the word that follows, which perverts or destroys the sense; and even lines are sometimes connected in the same way, thus:

Bu - ried in shadows of the night, We lie and

As sung, Bur - ie din - shadow---sof the nigh----Twe---lie

LEADING NOTES.

We can present a very common habit to the eye, of which many singers in former days were guilty. For instance, in performing Old Hundred, if the notes were written as sung, they would read thus (we hope to be pardoned for making use of a few notes of so venerable a tune as an example):

Be thou, O   God, ex - - alt - ed high

Here we find an unauthorized or unwritten note, that seems to be made a stepping-stone from which to leap to the following or written one; and perhaps many at the present day, if they should watch themselves critically, as they do their neighbors, would find that the habit was not yet extinct.

EMBELLISHMENTS.

The next practice we notice is that of retaining the melody in substance, but with variations at the will of the performer, thus:

Be thou, O   God, ex - - alt - ed   high

We have heard a different method of ornamenting tunes, rather more regular in its movement, but no more nearly confined to the original, — done by regular slides or triplets, so that a stranger would suppose the tune written in compound time, thus:

Be   thou, O   God, ex - - alt - - ed   high

Sung in this manner, or, more especially, when played on an organ, it would sound, to use the language of martial music, like "a double drag;" and, at other times, when played as we have heard it, this time-honored tune might be taken for a "hornpipe."

APPLICATION OF SLURS.

There were certain peculiarities in the style of enunciating music, within our recollection, which we would place on record, — so far as language can do it, — as a part of the history of music. Among the most notable, as well as the most ludicrous, was the mode of singing slurred notes. For example: in the tune of 34th Psalm, which we have mentioned as one of the first fugueing

tunes imported into this country, the following slur occurred, which
we have frequently heard sung, when young, as here represented;
but, to give it a more perfect representation, we must imagine a
powerful twang or nasal sound accompanying the performance.

My   hea - - - - - - rt and tongue employ
My   ha-wa-wa-wa-wa-wa-wart and tongue employ

REPEATED ACCENT IN SINGING.

We well remember, in after days, a practice of jerking and
dividing the notes and words, to correspond with the measure of
time. This habit seemed to be acquired by the energetic manner
with which time was beaten with the hand, which, if done with a
violent motion, is almost sure to affect the voice more or less. We
will try to illustrate what we wish to communicate, in the first
line of the tune of *Luton*, which, by the manner of singing and
accent, would read thus:

                With all   my pow'rs of   heart and tongue
Words sung thus, With au-awl my pow-ours of   ha-art and tou-unge

making the voice and words subject to the jerk of the hand at the
second beat, to a note of two beats, and made more emphatical than
the first. This habit was handed down through many generations
of singers; and we are mistaken if the same practice, though less
prominent, may not be heard at the present time in some churches.
Perhaps an example where dotted or pointed notes occur will
sound more natural, and be more easily understood.

BRATTLE STREET.

            While thee   I   seek, pro - tect - ing power
Sung thus, While the-ee I see-ek, pro - tect - ing pow-our

INAPPROPRIATE GRACES IN SINGING.

Should we stop here, the impression would naturally be that all has been perfection for many years past; but we are not prepared to sanction such a conclusion, for there seem to be some practices of later date equally worthy of rebuke.

We have told how our forefathers used to shake, torture and mutilate the notes of a tune. They, to gratify their fancy, ignorantly misrepresented the composer; but in after days, others politely, knowingly and exultingly, embellish and adorn the original notes of a tune with flowers that "in blooming die." Some practices may be admissible, and even proper, in one connection, but not in another. For instance, the step of a soldier under arms, although ever so graceful and noble in its place, is not such as would be imitated by a lady in going to church, or even in a ball-room. So the writhing of the body, tossing the head, and the intricate and rapid *ad libitums* of the voice, of splendid singers, which might please and amuse in a theatre, would be very inappropriate when exhibited in the performance of sacred words in the church. But when the same individuals are employed in both places, as is often the case, it is not strange that the same habits should be retained and exhibited, more or less, in both places. But, as it is said there is "no accounting for taste," perhaps what seems offensive to us may be the essence of beauty to others.

ABUSE OF THE LETTER *R*.

Another practice, which was in vogue but a few years since, was that of twir-r-r-ling, or whirling, one of the letters of the alphabet. This, of itself, to a certain extent, is rather pleasing; but, as we said before, when we begin to imitate, we pass the bounds of propriety, imperceptibly. In this habit the tongues of gentlemen could succeed but partially, therefore the ladies were the victors; and such was the struggle for mastery, that those who excelled could put to blush the sons and daughters of the Emerald Isle. The notes attached to this favored letter *R*, like the shaking of the notes by our forefathers, are indescribable on paper.

To describe the many freaks of the voice, in forming notes, articulating words, and adding unauthorized notes, while under the guidance of an untutored taste and tongue, would be as difficult a task as to describe the different emphases and cadences of public speakers.

GESTICULATION.

In addition to the habits contracted more or less by imitation, in the singing of tunes, and in the different methods of beating time with the hand, we have witnessed other imitated habits that affected the whole system.

We were knowing to the facts in the following account of extraordinary imitation in *action* while singing. A teacher of rather remarkable talents, some fifty years ago, taught much, had a remarkably fine voice, and taste which enabled him to give effect to words; and in school and individual performance his whole soul seemed to be wrapt up in his singing. He was viewed with wonder, all admiring his energy and inspiring manner before his scholars. In him all this appeared well, for he felt and acted it all naturally. His scholars, of course, particularly some that were preparing to teach others, imitated his motions, in some degree; for, to be considered popular teachers, they must, as much as possible, follow the example of their leader. We only know the result of the labors of one of them. He commenced teaching, with good success, and sustained a character worthy of the employment. He, of course, as I observed, must appear animated, excited, active, full of motions or gestures. Coming from the fountain-head, he must be imitated by his pupils. One of his pupils, a leader and chorister in church, who was of a tall, slender form, could act his part to perfection. He commenced teaching a school himself, and, after he had taught the rudiments and singing of some tunes, we were to finish the school. On entering the hall, we were soon handed a book, and the list of tunes that had been practised. The scholars were requested to turn to a particular tune, and the singing commenced. But, O!

the sight! Well might it have been supposed that all were taken suddenly with the St. Vitus' dance. All were in motion, turning and twisting in every direction. This was in the afternoon; we sung no more that afternoon. Before evening we saw the former teacher, and spoke with him on the subject; he acknowledged the impropriety, but had not been aware of it. All I asked of him was to go into school and keep himself still, and I would cure the rest. He did so, but told me afterwards that it required all his power of nerve to keep himself calm; and when he joined in singing, it seemed beyond his power. Such is the power of habit.

BAD HABITS NOT PERCEIVED BY OURSELVES.

No persons, in any art or profession, require friendly admonition in regard to bad habits more than singers, and perhaps none are so unwilling to receive it. The fact is, no one knows, neither can know, how his performance sounds to others; and many persevere in bad habits, which become still worse from day to day, till they are truly ridiculous, even themselves being judges, if they will allow their faults to be placed before them.

SAYING OF TOSI.

Tosi very judiciously says, "The correction of *friends* that have knowledge instructs very much; but still greater advantage is derived from *ill-natured critics*, for the more intent they are to discover defects, the greater benefit may be derived from them, and that, too, without any obligation." Many, apparently, who have sung for a long time, and, perhaps, have been extolled for their excellent voices and execution, if they subject themselves to the instruction of a competent teacher, are slow to believe that anything can be essentially wrong with them, and have neither patience nor inclination to make thorough work of reforming incorrect habits; and, consequently, when they leave their teacher, return imperceptibly to their former manner of singing. Every one knows that to learn we must feel the need of learning.

SAYING OF BATTISHILL.

Battishill, who was an excellent musician, used to address his scholars thus, when he could not correct their bad habits otherwise: "Are you a good-tempered fellow? Will you forgive me if I take you off?" A gentleman who was taught by him said he learned more by this pleasantry than he should have learned from half a year's lecturing.

SAYING OF A GERMAN VIOLONCELLO PLAYER.

An honest old German violoncello player used often kindly but earnestly to tell a famous singer he used to accompany, while hearing her songs, "Pray, madam, do dat passage over again, and ting (think) all de dime you sing." It is for the want of thought and observation that bad habits are contracted, and, consequently, words are repeated in music without any effect on ourselves or hearers.

CHAPTER XII.

EXPRESSION AND ADAPTATION.

Dr. Beattie's Saying. — Importance of Expression. — Hooker. — First Directions to Words. — Characters to indicate Expression. — Words must be Anticipated and Felt. — Old Style of Singing. — Want of Adaptation. — Difficulty of Adapting Tunes to Hymns. — Words for Particular Occasions. — Perceptible Improprieties. — A Traveller's Representation of a Performance. — Voices inadequate to the Music selected. — Pauses in Singing. — Observance of Punctuation. — Uniformity Necessary. — Conduct badly adapted. — Feelings adapted to the Subject.

DR. BEATTIE'S SAYING.

Expression, says Dr. Beattie, is allowed by all to be the chief excellence of singing. Without this, it may amuse the ear, it may give a little exercise to the mind of the hearer; it may, for a moment, withdraw our attention from the anxieties of life; it may show the performer's dexterity, and in these ways afford a slight pleasure; but, without engaging the affections, it can never yield any heart-felt satisfaction. The voices of singers may be in as perfect tune as the organ, and possess just as little feeling.

IMPORTANCE OF EXPRESSION.

An eminent musician once observed, that "to be a good singer, a *hundred* requisites were necessary; and one who had a good voice had ninety-nine of them, and the hundredth was a sublime conception of the import of the words and music." This is what is meant by expression, or pathos, in singing; without which, the ear may be gratified with harmonious sounds, or tickled with beautiful or rapid execution; but this is stopping far short of the true intent of church music. Rousseau says, the singer who sees noth-

14

ing but the notes of his part can be but ill prepared to catch
the spirit of the composer of either music or words; for, to give
expression, the singer must act in the same manner as if he were
not only performer, but composer, of the words and music.

HOOKER.

Hooker says, " In order to render the music of the sanctuary
what it ought to be, something more is necessary than a knowledge
of its elementary principles; that expression does not relate so
much to particular words, as to the precise idea and sentiment
conveyed by the whole sentence." You cannot change the tune
to correspond with all the changes of thought and feeling; but the
object may be in a good degree attained by varying the style of
performing the same tune. We have said that singing was double
oratory; for, to the sentiment of the words is added the power of
melodious sounds; and, if those who sing the praises of God would
take the same pains to give effect and expression to the words they
repeat in sacred song, as those who have cultivated their voices to
rehearse secular, frivolous, and sometimes blasphemous words, what
grand results might have been expected from this part of public
worship! A man who has a good voice has what is indispensable
to make a good singer; but he may fail of ever touching the feelings; while the man with less beauty and power of voice, with a
right conception of the music and sentiment, may cause hearers to
feel and admire. Music may be made to express grief, gratitude
and joy; but meanness, anger and malice, never. We make the
foregoing extracts and observations, to show how much importance
is attached to the subject by those best qualified to judge.

FIRST DIRECTIONS TO WORDS.

About fifty years ago a book of Psalms and Hymns was published, introducing, at the commencement of each, a [♭] flat or
[♯] sharp, to indicate the general character of the words. If a
sharp was there, the chorister named some cheerful tune, without
further examination; and the contrary if a flat was found. This,

at the time, was considered a convenience, and probably led to the introduction of the numerous characters since made use of, to indicate to the singer more definitely the sentiment and expression of each verse.

CHARACTERS TO INDICATE EXPRESSION.

The first attempt to introduce characters to direct the performer to give expression to words was in Worcester's Psalms and Hymns, published about 1812. We had somewhat to do with the subject. It was anticipated that the effect, in part, would be to produce *variation* rather than expression; and our expectations have been, to a great extent, verified. But it had in some respects its desired effect, for it turned the attention of singers to observe the import of words, who had hitherto sung on through all kinds of words, regardless of their meaning. We have felt much like the good man who was accused by an infidel of misquoting a passage of scripture in a religious meeting, saying "he had been looking in the Bible, and could find no passage just like it." He received in answer, "I thank God that I have been the means of making you look into the Bible once."

WORDS MUST BE •ANTICIPATED AND FELT.

Every one knows that, to give effect to words, the sentiment must be anticipated and felt. But those who follow these marked directions, without consulting their own feelings and judgment, will be sure to give a mechanical expression, always ineffective. For instance, when a line commences with some trifling words, but has near the close of it some expression of joy or praise, which led the compiler to place a mark to that effect at the beginning of the line, and at the sight of it we often hear the whole choir burst forth into an outrageous crash of sound, and expend most of their energy before arriving at the important word or words that led to the sign found at the beginning.

OLD STYLE OF SINGING.

Previous to the present century, it would seem that very little regard was paid in psalmody to the adaptation of music to the sentiment of the words, or to special occasions. Our memory carries us back some sixty years, to the days of genuine old-style singing, — the days when old St. Ann's, and St. Martin's, and a few similar tunes, were the only ones sung, and when singing schools and singing books were almost unknown. In imagination we recall the sound, as it impressed us in the days of childhood; and we wish that terms were in existence to convey an idea of the tone and manner. Their voices were tremendous in power, issuing from ample chests and lungs, invigorated by hard labor and simple food, and unrestrained by dress. They commenced a note in a cautious and proper manner, carefully swelling it, and with the swell shaking note and word to atoms; and so on from note to note, or word to word. It was no insignificant, tremulous voice, but grand, majestic and heart-stirring; and, when applied to such tunes as Old Hundred, Mear and Canterbury, everything around seemed to tremble.

WANT OF ADAPTATION.

To put the tune and words together, seemed to be all that was sought for. Hence, we find in old publications many solemn and plaintive words set to cheerful airs, and animated words set to minor music. And in the first books where words were applied to the notes of the tunes, which was about a century ago, we generally find the selection appropriate. At a funeral, or funeral service, the words, "Hark from the tombs," &c., were sung to the tune of "Funeral Thoughts;" and the words and tune so associated, that to sing those words to any other tune would disturb the devotion of a whole assembly. But the tunes that were introduced after this ancient music was driven into the shade had, with a few exceptions, so much jingle and confusion in their construction and in the application of words, that it made but little difference what the words were, for they were lost in the confusion of sounds. But there were even then exceptions occasional, in such tunes as Windham, Mortality, by Read; Lebanon, Emmaus, Brookfield, by Billings; Mentz and Arnheim, by Holyoke, and Poland and China, by Swan. The latter tune, in its construction calculated for cheerful words, having the words, "Why do we mourn departing friends," was formerly used at funerals, and stole the character of solemnity, and was so treated, showing the power of association. Besides, many of the psalms and hymns that were formerly used were either historical, didactic or doctrinal, — of such a character that it made but little difference what tune was applied to them; — but little force or effect could be added by musical sounds; for if the reader cannot make the hearer understand the import of language, it is in vain to attempt it by singing.

As it is of very little consequence what tune is made use of to drag through them, perhaps it would be advisable to adopt the practice of many heretofore, and sing those tunes which are performed with the least labor.

DIFFICULTY OF ADAPTING TUNES TO HYMNS.

The opinion has prevailed, which is very erroneous, that it required but little musical skill or taste to apply a plain psalm tune to words; but the fact is, one may learn to sing a recitative, song or chorus, well, by hearing or practising with others, when the music is specially written for the words, and yet not be able to apply in a proper manner a plain psalm tune to a hymn, where the sentiment varies in each verse. It requires no great skill to use words to sing a tune, but much skill, practice and attention, to be able to make use of the tune to give proper expression to words.

WORDS FOR PARTICULAR OCCASIONS.

After all, there was less inconsistency in adapting words to music, than in the application of words and music to particular occasions. We have known many strange and egregious improprieties of this kind. When there was any public occasion which required singing, such as an ordination or installation of a minister, dedication of a church, installation of a Masonic lodge, Fast, Thanksgiving, Christmas, &c., it seemed that, instead of selecting words appropriate for the occasion, the inquiry was, rather, what tune or tunes were the most popular, or would most please. We will mention one or two examples. When Judgment Hymn, the air said to have been written by Martin Luther, was first introduced before the public in this country, and performed by the Handel and Haydn Society, with the words, "Great God, what do I see and hear," &c., with instrumental accompaniments, the effect was powerful; and the fame of it soon spread through the country, and it being understood that it was not difficult to perform, copies were procured by a choir for the purpose of singing it at an ordination. Billings' "Anthem for Easter," words, "The Lord is risen indeed," was used, and considered proper, on all the foregoing occasions.

PERCEPTIBLE IMPROPRIETIES.

There are but few persons, however, that would not see and feel the impropriety of singing the words " That awful day will surely come" to such a tune as Coronation ; or to apply the words of Coronation, " All hail the power of Jesus' name," to such a tune as Windsor. It is, however, evident that the solemnity or vivacity of a tune does not depend altogether on its key, as some suppose. Tunes on a major key, that are kept within the compass of a few notes on the staff, such as Canterbury, York and Dresden, may be used to give expression to solemn words ; but, after all, much depends on the manner of performance, and the association of the words you have first heard applied to the tune.

A TRAVELLER'S REPRESENTATION OF A PERFORMANCE.

The inconsistencies of which we are treating are vividly represented in the following narrative, which we somewhere read, by a gentleman leisurely travelling on horseback from a city into the adjoining country. It was evidently intended as a burlesque, not only upon adaptation, but ignorant writers of music, and their mode and manner of instruction. The gentleman says : " Seeing a gathering at a school-house near the road, remote from any other building, I dismounted, tied my horse, approached the house, — inquired the occasion of the collection, — was told that their sing-ing-master had made an anthem for an ordination that was to take place in a few days, and that the singers had met to learn it. Being a stranger, the crowd that had gathered about the house to hear the performance politely made a passage for me, even into the interior. The singers, I found, all held a manuscript copy of what they were singing ; the leader, with his coat off, beating time with his head, both hands, and one foot. Knowing the impropriety of entering a room where singers are in the midst of rehearsing a tune, I held back at first ; but no, — as though they feared I should lose some important strain by delay, the spectators hurried me on to the sight and hearing of the performers. When they had got through, and sounded out the Amen, long and loud, the leader and author politely handed me a copy of the anthem ; and as their articulation was such that I had not been able to dis-tinguish a single word of what I had heard sung, I therefore set about reading them, and found, to my astonishment, that they were the familiar words of boyhood, being a fable taken from an old spelling-book, commencing as follows : ' An old man found a rude boy upon one of his trees, stealing apples, and desired him to come down,' &c. They soon commenced the anthem again. I heard it through ; my feelings sometimes disposed me to laugh, sometimes to weep ; taking the words and music, and mode of singing, alto-gether, it was an amusing scene. I retired, after a few necessary compliments for their politeness, mounted my horse, went on my way ; and, on reflection, concluded that I had known music and words on other occasions, although not quite so unpoetical, still about as illy applicable to the time, place and circumstances, for which they were learning the tune."

VOICES INADEQUATE TO MUSIC SELECTED.

Sometimes a body of singers will attempt to perform musical pieces with utterly inadequate means. Select music, which requires a multitude of voices and powerful instrumental accompaniments, will be attempted by a few inefficient voices, unsupported by instruments. We have heard the anthem, or great chorus, "Glory be to God on high," commenced, and sung to the end, by six or eight students of a college, on commencement evening; and, being disappointed in a player on the piano, as well as a female singer, where those little symphonies occur between the words "peace on earth," some of the singers actually tumtum'd them with their voices. Whatever their skill might have been, it is evident courage was not wanting; on their views of adaptation of music to voices there needs no comment.

PAUSES IN SINGING.

Pauses in singing are of two kinds, — actual suspension of sound, called a rest, either written or imagined, or the prolongation of a note, called a hold. In addition to these there may be a pause more or less prolonged, according to the taste of the leader, at the close of a line of poetry in choral music; but the latter is not always admissible; as we have before shown that, by reason of a peculiar connection of the words in successive lines, the sense would be perverted by a pause.

OBSERVANCE OF PUNCTUATION.

There is a great difference in practice, if not in theory, in regard to the notice taken of the *punctuation* of the words. Some take very little notice of it in singing; others sometimes observe stops, and again others pass them unnoticed; while others give a well-timed and reading-like suspension of voice, without labor, which is always pleasing. Sometimes the voices stop, while the organ or instruments do not. Then, again, we hear choirs and organ stop so abruptly that one would be led to suppose that they were suddenly suffocated. But one thing must be obvious; that, to prevent confusion, strict conformity to a leader or organist, or both, is necessary; for it is not to be expected that all will have the same ideas, in regard to this subject, any more in singing than in reading; and, to be a good singer, it is necessary to hear, as well as sing. The old proverb, that " A man has two ears, and but one tongue, and that while he uses the latter he must hear with *both* ears," if necessary in talking, is doubly so in singing.

UNIFORMITY NECESSARY.

Without uniformity in the manner of singing and giving expression, there can be no great effect. It is, however, hardly too much to say, that it is better to be united in a wrong manner than be divided about the right; therefore it is necessary, after all, that singers, as we have said, have their ears open, and with a ready heart, mind and voice, "follow their leader," if his manner is tolerable, in speaking words, in movement, accent, and mode of expressing sentiment.

CONDUCT BADLY ADAPTED.

When we speak of adaptation of words and music, no one disputes the propriety of strictly conforming to reason and taste, for the purpose of giving the desired effect, on any given occasion. We feel constrained to say, however, in addition, that we have witnessed occasions where the music and words were well chosen, but the conduct of the performers was little in keeping with the performance of sacred music, on a solemn occasion. The following is a painful instance.

We were once invited to attend the dedication of a church and ordination of a minister at the same time and place, not forty miles from Boston, with a society of singers which we have had occasion to mention with much interest; — most of the voices which then took a part are now stilled in death, and we forbear to mention names. It is enough to say that a great proportion of the members were professional men, and such, in those days, were especially more exposed to pernicious beverage. When we arrived at the place of rehearsal, which was about a hundred rods from the newly-erected house, we found the members gathered, the hall of rehearsal in readiness, — but a majority were engaged, not exactly in playing on glassichords, nor after the fashion of the Bellringers, to make tunes, for they had but one glass to a man to jingle. Every one, according to their own notion of time, stirred the delicious draught. They had been travelling all the morning, were fatigued, and such potations were regarded as really necessary on such occasions. This being over, all were called to a rehearsal ; this being in part accomplished, word was received that all was ready at the meeting-house. Books were closed, and many again repaired to the refreshment room ; and one after another, apparently with lingering steps, moved toward the house of worship. Such of the clergymen as were not expected to take a part in the pulpit, took their seats with the singers in the gallery. The exercises being ended, all. returned to the place of rehearsal with cheerful steps, where the same scene was acted over again. We saw many of them on their way home, but we forbear to describe the condition of some.

Suffice it to say, that it was at the period when the use of intoxicating drink had well-nigh destroyed both good and bad together ; and, from that very day, those serious individuals, who had taken a part in the motley exercises, impressed with the inconsistency of the custom of the times, set about laboring in the pulpit, and by the way, to convince others of the awful consequences to both soul and body ; being among the first who took an active part in the cause of temperance. We presume that every reader will concede that the *conduct* and *example* of these individuals, on this occasion, were not well adapted to the duties they performed.

FEELINGS ADAPTED TO THE SUBJECT.

How often do we hear the most solemn words rehearsed in music, when the countenance and apparent indifference of the performer, or his entire attention to reading the notes, to the neglect of the words, lead you to conclude that neither words nor music will produce any marked effect!

The words we sing must be so clearly apprehended-and felt as to make them our own. We must speak them out; for the words will not, without our aid, make any impression on our own feelings, or the hearts of others. Reason teaches us that, if words are sacred, the mind should be directed toward the Being we address, and carried away from man and earth, and from all thought of making a display of musical talent. If the words are solemn and sublime, the mind should be fixed on the grand and awful scenes which time and eternity present. If plaintive or pathetic, we should bring the scenes they are intended to represent home to our own hearts. If supplicatory, our minds should be impressed with the fact that it is as solemn to address the throne of grace in sacred song, as to use the same language in the voice of prayer. With these feelings and views, individuals and choirs can scarcely fail of giving that kind of expression which will do good; and without them all is solemn mockery.

CHAPTER XIII.

INSTRUMENTS OF MUSIC.

Puritan Fathers rejected Instruments. — Bass-viols introduced in Billings' day. — Human Voice uncertain in Giving the Pitch of a Tune. — Pitch-pipe the first Instrument used. — Tuning-fork and Brass Reed. — Opposition to the Bass-viol or Violoncello. — Extreme Case of Opposition. — Different Instruments introduced. — Flute, Hautboy, Clarinet,. Bassoon. — Perplexities attending them. — Instrumental Accompaniments. — Confusion of Instruments. — Interludes. — Privilege of Players on Instruments. — History of Organs. — First Organ built in America. — First Imported Organ. — Its History. — Organs astonished all. — Former Objections to Organs. — Change in Playing it. — Scarcity of Organists. — Organists and Singers not moving together. — Advantage of having the Organ move in advance. — Interludes and Voluntaries. — Instruments attempt to imitate the Organ.

PURITAN FATHERS REJECTED INSTRUMENTS OF MUSIC.

Our Puritan fathers, when they left their native shores, that they might escape a religion of forms, naturally condemned and avoided all the outward show of the service of the Church of England; and with usages which to them appeared superfluous, and which they had been accustomed to hear, were also instruments of music, — organs in particular, — but all, of every description, were discarded, as a part and parcel of unsanctified and unwarranted abuses of the pure worship of the followers of the meek and lowly Jesus. Whatever other use they might have made of musical instruments, for the first hundred years after they landed it is certain that no one was allowed to be heard in the house of prayer.

BASS-VIOL INTRODUCED.

About the commencement of Billings' career, we find that the bass-viol (now called violoncello) was used in his schools and concerts of sacred music, and to accompany the singer of songs. This simple and grave instrument, however, created astonishment in some, alarm and disgust in others, and some few were delighted with it; but, generally, it was considered unfit to have a place within the walls of a church.

HUMAN VOICE UNCERTAIN IN GIVING THE PITCH OF A TUNE.

As it *was*, and is *now*, it probably always will be, a matter of uncertainty, which no practice or skill can make sure, to be able directly, and without failure, to give the exact sound of a given note or letter at any moment, with the human voice. Therefore, after schools began to multiply, and with them parts were added to the melody, it made it more and more necessary that tunes should have their proper pitch, to keep all the notes within the compass of the voice; and that some means should be devised to make the sound, or pitch, *certain* and *correct*.

PITCH-PIPE FIRST INSTRUMENT USED.

The first instrument to effect this object, in church, that we know of, was what was called a *pitch-pipe*. This was a box six or eight inches in length, about four wide, and one thick; at one end a mouth-piece; in the inside a slide that moved up and down, having the letters of the octave on one edge, so that by moving the slide to any one of these letters, then blowing into the mouth-piece, the sound of the letter was produced. This simple *sound* had to be made cautiously, and the pitch to the other parts carefully found, and dexterously handed round to the several parts, to prevent detection, and consequent reproof from the fathers, for sounding an instrument in church. We may wonder that a sound so trifling should disturb any one, eighty or ninety years ago; or you will perhaps think it still more strange, when told that the same prejudices existed in the queen city of Ohio (Cincinnati) only seventeen years ago, a place that is regarded as a pattern for all the west, when and where the same scenes and prejudices were encountered as in New England seventy years ago.

TUNING-FORK AND BRASS REED.

The next instrument was a *tuning-fork*. This was made of steel, with a handle, and two parallel branches a. one end ; when struck against any hard substance, it would vibrate, and, by placing it to the ear, give the sound of one letter, which was usually G, A, or C. This was of no more utility than the pipe, but more convenient to carry about. After that, a small brass tube, with a reed, which also sounded but one note, was and is now used to regulate the pitch of tunes ; also to tune other instruments by, being so constructed that it can be held in the mouth and sounded while tuning a stringed or keyed instrument, and the sound continued through the operation.

OPPOSITION TO THE BASS-VIOL OR VIOLONCELLO.

About the commencement, and even long before the present century, the bass-viol was here and there introduced into churches. It was the grand entering-wedge that opened the way for all other instruments. Although the generation that left England with their strong prejudices against the use of instruments in the church had passed away, still the story, as told by their fathers, was received, and with it the same feelings of opposition. The opposition manifested at its first appearance and sound would hardly be now credited. Suffice it to say, that, for a long time, it was so strong and bitter, that in consequence of it many churches had well-nigh been rent asunder. Nothing could reconcile individuals, in some instances, but an entire expulsion of the instrument from sight and hearing. There is no accounting for the opinions and prejudices of mankind. The present generation look back, and talk of those who indulged these prejudices as bigoted, narrow-minded, and the like, and pronounce it the result of the ignorance and superstition of by-gone days. But human nature is still the same, and we need not go far, at the present day, to find the same spirit. Many are as tenacious about changing a hymn-book that they have used some fifteen or twenty years, as our forefathers were, who had used the same book a hundred years, — so long that the book was looked upon by the multitude as a holy book, sacred and inspired, like the Bible.

A history of the battles fought *by* or *with* the innocent bass-viol, sometimes victorious at once, then again driven from the field, then renewing its attacks, till finally opposition was rather worried out than reconciled, would be more ludicrous and laughable than could be furnished in fiction by the most fruitful imagination. Some, at the sound, would run out of the meeting-house; others immediately dissolve their connection with the church and congregation; others lay their grievance before the church or town, praying to have the idol-instrument banished, asserting that it was of the same form as the fiddle they danced after when young, only a little larger. It was opposed, like all other innovations or improvements, on the ground of *conscience*, which is a convenient pretext for some other word. that would much better express the truth.

We will dismiss this instrument, only mentioning one extreme case of prejudice and ignorance, that cured itself. For, if we should attempt to relate them all, generally and truthfully, it would appear that the battles were fought with no less vigor, and far less consistency, or even Christian spirit, than were the battles of the Revolution.

EXTREME CASE OF OPPOSITION CURED.

Not more than twenty years ago, in a town now a city, was a very respectable church, as it regards wealth, piety, or general intelligence ; but which had never, in any respect, stepped out of the track of their fathers, in regard to modes, forms and customs, of religious worship. A chorister, or leader, stood in front of the pulpit and " raised the tune," and those that had skill, or a *mind* to sing, followed after as they could. By and by, a violoncello-player, who was also a good singer, from a foreign country, came among them. He was of the same denomination, but in his native country had broken loose from the fetters of old customs. Of course, he was uneasy under the singing administration. He first obtained consent for a few singers to sit together in the front gallery. This grieved many, but was soon overlooked. He next proposed to play the violoncello; at which all started with amazement, that he, being a professor of religion, should even suggest such a thing. After waiting till all was calm, he, one Sabbath morning, before the services commenced, placed his viol under a seat, and when they sung, played, keeping it out of sight. At noon all praised the singing, but no one knew of the hidden aid. But, unfortunately, some boys saw it, and gave information; consternation ran through the ranks, particularly of the aged. The consequence was, that a vestry meeting was called, and a committee chosen to wait on the aggrieving brother. They called on him the next day at his shop, told him their errand, expressed their surprise that he should, against all the principles of propriety and religion, carry that instrument in the form of a fiddle into the church. He mildly answered that he thought they were laboring under a mistake in regard to the instrument,— that he had it made in his own country for the express purpose of playing church-music, and had used it for that purpose many years. And he had named it a " Godly Viol," and thought he could satisfy them of the fact that it was not like other viols. He brought the viol forward, played and sung several tunes, which he was capable of doing in the most touching manner. The committee felt the power of the music, and, looking at each other, said " There can be no harm in that, I am sure ; " and consequently reported that it was " a Godly viol," — and however incredible the account may seem, it worked a perfect cure for the prejudice. Soon after, other instruments were introduced, and then the organ.

DIFFERENT INSTRUMENTS INTRODUCED.

Man is restless. When he has accomplished an object, even though it be through violent opposition, he is then looking for something new to occupy his mind and will. After the bass-viol had found an unmolested resting-place in most of the churches, all the lovers of music were in search of some other instrument to accompany it. Well may the lovers of music be classed with those who cry " Give! give! "

THE FLUTE.

The flute was next introduced. It was not only the cheapest, but the most convenient for immediate use; for in those days the instrument had but one key, and the fingering differed so little from that of the fife, that the militia fifers could manage it with but little practice, although the flats and sharps, if they could have spoken, would probably have accused the performer of grossly slighting them. Still, nothing was noticed by the hearers, for their attention was directed to the sound of some of the prominent notes, rather than to the perfection of the tones.

HAUTBOY.

The next instrument was the hautboy, the fingering much the same as the flute; but the wind, being communicated through a delicate reed, required a correct ear, and a very considerable degree of skill, to manage it; also, in unskilful hands, it was subject to squeaking and squalling; therefore, it did not receive very much favor or attention, but was looked upon as of doubtful character.

CLARINET.

After the *hautboy* came the *clarinet*. This instrument astonished every beholder, not so much, perhaps, on account of its sound, as its machinery. One that could manage the keys of a clarinet, forty-five years ago, so as to play a tune, was one of the wonders of the age. Children of all ages would crowd around the performer, and wonder and admire when the keys were moved.

BASSOON.

After this came the bassoon. This was considered the climax of instruments for bass, coinciding so well with the human voice and bass-viol in church music, and having such power in a band of instruments, that for many years it had general favor.

PERPLEXITIES ATTENDING THEM.

In all the foregoing instruments, in addition to the want of skill in fingering, to make the semitones, the instruments themselves were usually purchased second-hand, and probably never correct. Therefore, to make these harmonize, in unskilful hands, would require the skill and patience even of a professor of music at the present day. To tune the bass-viol with these variable instruments caused much necessary and more unnecessary sawing and snapping of strings and squeaking of the wind instruments, to the no small annoyance of hearers, especially when assembled or assembling in a congregation. This exercise of tuning could be borne with, for once, at the commencement of worship ; but this was not the end, — they must be tried and proved before each singing.

These instruments were, notwithstanding, calculated to please the ear. The young heard with admiration. Soon came a struggle between voices and instruments ; — not only so, but instruments struggled for mastery among themselves ; each wished to have his own instrument heard, and, as he acquired skill, no regard was paid to the particular standing of the letter or notes on the staff, but each that could, must soar away to find the letter in some unknown regions above, or sink as far below. The strings of the double-bass, when that was introduced, must be sawed with such violence that the crash of the string on the finger-board made a more conspicuous noise than the vibration. This display, added to the tuning of the instruments, while the minister was reading the hymn, if not during other services, must have been of wonderful assistance to his devotional feelings !

INSTRUMENTAL ACCOMPANIMENTS.

These instrumental accompaniments prevailed in New England from the entrance of the bass-viol on the stage, increasing gradually, as they were introduced into this country, until at last came the violin, formerly called fiddle, and in the hands of many at the present day is worthy of no better name. The sound of this instrument awakened associations not very favorable to devotion, with the aged particularly, but joy and gladness to the young. But what could be done? They had suffered other instruments to be introduced, one after another, without complaint, from the bass-viol to those of tremendous martial blast, and now the fiddle was there. When it was first heard, many *felt*, if they did not *exclaim*, " That Satan came also among them."

CONFUSION OF INSTRUMENTS.

The perplexity and parade of such a heterogeneous collection of instruments soon became irksome. All were convinced that solemnity and devotion were in many instances driven out of the church ; but the instruments were *there*, and how could they be removed, was the question. There was but one alternative, and that was, to put an organ in their stead. After that was done, many persisted in showing themselves, with their favorite instrument, at its side, until they found it futile to try to make a display, or contend with or add to the sound of the organ.

PLAYING OF INTERLUDES, ETC.

We shall not enter into particulars in regard to this noble instrument; but, in connection with other instruments, speak of voluntaries and interludes ; or, in other words, playing the congregation into church, into the tunes, and out of church. The manner and continuance of this practice is left for judgment or fancy, or both, to dictate ; and if no advantage is derived by the congregation, in using the organ for this purpose, it certainly gives the performer an opportunity of displaying his skill, as well as to recommend the organ-builder. But we leave this king of instruments, and its appropriate powers, uses and abuses, to speak for itself.

These exercises having been heard as performed on the organ, that propensity to imitate, and not to be outdone, is called into action, by players on instruments, where there is no organ ; and human nature must be indulged, and try its skill at these organ appendages ;

and if but a few instruments are collected, those few must go through the ceremony.

We have heard all the routine of playing the tune before commencing the singing, and interludes between the verses, by a single violoncello. But this, being done by a skilful hand, was, on the whole, rather interesting.

We have heard the same exercise performed by any number of different instruments, from one to a dozen.

When there is a great number of instruments, they are deprived of the privilege of extemporizing, as organists do; for, if every one should follow fancy, they would neither harmonize nor end together. Therefore, they have to confine themselves, however reluctantly, to the closing line or lines of the tune for the interludes. Still, this gives an opportunity for those who operate on the highest-toned instruments, while the bass are sounding their simple notes, to trill, slur, slide, and add an innumerable multitude of imaginary notes, and keep up a continual chase, obliging the bass instruments to hold on the last note, and wait for their arrival. Such-like performances have a tendency to call forth many compliments, such as, That was beautiful, fine, sweet, capital, — words not very appropriate to apply to religious services.

But the most attracting, if we may be permitted to use the expression, was where there were *four fiddles*, and no other instruments. These took the place of an organ, and went through all the ceremonies very precisely. The effect and solemnity we will leave for some one to describe who was more edified, and could appreciate its beauties better than ourselves.

PRIVILEGE OF PLAYERS ON INSTRUMENTS.

It was in vain to make any objections to the display of instruments; for this was the time for them to show their skill, and this was their only inducement. We say this advisedly, for we have known many instances where the musicians refused to play at all, unless they could be allowed this privilege.

HISTORY OF THE ORGAN.

As the organ, through all ages, has had a name more conspicuous than any other instrument, it deserves more than a passing notice. It is of great antiquity. An instrument of the same name, whatever might have been its construction, was used in the early history of the worship of God in his earthly temples.

In A. D. 757, we have an account that Constantine the Great presented an organ to Pepin, King of France.

During the tenth century the use of the organ became general in Germany, Italy and England, but differed materially from the organ of our day. A description, written in poetry, is given by *Wolsten*, a monk, of an organ in the cathedral of the city of Winchester, as having twenty-six pairs of bellows, requiring seventy men with ceaseless toil to blow, closing with these lines :

> Of which four hundred pipes in order rise,
> To bellow forth the blast the chest provides.

The construction of the organ reached great perfection in the eighteenth century, and the eagerness to discover new combinations of harmony caused a neglect of melody, which, perhaps, is somewhat the case, at the present day.

FIRST ORGAN BUILT IN AMERICA.

The first organ made in this country was by Edward Bromfield, of Boston, in 1745. He is said to have been well skilled in music, and, for exercise and recreation, with his own hands made a most accurate organ, with two rows of keys, but died before completing it in full, excelling in workmanship anything of the kind brought from England, he having only looked into one, two or three times. He was born in Boston 1723, entered Harvard College 1738, died August 18th, 1746.

THE FIRST AMERICAN ORGAN.

The first organ used in New England, if not in America, was in Boston, in what was then called Queen's Chapel, at the corner of

Tremont and School streets. It was imported in August, 1713, and presented by Thomas Brattle, Esq. It is said that the prejudice of the multitude against the instrument was so great that it stood unpacked in the porch seven months; but was finally put up and used (at the close of Queen Anne's reign, the chapel took the name of King's) until 1756. Then it was sold to St. Paul's Church, Newburyport, and there used eighty years. In 1836 it was sold to St. John's church, Portsmouth, N. H., for about four hundred and fifty dollars, put in a new case, and has been used ever since.

ITS HISTORY.

Its historian, in the Portsmouth Journal, says, "Could it give a history of itself, it could tell of the events of the reign of five kings on the throne, before Victoria ascended it. It could tell you that, when it commenced its notes in Boston, but one newspaper was published in the colonies, to proclaim its arrival. It could tell you of a little boy who came to listen to its tones, — the same that afterwards harnessed the lightning. Also, that at the age of eighty-four it sounded the dirge of Washington. Sacred, however, to the holy purpose for which it was erected, it has been a looker-on, not a participator, in the events of the world."

ORGANS ASTONISH ALL.

At the commencement of the present century, there were but few organs in the country. These were among the wonders of the age. The sound of this instrument, to an unaccustomed ear, was calculated to surprise, astonish and delight, all who had souls for music. And whenever a person from the country visited Boston, when he returned, one of the first questions asked him was, Did you go to hear the organ? And if his answer was in the negative, he was considered wanting in taste, and as having neglected to examine one of the principal curiosities of the city.

There is a glorious majesty of sound with which an organ fills the house of prayer. Martial bravery, love, joy, and other feelings of nature, have each their peculiar instruments of sound to excite them. And the connection between religion and the organ, when properly managed, is something more than fanciful. Twenty or thirty years ago, when the theory and practice of music became a subject of interest in this country, among other improvements in church music, the use of the organ was recommended. The principal objection — and that was almost universal — was that there was too much noise made on them, as they had been heard.

FORMER OBJECTIONS TO ORGANS.

This was conceded by its advocates, and a remedy prescribed; which was, to make use of small organs, and those played lightly, just to accompany the voices, never to be made conspicuous, but moving gently along, bearing up and sustaining the vocal parts. The experiment was soon commenced in Boston, and in many towns through the country, and the doctrine for several years adhered to, and made to accommodate the mode of singing introduced at the same time, which was of such a peculiar staccato style, that piano-players had very little change to make in their touch of the keys.

CHANGE IN PLAYING IT.

But this manner of suppressing, or keeping back, the tones and power of the organ, could not long satisfy the taste and ambition of organists; and those who had advocated the doctrine of soft playing were observed, either by accident or design, gradually to mark their performance with crescendo, from Sabbath to Sabbath. By and by all restraint was thrown aside, and the struggle was for the organ of the greatest power. The small organs were set aside to make room for thunder tones, still more and more powerful, till an organ was *worthless* that would not make the granite walls of a church tremble, at times, when used in full strength. And many times now, when the doxology is sung, at the close of worship, we hear such a crash of sound on the organ, that, the choir and the whole congregation joining, could no more make words intelligible, than would be the words of a public speaker in the midst of roaring artillery. This may satisfy those who are more pleased with *noise* than *sense*.

DIFFICULTY OF PROCURING GOOD ORGANISTS.

When the rapid introduction of organs took place, it was not so difficult to procure the organs as to provide competent organists. It was represented by those who were interested that any one might, in a short time, qualify himself to play plain psalmody; consequently, young ladies and gentlemen, old men and maidens, made the attempt. But it was found not to be the work of a day, or a month, to learn to manage an organ so as to satisfy singers or hearers. Some one, perhaps, would attempt, with little experience in execution, time or harmony, the singers and organist hobbling along in sweet confusion. Complaints are made; the organist is mortified, if not provoked; stays away from church,— no organist. The waiting eyes and ears of the congregation are disappointed. The chorister perhaps makes use of the organ to sound a single note, for the key of the tune about to be sung, then sings on faintly through the hymn. There stands the organ,— and nothing so great a damper to singers and hearers as the presence of a silent organ. But these difficulties have in a great measure been overcome. Competent organists are to be found, so far as execution is concerned.

ORGANS AND SINGERS NOT MOVING TOGETHER.

After nearly fifty years' confinement to choirs on the Sabbath, we have, for four or five years last past, had an opportunity of visiting many different churches on public occasions, sometimes on the Sabbath, both in towns and cities, and have heard choirs and organists of every degree of skill perform. We are aware that we are not qualified to criticize; and hardly dare to give an opinion, much less to give directions, or to prescribe remedies for what seems to us erroneous. One thing we do know, — that there is a marked difference in players and singers, when performing together or separate.

We have heard, as we have said before, many organists who seemed to carry a choir gently along, bearing them up; and, instead of placing the crash of the organ before the voices, and obliging them to fight their way not *with* but *after* them, the organ lays a foundation, and sustains the harmony, and even seems to assist them in speaking and giving expression to words and sentiment, altogether making a solid body of harmonious and devotional sound.

The same cannot be said in all cases. In some instances may be heard the organ distinctly before the voices, as though afraid the singers would fail to sustain themselves, or would fail in each succeeding note; or else that the singers are destitute of power or disposition to be prompt. Where the fault lies is not for us to say; but the fact that such performances are to be heard, we have no fear will be contradicted.

We have been astonished that good singers and hearers — judges of music — should be drawn so imperceptibly into this habit that neither are aware of the fact.

ADVANTAGE OF HAVING THE ORGAN MOVE IN ADVANCE.

Perhaps we ought to mention that by experience we have found this manner of performance was not without its benefits, which, perhaps, may compensate for all the clashing of feelings, where the organ and singers move in separate columns. We have attended churches where tunes we never heard before were sung, and soon perceived that we could sing them just as well as though they were perfectly familiar; for the organ gave every note so distinctly before the voices, that we were prepared to join the vocal part when the words were spoken. This is certainly a convenience; but whether all former rules of harmonious music ought to be sacrificed for this one benefit is the question. At any rate, to be able to join in this manner is the only way one can be reconciled. Still, many times the singing and playing were, in their separate capacity, beautiful. We suppose no one who reads, if he believes, will either justify or own any part or lot in the matter. But, as we have before said, we conceive that the grand secret and excellence of a leader or organist is to possess the talent and power of carrying the choir by his side, not dragging them.

In our history of schools, choirs, &c., it was observed that, according to our hearing, the voices were not always prompt with the organ. It was not asserted which was in fault; we only related the fact as belonging to the history of church music near the middle of the nineteenth century, and leave the parties concerned to settle the variance among themselves, if true ; if not, then it will be matter of record hereafter that the historian of Church Music in America in 1852 was mistaken.

We have one more suggestion to make, which does not concern any parties in the musical world, but is a matter to be settled by organists between their right and left hand, when at variance, — when the left hand is suffered rather insultingly to make every note distinctly before the right hand is suffered to be heard. This may or may not happen where the voices, besides, are by themselves; but when it does, it would be difficult to describe in words the effect produced. All this may be said to be the work of imagination ; but if so, — not considering ourselves competent to judge of accompaniments, — suffice it for us to say, that in vocal music alone this hobbling of one part after another would be painful even to an uncultivated ear.

INTERLUDES AND VOLUNTARIES.

Since the introduction of the bass-viol, perhaps nothing has caused so much speculation, observation, and in some cases unpleasant feelings, as interludes and voluntaries. This arises, perhaps, not so much from their performance as their abuse. It is, however, asked, and easier asked than answered, What is their use ? If we could always hear them played as appropriately as we do in many congregations, loving music as we do, we should not hesitate to give a decided and hearty opinion in their favor ; and if we express a doubt in regard to their expediency, we know we shall be accused of bigotry, wanting in taste, &c. But, in many instances, we would rather dispense with this part of the performance altogether, however pleasing to the ear, than to hear the uncouth, unmeaning, disconnected and inapplicable sounds many times introduced by players on instruments and organs. For instance, when we hear, as we have, voluntaries, made up of a mixture of parts of songs, marches, waltzes, &c.,— or while the minister and congregation are waiting, to hear Hallelujah Chorus played from beginning to end, for a voluntary and interludes more unmeaning and flighty than the music of the street organ-grinder, — we are forced to the conclusion that much of the time spent in listening to this part of — I was going to say public worship, — but I can only say, this part of the ceremony of the church, will be recorded as *time lost*.

INSTRUMENTS ATTEMPT TO IMITATE THE ORGAN.

As formerly the organ was taken as a pattern for all instruments, it gave an excellent opportunity and excuse for players on instruments to display their skill; and we do not hesitate to say that we have heard even instruments of different kinds united, and the time, tone and manner, so executed as to give a surprisingly pleasing and solemn effect. But far otherwise when we have seen a host of players from the martial band with all their instruments, calculated by their triumphant blast to animate the soldier on his way to the training or battle-field, and the taste of the players never softened below the animated marches of the day. When we see these come into the church, and commence accompanying the solemn or pathetic strains of church music, and add their introductions and interludes, according to their training and manner of playing, we tremble for the cause of devotion.

CHAPTER XIV

SOCIETIES, ACADEMIES, CONVENTIONS AND CONCERTS.

Our Fathers' Meetings for Singing. — Billings' Concerts, by Schools and Socie-
ties. — Other Teachers followed his Example. — Choirs formed into Societies.
— Pecuniary Concerns. — Want of Patronage. — Deception. — Particulars
of N. H. Musical Society. — Instruments in those Days. — Handel and
Haydn Society. — Billings and Holden Society and others. — Conventions. —
Object of Conventions. — Effect of Secular Music with Sacred. — Concerts of
Sacred and Secular Music. — Advertisements for Concerts. — A Dialogue. —
Good Accomplished.

OUR FATHERS' MEETINGS FOR SINGING.

We find, in the history of music of the eighteenth century, that
there were occasional meetings for the practice of sacred music ;
but how extensive, how managed, and whether called schools, or
societies, or associations, or even by any name, we have no information ; but we presume they were merely for mutual benefit and
gratification, and probably would no more compare with the schools
and societies of the present day, than the musical instruments in
scripture times would compare with instruments of the same name
in 1850.

CONCERTS BY SCHOOLS AND SOCIETIES.

The new style of music, introduced by Billings', created such an
excitement, that all who had a natural talent for music enlisted in
the cause ; and the desire of the remainder to hear was no less
universal.

Mention has been made of the crowds that flocked to hear his

schools and concerts.   These exhibitions we know were thronged :
but how well they were patronized, in a pecuniary point of view, we
have not been able to learn.   It is, however, ascertained that the
secret of selling tickets had not then been learned, but contributions
were depended on ; and we may safely calculate that, unless a mixed
multitude of hearers were more liberal than they are at the present day, Billings was never made rich by his concerts, — at any
rate, he lived and died a poor man.

OTHER TEACHERS FOLLOWED HIS EXAMPLE.

New teachers sprang up and followed his example, in different
parts of New England ; and the same practice prevailed of exhibit-
ing their attainments and skill, for the gratification of themselves
and the public.

Although there were several regular societies known to have
been formed about the commencement of the present century, some
of them for the practice of a species of music different from that
which had been manufactured in the mill of Billings & Co., still
there was none that took a decided and prominent stand till about
the time of the establishment of the Salem and Middlesex Societies.

From personal knowledge, we have reason to believe that the
professed object of these last-mentioned societies was to introduce
music of as high order as could be obtained at that time, and that
they exerted themselves to the utmost, to effect their purpose. But
they were prevented from carrying out the exhibition of its merits,
by the want of experience, skill, means and numbers ; for these
societies were formed principally by those who were what might
be called old singers ; and other generations had sprung up, a majority of which, as a whole, took no part nor lot in the reform.
Therefore it was at first with some difficulty that sufficient numbers and strength of voice could be obtained for expression and
execution such as they aspired to ; but their exertions, public
addresses and performances, laid a foundation for after progress,
and have had a powerful influence on music in America.

16*

CHOIRS FORMED INTO SOCIETIES.

Singers of a single church and congregation soon began to form themselves into regular societies, assuming some title significant of their object, — generally selecting the name of some great author, such as Handel, Haydn, Mozart, or Lockhart. The most limited of these societies must have rules and regulations, leaders and officers. Many times, legal and ecclesiastical aid was called in, to make every article according to the rules of law and order. And with their constitution in hand, signed by those who were considered worthy and well qualified, they went to work systematically. For a considerable time all would probably look fair and prosperous; but, after all this formality, they were no better singers than before. *Fines*, for neglect, were established by their by-laws. Soon, some would be reported as transgressors of some article of the constitution. A discussion ensues; time intended for practice is consumed, — so that, with a constitution well officered and manned, singing, the main object, was too often neglected, and the time mostly occupied by those who were anxious to display their talent for debating. So that experience has taught those concerned in singing, that unless members will do all in their power, voluntarily and cheerfully, to promote the interest of church music in a choir or society, no written rules will compel them; and that no form, ceremony or name, will make singers better, without practice; so that the fewer the rules and regulations to bind singing men and women to do that which it is their duty to do, without constraint, the better.

SMALL SOCIETIES TRIBUTARY TO LARGE ONES.

These provincial singing societies and exhibitions have been but as tributary streams to supply some great central fountains, such as the Handel and Haydn Society, in Boston, the Sacred Music Society, in New York, &c. The small beginnings, such as the Middlesex and Salem Societies; the Hubbard Society, at Dartmouth College; the Lockhart, at Andover; the New Hampshire

Musical Society, and hundreds of others, have had their day of action, and their influence. They have effected their object, and most of them have dissolved their connection and name. The same exertions and the same results have been spreading further back through the country, from year to year; and in some parts of the land the same scenes are now being acted which were familiar in New England thirty or forty years ago.

PECUNIARY CONCERNS.

It is worthy of remark, where societies have been formed on a somewhat extensive scale, embracing the singers of different choirs and associations, with or without an act of incorporation to protect the property held in common, such as books, instruments, funds, &c., that when they came to close the concern, with a very few exceptions, they have found themselves minus funds, minus books, and minus members to pay arrearages. Of this fact the writer has had an opportunity of knowing, having had the honor of presiding over twenty-one regularly organized and constitutional-ized societies.

WANT OF PATRONAGE.

Through New England, hearers and spectators of every descrip-tion were not wanting at rehearsals, who would talk kindly, extol the exertions to improve sacred music, and when an exhibition was about to take place wish them prosperity; but when the con-tribution box, or tickets, were presented, they had too much of the spirit of " Be ye warmed, and be ye clothed," at heart, to afford any substantial aid.

DECEPTION.

It has been ascertained that in some instances, —*few*, I will say, — members of societies, after meeting with the society to prac-tise or rehearse, immediately before a public exhibition, having received a ticket as member, and two or three others to pass their friends, have sold them all, and gone their way.

At other times, it would be ·found that there was a full house, and but little money taken; when, on investigation, it was ascertained that the printer's boys had made use of the types, and printed and sold tickets at a reduced price, on their own account. Therefore, there was nothing to console members, after all efforts, but the hope that good had been done.

PARTICULARS OF THE N. H. MUSICAL SOCIETY.

We have alluded to the New Hampshire Musical Society, formed not many years after the Middlesex and Salem, which deserves a passing notice; more especially, as some of the incidents attending its operations will apply to almost all societies or musical associations that existed at the time. This society embraced the whole state, or rather the principal singers in the state were invited to unite their influence and labors, in order that they might excite a general interest in church music. As many of its members had to travel a great distance, the society continued in session two or three days; all but the last of which were devoted to rehearsing, in preparation for singing in public. After meeting once a year, for some ten or twelve years, in different parts of the state, practising and publicly rehearsing, with apparent success, the society dissolved, by mutual consent, having accomplished all it ever expected.

INSTRUMENTS IN THOSE DAYS.

While this society was in operation, organs had not yet visited that state, except one or two in or near Portsmouth. The society, therefore, at their exhibitions, was under the necessity of calling in the aid of such instruments as were then extant, such as the flute, clarinet, violin, bass-viol, bassoon and double-bass. The latter instrument was not in use till near the close of the meetings of the society. And not only may the scarcity of the instrument, but the perseverance of some worthy men and members to promote the cause, be judged of, when we say that Dr. R. D. Mussey, then medical professor of Dartmouth College, — now professor at Cincinnati, Ohio, — possessing a double-bass viol, and skill to perform on it, to accommodate and gratify the society and the public, conveyed, or caused to be conveyed, this cumbrous instrument, through the state, from his residence, at Hanover, on Connecticut river, to Portsmouth, on the sea-shore.

HANDEL AND HAYDN SOCIETY.

The Handel and Haydn Society was established in Boston about forty years ago, — the first society in America formed on a broad scale.

Although its beginnings were comparatively small, it was, notwithstanding, for many years the " wonder of the nation ; " and all the lovers of music, at home and abroad, when opportunity presented, resorted to their concerts, as the climax of musical performance. In this society was the grand concentration of the musical talent, not only of Boston, but for twenty miles around. It was a glorious era to the lovers of harmony. Such was the excitement of the hearers and enthusiasm of the performers, that there is nothing to compare with it at the present day. It is not pretended that the execution would compare with what we now hear ; but it was far superior to anything of the kind in those days ; and, however simple the music, compared with that performed by the society for some years past, still the contrast between performances of the society in that day, and those of churches and other societies, was far greater than is now heard. This society was the grand fountain into which all other minor societies flowed ; and the spirit which was there imbibed spread through the land, and, although other societies and associations have sprung up since, and done well, this ancient and honorable society has held, and still holds, a prominent name and place among the musical institutions of the country.

Its first prominent meetings were held in Boylston Hall, over Boylston Market, which was then one of the largest in Boston. Afterwards the Melodeon was fitted to accommodate them, and has been occupied ever since. Soon after its establishment, it was found to be necessary for them to select and publish music for their accommodation. The "Old Colony Collection," first and second volumes, was printed, and afterwards other collections of anthems, oratorios, &c. It would be pleasing, would our limits permit, to give a more particular history of its doings; but we forbear, knowing that many similar societies, that have since sprung up in different parts of the country, deserve similar praise and notice for their exertions to promote sacred music. We therefore must be satisfied with giving the names of those who have taken a prominent part in its movements, and acted as Presidents of the society, namely, Col. Webb, A. Winchester, Holt, Rogerson, L. Mason, C. Zeuner, B. Brown, S. Richardson, C. Lovett, J. Chickering, J. Bigelow, and the present year, Meriam. Of the original members, a great proportion have passed from the stage of life, and but here and there one is seen in their ranks. It may well be styled the father of sacred music societies, and has outlived most of its descendants.

BILLINGS AND HOLDEN SOCIETY.

We ought not, perhaps, to omit mentioning that, some ten or twelve years ago, many respectable singers and musicians, partly for amusement, and partly for the purpose of reviving old associations, and giving an opportunity for the curious, who had a desire to hear the tunes sung by their fathers and mothers, of which they had heard so much, and others, who really preferred them, formed a society, in Boston, by the name of the "Billings and Holden Society," and confined themselves principally to the music of Billings and those that followed him. They went on prosperously for a number of years, to the edification of some, and the amusement of others. They published a collection of music, much of it of American production in the eighteenth century, with many good compositions interspersed. It was, on the whole, a useful book. Other societies have been organized in Boston, similar to that of the Handel and Haydn, — perhaps equally respectable in talent, if less in numbers, — such as the Beethoven Society, Musical Fund Society, Musical Education Society.

In Salem, a society by the name of the Mozart Society has been creditably sustained for nearly thirty years; in Cambridge, Andover, Hartford, New Haven, Conn., Hanover, N. H. In New York, many, besides the Sacred Music Society. All these have exerted a favorable influence in the musical community. All have had more or fewer public exhibitions, to gratify themselves and the public.

COMPETITION.

Academies, societies and conventions, have been multiplied; and at the same time worthy and well-qualified professors have been found to conduct them. There has been a struggling for mastery by different professors, not to say competitors; so that, at times, they seemed in danger of clashing with each other. These waves of opposition, although they sometimes rose high, had a tendency to keep all hands on deck at work, till the storm has subsided, and all have improved by the exercise.

CONVENTIONS.

Since the Boston Academy was established, the efforts and combinations of the lovers of music have assumed a different name, and somewhat of a different character. Instead of *society*, the name *convention* is applied. Instead of being composed of members who have been admitted by election, on the possession of certain qualifications, who elected their own officers and leaders, certain distinguished professors have been the sole managers, have assumed the whole responsibility, and have invited everybody to join. Other conventions have been formed in Boston, besides the Academy, heretofore known as Baker & Woodbury's, Johnson and others, and, the present year, Johnson & Baker. The professors of all these, and other similar institutions, have, for several years past, been called to meet conventions of musical amateurs, in many of the principal towns and cities in the Northern and Western States, which have been attended with much interest, — much musical talent being developed and improved. Churches and congregations interested in the promotion of church music, seeing the good effects of these meetings, lend their aid and influence in the cause.

OBJECT OF CONVENTIONS.

The proposed object of these conventions has been the improvement of sacred music. But the practice of secular music has been made a part of the exercises. The propriety of this introduction of secular music has become a question among those who have the interests of sacred music most at heart. To give due exercise to the voice, and make a finished singer, all kinds of music and musical exercises are necessary; and, so far, secular music becomes almost indispensable. To vary the exercises of a long session, so as to avoid weariness and listlessness, is also a matter of no small importance.

EFFECT OF SECULAR MUSIC MIXED WITH SACRED.

But we have watched with peculiar solicitude, at these conventions, when the books lie promiscuously together, and are used alternately every few hours, to see the longing eyes and evidently itching ears of a majority, to use the book that has written on the outside, "Songs, Duets, Madrigals, &c.," and take them up with cheerful countenance, while those marked "Church Music" will be moved by the same hands slowly, and sung apparently with little interest. This would sometimes raise a doubt as to the judiciousness of the course.

But all this could be easily acquiesced in, did the result stop here. May it not be the case that teachers go out from the conventions into the country for the purpose of teaching sacred music for the benefit of a church? They introduce the same exercises, having the best authority for so doing; and the object of the school, in many instances, becomes in a great measure perverted.

CONCERTS OF SACRED AND SECULAR MUSIC.

The end is not yet, — concerts or exhibitions, by schools and societies, are now rarely performed without the use of some words or music that were never intended to be rehearsed in a house consecrated to the service of God. Within a few years past, travelling companies, clubs or families, have almost superseded all other public exhibitions of music. With some name attached, they proclaim themselves in large letters, so that the first object that attracts the eye of a traveller, as he enters a town, village or city, is a placard, in large letters, pasted on every post, fence and door, giving notice of these wonderful performances, suited to the tastes of all classes in society.

ADVERTISEMENTS OF CONCERTS.

Advertisements may be seen, announcing "Sacred Concert," "Concert of Sacred and Secular Music," "Secular Music,— Songs, Duets, Quartets and Choruses, — Indian and Negro Songs," to be performed by some select company or family.

Many of these concerts consist of music chaste and worthy of patronage; others, by good and superior execution and harmony, are pleasant to the ear. Some, astonishing and amusing; others, the singing, talking, and acting of *negro* to the life, — the more comical the better patronized; and if it be true that the character of a nation is formed or known by the popular songs of the day, what would be the established character of America?

Although our principal object is to treat of sacred music, still, we are obliged to step aside, now and then, and notice other kinds of music that come in contact with our subject; and our allusion to them is not to object to the practice of any of the concerts mentioned, for the listening to many, or all of them, to say the least, is innocent amusement; and, as there is a time to laugh and a time to cry, we know of no more feasible way than to attend some of the popular concerts to accomplish both. But when sacred, secular and nonsensical music are mixed together, we hesitate. We cannot see the difference, so far as propriety is concerned, between a notice of a concert of sacred and secular music, and one for a meeting for prayer and a political caucus.

17

DIALOGUE.

When seeing and hearing these performances so prevalent, the reflection crosses the mind, What would a Handel, or a Haydn, or any of the great masters, think, were they permitted to revisit the earth ? He would have a right to expect that music of a sublime character, such as he left, would now be practised ; and that the spirit of music had moved onward, and that his ears would be delighted, his soul ravished, by the glorious strains of anthems and oratorios of those that followed him.

Suppose him to inquire of some one, whose feelings and voice had never been trained to music and words like " I know that my Redeemer liveth," — we are naturally led, in imagination, to conceive a dialogue something like the following : —

Visitor. — Friend, my stay must be short; can you direct me where I can hear some of your best modern music performed ?

Answer. — We have sacred music of the highest order, published from year to year; but it is not so well patronized as music of a lighter character, at the present day ; of course, it is not so easy to collect a company to perform it.

Visitor. — (*Inquires with earnestness.*) — Can I have the privilege of hearing some of the late publications, written since my exit ?

Answer. — I could easily collect a company of singers to perform some of the popular music of the day.

Visitor. — Can I hear an organ ?

Answer. — Well, the music to which I allude does not require an organ to accompany ·it ; a pianoforte, or some light instruments, answer all the purposes, — and, in some instances, no accompaniment is necessary to give effect ; nothing more, indeed, than a couple of dry bones, to rattle between the fingers.

With this answer, we feel assured his stay would be short.

GOOD ACCOMPLISHED.

Of the advantages derived from these musical associations, no one can form an estimate. By their meetings and exercises they have given a general impulse to the cause of sacred music, which no one that has witnessed their progress will deny. Many who before were indifferent to its benefits or charms have been induced to apply themselves to the theory and practice of music, both vocal and instrumental, who, had not such means been employed, would have been ignorant of both to the present day. Also, from the habit of singing with restrained, unmeaning tones, by the attention that has been given to the cultivation of the voice, talents and voices have been developed which would otherwise have remained dormant. Besides, by the private and public practice of individuals, and in consequence of the general knowledge attained of music and its application to words, they have become not only masters of sounds, but of their own feelings, when attempting to exhibit music in its true light; so that solos and duets are now sung without hesitation by single voices, without fear of failure, either by the performer or hearer. It has been mentioned that teachers of sacred music were few, and not all of these few possessing unexceptionable character. Not so at the present time. These institutions have caused a multitude of young men and women to qualify themselves to teach others; so that in New England alone may be found a sufficient number of reputable and well-qualified persons, if they choose to enlist in the service, to supply the wants of the whole country. At the time aforementioned, scarcely a native American could be found who knew, or pretended to know, anything of the laws of harmony in music; but now, through these instrumentalities, or from personal application, or both, we find those on every side so well versed in the science of music as not only to be judges of its correctness, but able to write music also, much of which will compare favorably with tunes of the same character in Europe. If the same spirit of improvement continues to prevail, for thirty years to come, as during the thirty years last past, grand and sublime anthems, masses and oratorios, may be expected from the pens and imaginations of Americans.

CHAPTER XV.

CHURCHES, MINISTERS AND CONGREGATIONS.

Music in Churches improved. — Inattention of Congregations to Singing. — Worshipping God by Proxy. — Foreigner's Visit to an American Church. — Reasons for hiring Theatrical Singers. — Reasons for the Young undervaluing Singing in the Church. — Errors of Clergymen. — Complaints and Perplexities. — Ministers' Connection with Singers. — Inappropriate Words. — Attitude in Singing. — Likes and Dislikes of Hearers. — Complaints about the Manner of Singing. — Of the Tunes sung. — Of Chants and Anthems.— Of Expression in Words and Music. — Of Organists. — Promiscuous Singing in Congregations.

MUSIC IN CHURCHES IMPROVED.

From the landing of the Pilgrims until near the period of the American Revolution, that part of public worship called singing was in the hands and under the control of the church, and treated as a solemn act of worship. Tunes and performers then assumed an entirely different character. The apparent causes of the change have been mentioned, together with the struggles of the few against the many, until the restoration of music, as an act of worship, so far, at least, as *external* appearance is concerned.

INATTENTION OF CONGREGATIONS TO SINGING.

But, in many assemblies for religious worship, though there may be a death-like stillness while prayer is offered, so soon as singing commenced, although accompanied with the most solemn words, — how is the scene changed! All restraint, either as to attitude or demeanor, is at an end; and, as you cast your eye around on the congregation, all is listlessness.

If singing is a part of worship, the inquiry naturally arises, Why is not the same interest taken by the friends of religion to sustain it, as there is in the exercises of prayer and preaching? We have waited a long life for an answer to this question, but it has not yet been given.

We cannot but think that great and solemn must be the account which many individuals must give in regard to this part of public worship. How often does what is *called* sacred music evidently administer only to the vanity of the performer, and gratification of the hearer, even at the present day!

QUAKERS LESS GUILTY.

The idea frequently suggests itself, whether the Quakers are not much more consistent, in meditating the praises of God, than those who with voices make a loud noise, sometimes evidently to feed their pride. Well may we shrink from the comparison. And, if the doctrine be true, that all are capable of preparing themselves to join and assist in this part of worship, how can we delegate to others the act of praising God?

WORSHIPPING GOD BY PROXY.

Can we worship God by proxy? We have reason to fear that the reply, made by a good man, who asked a professional gentleman whether he heard the extraordinary preacher the Sabbath previous, will apply to many. The gentleman said he did not attend to hear him himself, but he always sent his wife to church, and in that way worshipped by *proxy*. " Yes," answered the good man, " and in that way, if any, you will probably go to heaven."

We find it difficult to present this subject in any form, without touching some tender, and perhaps forbidden, spot. Our hope is, that whatever we may be led to say from experience or observation will only apply as matters of past history.

FOREIGNER'S VISIT TO AN AMERICAN CHURCH.

Let us, however, draw a picture from imagination, the like of which has, in fact, many times happened in substance, if not in every particular.

Let us suppose a foreigner on a visit to America, unacquainted with our modes of worship, to make inquiry in regard to the forms of worship in our churches. He is told that the exercises consist of prayer, praise and preaching. That praying and preaching were conducted by a teacher, or minister, of acknowledged piety, regularly chosen and inducted into office for that purpose; thoroughly educated, so as to be able to explain and defend the doctrines of the word of God. In regard to the other act of worship, — namely, that of singing, — the stranger must be informed that it is performed by an indefinite number of persons, who, without particular regard to age, education or character, voluntarily associate themselves together for the purpose, to sing the words that are dictated by the minister from the pulpit, on the Sabbath. He goes to church, — sees the man of God in his place, who reads the Scriptures, — prays. All is solemn and appropriate. The psalm or hymn is to be announced, and he says, " Let us continue the worship of God by singing." The hymn is read. The stranger expects, and has a right to expect, the same solemnity, in this performance, as in that which has preceded. He looks where other eyes are directed, and there sees a number of young persons, apparently in confusion, partly hidden by a curtain, preparing for some exploit. By and by he hears, perhaps, the sound of instruments similar to those he had heard before at the theatre, — if he had ever been there. The singers catch the sound, — they rise, and thoughtlessly commence, and continue the exercises as directed. Nothing in the air of the performers or in the style of performance gives any indication of solemnity, that can, in his mind, possibly connect this service to what he has heard before. The sermon is heard, and, unless some happen to fall asleep, attention is pretty general to the word preached. Perhaps he recognizes, among the singers, individuals whom he had seen taking an active part on the stage of a theatre. He might, at least, with propriety, admit to be true, what foreigners frequently say of Americans, that they have no trade in *particular*, but *could* turn their hand to any and every thing.

REASONS FOR HIRING THEATRICAL SINGERS.

Should he ask how it happens that singers employed in theatrical performances are employed also to assist the minister in the worship of God, he would probably be told that voluntary choirs are so irregular and contentious, and, withal, so incapable of giving very refined singing, that it is found to be less trouble, and more gratifying, to hire a few accomplished singers, and have the thing done scientifically.

If he were informed that churches were composed of those who profess to be, in a peculiar sense, the followers of Christ,— who had bound themselves, by mutual covenant, to promote the pure worship of God on earth, especially in the church with which they had connected themselves, — would he not naturally reason that it was the duty of these professors to *sing*, as well as pray, and to see that this part of worship is properly performed ? Would he not inquire, Cannot Christians sing ? If so, can they delegate to others the duty that belongs to themselves ? Let every Christian answer the question for himself.

REASONS FOR THE YOUNG UNDERVALUING SINGING IN THE CHURCH.

Although members of the church, and other men of influence, have, by their example in not taking a part, given occasion for the young to regard singing in the church as of little consequence, still more have they many times disheartened those who did sing, by their dictations and complaints. Their language was, perhaps, " You are a quarrelsome set of beings ; go on your own way." And the young had it their own way, in every sense of the word.

ERRORS OF CLERGYMEN.

No better evidence is needed that ministers too seldom place a due estimate on this act of worship, than the fact that, instead of having any appearance of joining in the words or music, many take the opportunity, during the singing, to adjust everything about them. The manuscript sermon is put in order ; a chapter in the Bible is found, and a hymn, to be read next; and perhaps he beckons to the sexton, and gives some directions in regard to the doors and windows.

COMPLAINTS AND PERPLEXITIES.

There are many other practices, not to say inconsistencies, which have justly led singers to suppose that their performance was a sort of respite from worship, rather than one of its acts. Among others, it has been customary, after the reading of the last hymn, to give directions to take a contribution while the hymn was being sung. We have known instances, where the singers were, in our opinion, more consistent than the preacher, and avoided singing till the collection was concluded, much to the astonishment of the preacher and congregation. But, if singing is an act of worship, why might not the minister as well say, " I wish you to take up the contribution while I am praying " ? In some respects, the latter would be more consistent; for the jingling of money sounds far more discordant with singing than with the voice of a single speaker. We can only reconcile such things on the ground that *custom*, not judgment, has suffered it to take place.

There are one or two other matters of inconvenience, which are not thought of, and perhaps not known, by many. When a psalm or hymn is given out, instead of mentioning the verses to be omitted (if any), the clergyman reads the whole. The chorister is all the while busily engaged in selecting a tune applicable to the hymn as a whole. Some of the verses are pathetic, perhaps, and some cheerful. He names a tune that he thinks will best accommodate a majority of the words, when lo! in the midst of the confusion to find book, page and tune, the minister says, Please to omit such and such verses, — the very verses, perhaps, that have influenced the chorister in his selection. Now all is wrong. The singers have been so intent on their search, that they have not all heard the directions, and rise and sing; and, besides the inappropriate tune, they are soon, Babel-like, some singing one verse, some another.

It is not uncommon for ministers merely to name some one or more of the hymns, and perhaps read the first line; and, unless the singers have had the hymns given them previously, there must be some considerable time before they can be prepared; and there is nothing more painful to a congregation than waiting in silent suspense for any exercise.

MINISTER'S CONNECTION WITH SINGERS.

We have already alluded to the strange distance there was formerly between the minister and singers, nor has it wholly disappeared at this day. Every one sees the necessity of coöperation between the minister and singers, or at least the chorister, that all things may be done "decently and in order." To prevent confusion and mistakes, the latter should be supplied with the hymns and stanzas to be sung. Until the last thirty years this was never done; and if a choir wished to sing a select piece, and sent the words to the minister, it was quite likely to be considered as a gross assumption for the singers to undertake to dictate to him. The custom of sending the sexton to the pulpit, to wait a long time till the hymns are selected, besides keeping him from his appropriate duties, is by no means pleasant to a waiting congregation. This may seem necessary, in case a stranger officiates. But we regard singers as inexcusable for the want of so much preparation, on their part, as may enable them to apply two or three tunes to words of any metre, without having the exact hymn beforehand. Obtain the hymns, if convenient; if not, never delay a whole congregation to procure them.

ATTITUDE IN SINGING.

The restoration of old, chaste music, about 1808, awakened an interest in singers of preceding generations. Ministers and churches were satisfied that poor singing made a miserable congregation; and, as one writer says, made an open window for the preacher's instruction to escape. It was now fondly anticipated that a generation of singers would rise up and sing. — *Rise up and sing*, did we say ? This might be said of some congregations now, as it was of those who sung praises to God in the days of the patriarchs and prophets ; but is entirely inapplicable to religious meetings in these days, where worshippers take their seats when they enter the vestry or place of worship, and many of them never rise till the closing benediction or doxology. This custom has not been of long continuance ; and we believe that, if Christians were awake to the best interests of their own souls, and the souls of sinners, they would not sluggishly sit and sing, when neither the voice nor the spirit of the song seems to rise above the seats on which they sit. Besides, to enter a crowded and perhaps ill-ventilated apartment, wearing an unusual quantity of clothing, and coming from the noise and bustle of active duty, to sit down immovably and silently for an hour or two, must inevitably produce languor and stupor. No wonder that religious meetings seem dull, — that preachers see so many of their audience nodding, — or that so many find it difficult to break the spell, and rise from their seats, to take part in social meetings, while such a practice prevails.

DR. ROMAINE.

Dr. Romaine, in speaking of the abuses of psalmody, says, " The posture generally used among us in singing to me is very offensive. Suppose there had been nothing said about it in scripture, is it respectful and becoming to sit down to sing ? Does the person that pays homage *sit*, or he who receives it ? But it is not left to ourselves, or to what we may think right or wrong. The case is decided in the scripture. The singers and musicians stood when they performed in the temple service, and so did all the people, — 2 Chron. 5 : 12. It is recommended in scripture (Ps. 124–135), and practised by laity and clergymen.

CHURCHES AND CONGREGATIONS CONNECTED.

In speaking of churches and congregations, we are constrained to speak. of them as one; for churches, as such, have seldom taken any distinct interest or direction of this part of worship; therefore, when schools, choirs, or associations for the advancement of the cause, have been instituted, all mix together, without distinction; all appear to have been impelled by the love of music, rather than that of duty; consequently, very little has been done directly or willingly by those who were not moved by the harmony of sounds.

LIKES AND DISLIKES OF HEARERS.

Of all things in this uneasy world, nothing is more at variance than the opinions and tastes of the performers and hearers of music. Their ears differ as much as their voices and faces. It may be possible to find some one tune that is so universally pronounced *good* that no one dares deny or condemn it; but no one supposes that equal· pleasure is enjoyed by all in hearing it; nay, if the truth were known, it would be found that many had no pleasure in it. But let any one who has taught and led singing for any number of years, relate the salutations addressed to him by the multitude in regard to the likes and dislikes of hearers, and it will furnish a picture of human ears and tastes, if not of nature, quite varied, and show better than anything else the trials and perplexities of choristers, as well as the impossibility of satisfying even the members of one congregation. And would that the picture might serve to terminate the never-ending criticisms of those who never take any part in music, but to give their opinions, — and generally without knowledge !

COMPLAINTS OF THE MANNER OF SINGING.

We venture to say that the following observations will sound familiar to all leaders of choirs, and even to many who have only taken a humble part in them. When they leave the church, the inquiry will be first, perhaps, What was that tune you sung last ?

It was an awfully dragging affair.   Another says, The last tune
you sung was a capital tune, but I think you sang it rather too
fast for music so grand and majestic.   Another says, They sang
altogether too soft; I love to hear singing spoken out with energy,
and move on with animation.   Another, I think the choir sing
too loud; if the tune had been sung softer, the words would have
been heard *distinctly*.   Another, The air was so low that there did
not seem to be much music in it; I like to hear tunes where the
voices run high, so that Miss —— can have a chance to show off
her voice; for we don't want to hire her for nothing.   Another,
I was pleased in regard to the tune, the harmony was so well
blended, and the parts kept in their proper relations; it is dis-
tressing to hear one part soaring above another. These and a thousand similar observations might be mentioned.

COMPLAINTS OF TUNES SUNG.

Then, in regard to the tunes in general : A friend meets you,
and observes, You seem to have a good choir, but the singing does
not go off with so much life as when Mr. B—— was chorister.
Another, Your singing is well enough, but you have a poor set of
tunes.   Another, You sing too fast, altogether; such rapid music
was never intended for the church. Another, I wish you would sing
tunes that have more solos and duets.   I want to hear Mr. C.
and Mr. D.'s voices more.   Another, I hope in mercy you will
avoid singing tunes with solos and duets in church; I consider
them entirely inconsistent with the spirit of devotion; to select
some one or two of the choir to show off their airs in the house of
worship, while others of the choir stand mute, as though they did
not approve of the sentiment of the words, just as I have known
those who did not believe in the trinity keep silence when the
words Father, Son and Holy Ghost, occurred in a doxology.   One
says, I was glad to hear you sing one tune that sounded somewhat
like tunes I heard when a boy, — I mean where one part comes
in after another, — it reminds me of good old times.   But
another expresses astonishment that the present enlightened gen-

eration of singers should stoop so low, as to revive or introduce tunes similar, if not the same, as those sung where the words were scattered in every direction. Thus much may suffice to give an idea of some of the trials that have been passed through, and that may be expected hereafter ; for ears and tastes continue the same.

OPINIONS OF CHANTS AND ANTHEMS.

We will venture a little further, and hear something about chants and anthems.

We hear it said by some, What sense is there in those *chants ?* There does not seem to be any tune to them. Then, again, it used to be said, Well, you are going on, step by step, introducing Episcopalian or Roman Catholic service ; we shall, if you continue, soon expect to see images in the church. Another, How beautiful and devotional is this chanting, when the words and sentiment can be so perfectly understood ! One can almost realize, in imagination, the heavenly host chanting, Glory be to the Father, &c.

Then, again, the chorister is often accosted as follows : Why don't you sing more select music and anthems ? We used to hear them often, but now, for some cause, you have almost discarded them ; there is nothing more reviving and animating than a good lively anthem, at the close of service. But another one says, I was distressed and mortified, that after so solemn a sermon as we had last Sabbath, you should undertake to perform an anthem ; I think it was calculated to dissipate all the serious impressions made by the preaching. I hope I shall never hear anything of the kind again, unless it is some piece of music where the words exactly correspond with the subject of the sermon.

OF EXPRESSION IN WORDS AND MUSIC.

There are observations, however, still more trying. A leader has, for a whole evening, been training and preparing the voices, ears and feelings of his choir, to give expression to the words intended to be sung on the following Sabbath. They are of various characters, — some spirited, some pathetic. They have been executed in church to his satisfaction. He meets, in passing out, one who knows and appreciates good and appropriate singing, and who, with a tear glistening in his eye, says, That was delightful,— any one who could not feel the power of such music must have a heart of stone. He passes quietly on for a few steps, when some one comes rushing on behind him, and accosts him with the question, in which, probably, one-half the congregation would have joined, What was the matter with your singers? They "got out," two or three times, did n't they? If he is asked whether he noticed the sentiment of the words that caused the change, the answer would be, No, I heard the minister read the words, and that was enough; I attend to the singing afterwards.

OF THE ORGANIST.

In regard to the organist, there is less knowledge, and, if possible, more complaints, or diversity of opinion. Each one in the congregation gives his decided opinion, and considers himself a competent judge; and the poor organist has all kinds of exclamations heaped upon him, such as, That was horrid! how tame his playing! what miserable interludes! Why did he play such long interludes? it made me nervous. Another, Why does he make his interludes so short? They are so sweet I never should be tired of hearing them. One thinks they were too loud; another, too soft. And in regard to the voluntary, all the same,— too long, or too short, — too loud, or too soft, — too lively, or too solemn, and so on.

PROMISCUOUS SINGING IN CONGREGATIONS.

We have only one more presentation of the church and congregation to make, and that relates to the assistance rendered, or attempted, in joining as a congregation with the choir. We have spoken of their sayings; but they have doings also, worthy of notice, some of which it seems proper to present. If we are asked, Is congregational singing desirable? we answer, yes; but not till all, or a majority, have learned to sing. It requires more skill and independence for one to sing sitting remote from a choir, than to be one among them. There are many tunes of a choral character, where the notes are of equal or nearly equal measure, where those who can sing may join all over the church, without much hesitation; but in music of a mixed character, especially where the words are changing in spirit and sentiment, and the choir has been trained to a particular manner or movement, to give expression to music and words, the best of singers, separate from the choir, will often find himself beginning or finishing some words solus. But we have little to fear from this class; they soon learn either to proceed with care, or become hearers only. Another class of persons *always* sing, not knowing what they sing. Their voices will generally be found following after the *air* of a tune, but not sure to be there; it is quite as likely that some other part, having some prominent note or notes, will have their company, not in either case with others, but stepping in their steps. And what can there be more annoying, when a solo or duet occurs in a tune adapted to a psalm or hymn, and assigned to single voices in the choir, than to hear one, two, or more voices, here and there in the congregation below; dragging after, heedless themselves, but not unheeded by those who have any sense of propriety, within hearing.

We have one more class to mention, but we are at a loss what to say or how to describe them among singers. We cannot expect that anything we can say will avail much, for they are a class that do not know enough to be aware that they know nothing about singing; of course, they mumble and jumble over the words in an unknown noise and tongue. And if they have the spirit of singing within, they have no understanding without. Yet nothing can induce them to desist. They say, they *wish* to sing, they *love* to sing, they are *commanded* to sing, and have a *right* to sing; and, if their manner is not so refined, they must do their duty. This class of hangers-on are, of all grades, the worst, beginning with those who have voices to follow after others, down to those who can sound but one note. We have known many, who had pews near such plodding singers, remove to another part of the church, to avoid the annoyance; but not always freed, for others were found elsewhere. We have sometimes thought that it would be well to have a committee in every church to admonish and advise with those who disturbed the devotion of others by their disorderly singing.

There are, at the present day, customs prevailing in worshipping assemblies, in which all are more or less interested. In some congregations it is customary to have spacious seats for singing choirs, and to have them well filled, so that, occasionally, at least, they can sound forth the praises of God in grand chorus; and by so doing, give evidence that this part of worship is appreciated by the church and congregation. Others say, *Quartette* singing is best; four singers make the *sweetest* music; and seats are provided accordingly. Some think it desirable that this part of public worship should be led by a professor of religion. Others say, No matter who leads, if they do but make *splendid* singing. Some choirs, to give an opportunity for the congregation to join their voices, occasionally select some familiar tune; while others, particularly where there are but few singers, virtually say, Let us sing something new, so as to keep the congregation attentive.

The attitude of congregations, while singing is performed, is various. Some rise, turn round, and face the singers. Others think, or say, This method has too much the appearance of worshipping the choir; consequently, contend for the opposite position; but, as it is natural to direct the eye to the point whence the sound to which we listen comes, some will involuntarily turn part way round; others turn their head, looking over the shoulder; others turning quite round. In all cases many individuals remain seated; some whole congregations keep their seats, till the singing of the doxology. The foregoing customs are recorded as matters of fact, existing at the present day. Whether uniformity is attainable or desirable, is a question for the public to decide.

CHAPTER XVI.

EFFECTS OF MUSIC.

Music God's Gift to Man for a Sacred Purpose. — Extract. — Different Effects of Music. — Effects in Scripture Times. — Sayings of Martin Luther. — Dr. Pomeroy's Description of Music in Constantinople. — Effect at the Performance of Handel's Messiah. — Of a Band of Music on Savages. — Barbarous Conquerors subdued. — Singing at the Siege of York. — Music at the Battle of Quebec. — Among the Ancients. — Peruvian Indians. — Law-suits settled in Greenland. — Of National ·Music. — Cases of Insanity cured. — Secular Music in the Days of our Fathers. — Want of Knowledge in Music. — Of a Sultan at Constantinople. — Of Ostinelli's Performance. — False Notions of Music. — Effect lost mixed with Talking. — Effect of Different Instruments. — Vocal Music of Different Character produces Different Effects. — Music in the Theatre. — Church Music outlives all other Kinds.— Effects of Bad Congregational Singing. — Good Congregational Singing. — Conventions of Singers. — Conventions of Churches. — Effect on an Individual. — Singing of Children. — Effects on Preachers of the Gospel. — Of a Single Voice. — Effect in a Clergyman's Family. — The Nobleman's Daughter. — Effect on the Bed of Death, and at a Funeral. — Importance of Music in the World.

MUSIC GOD'S GIFT TO MAN FOR A SACRED PURPOSE.

MUSIC was communicated to man for noble and sacred purposes, and to produce important effects on society generally, conveying sentiments of passion, to heighten the emotions of sorrow and joy, refining the feelings, elevating the affections, softening the obdurate heart, directing the mind of man towards heaven. The effects of music in its highest sense are beautifully described in the following lines :

EXTRACT.

" When Israel's king was troubled, her soft hand,
Put close but gently to his gloomy breast,

18*

Reached the dark spirit there, and laid it still,
Bound by the chords a shepherd's minstrel swept.
And since her countless thousands she has brought
To heaven's mild kingdom, happy captives, led
By those sweet glowing strains of David's lyre.
But, O ! her richest, dearest notes to man,
In strains aërial over Bethlehem poured,
When He, whose brightness is the light of heaven,
To earth descended for a mortal form,
Laid by his glory, save one radiant mark,
That moved through space, and o'er the infant hung.
He summoned music to attend him,
Announcing peace below.
  He called her, too,
To sweeten that sad supper, and to twine
Her mantle round him, and his few grieved friends,
To join the mournful spirits with the hymn,
Ere to the Mount of Olives he went out,
So sorrowful.
  And now his blessed word,
A sacred pledge, is left to dying man,
That at his second coming, in his power,
Music shall still be with him, and her voice
Sound through the tombs, and wake the dead to life.
  Then will her mission out of heaven be o'er,
Her end achieved, her parents found again,
Her place forever near the throne of God.''

DIFFERENT EFFECTS OF MUSIC.

The different effects, caused by different instruments made use of, the construction of music, and the different tone given in performing it by the voice and instruments, added to the peculiarity of the different occasions in which it is employed, are mysterious, and prove that music of itself, but more especially when connected with words, has a power beyond conception.

EFFECTS IN SCRIPTURE TIMES.

The effects of music, in the days of the prophets and patriarchs, on the multitude, must have been very wonderful. That we may be led to contemplate, from time to time, a history of its effects, let us, for a moment, cast our minds backward, in the history of man.

Think of that scene, which will ever present itself vividly in the imagination of every believer in Holy Writ, when Miriam, the prophetess, took a timbrel in her hand, and the women followed her with the same instrument, which roused the host of Israelites, who rose and sung as they were directed, the burden of their song being an expression of gratitude to God for the glorious triumph wrought by him in their deliverance. Think of the scene when David returned from the Philistines, when all the singers came out of the cities to meet Saul, with timbrels and with joy. Also, when David and all Israel appeared before God, with singing, playing with harps, with psalteries, timbrels, cymbals and trumpets, at the dedication of the walls of Jerusalem, where the Levites were sought out of all their places, to bring them together to Jerusalem, to keep the dedication with gladness. What a wonderful effect must this display of music have had on the mighty host that were within hearing!

It seems almost needless to mention the effect of David's harp in dispelling evil spirits from Saul; for we presume the fact will present itself to every reader, even before we mention it.

SAYINGS OF MARTIN LUTHER.

" Music," says Martin Luther, " has ever been my delight; it has always excited and moved me, so as to give me a greater desire to preach.

" I have always been fond of music. He who undertakes this art is the right sort of a man, and is fit for anything else. It is needful that music should be taught in schools. A schoolmaster . must be able to sing, or I do not think much of him. Music cometh near to theology; I would not exchange my little knowledge of it for much money. The young should be constantly exercised in this art, for it refines and improves men. Singing is the best of arts and exercises; it is not of a worldly character, and it is an antidote for all contentions and quarrels. Singers are not gloomy, but joyful, and sing their cares away. There can be no doubt that in minds which are affected by music are the seeds of much that is good ; and those who are not affected by it I regard as stocks and stones. Music effecteth what theology alone can effect besides : It giveth peace and a joyful mind. Therefore, the prophets have employed no art as they have music, inasmuch as they have put their theology not into geometry, arithmetic or astronomy, but into music. Hence it cometh, that by teaching the truth in psalms and hymns, they have joined theology and music in close union."

DR. POMEROY'S DESCRIPTION OF MUSIC IN CONSTANTINOPLE.

Dr. Pomeroy said he attended an Armenian church, a few years ago, at Constantinople ; was pleased with their singing, although he could not understand the words. They all sung the same part, and while singing the hymn they had their eyes closed; and as they sung the tears trickled down many cheeks. On inquiry what the hymn was, one of the missionaries informed him that it was " Rock of ages, cleft for me." He observes, in connection, that "most members of our American churches take precious good care that the singing should have no such effect on them."

EFFECT AT THE PERFORMANCE OF HANDEL'S MESSIAH.

However indifferent the mass of hearers, even at the present day, to sacred music, when well performed, we know that since the days of David, if the history of the performance of some of Handel's oratorios be true, there has been music performed, so grand, so powerful, and so perfect, as to raise a whole audience of thousands to their feet, unconscious of the time when they rose.

EFFECT OF A BAND OF MUSIC ON SAVAGES.

The band that passes through the street will draw every family to the window ; and the flute's soft notes, floating o'er the still waters in a summer evening, will cause the Indian to lift his paddle from the water, and let his canoe drift noiselessly down the stream.

And the proudest monarch on earth will kneel and weep during some of the strains of the mighty organ and choir, as they perform the Messiah. The poor Indian and Hottentot weep under the influence of music, and give positive evidence of their susceptibility to the milder passions and emotions. And all the nations of the earth associate music with the joys of a future state of existence.

BARBAROUS CONQUERORS SUBDUED.

The barbarous conqueror's heart is not proof against the softening power of music. When Murad IV. had taken Bagdad by assault, in 1637, he ordered a general massacre of the inhabitants. One Persian alone dared to raise his voice; — he demanded to be conducted to the emperor, as having something of importance to communicate to him before he died. Having prostrated himself at the feet of Murad, Scakculi — for that was the Persian's name — cried, with his face to the earth, " Destroy not, O Sultan, with me, an art of more value than the whole empire; listen to my songs, and then thou shalt command my death." Murad consented. Scakculi drew from under his robe a little harp, and poured forth, extempore, a sort of romance on the ruins of Bagdad. The stern Murad, in spite of the shame which a Turk feels in betraying the least emotion, was melted into tears, and commanded the massacre to be stopped.

SINGING AT THE SIEGE OF YORK.

Master M. tells us that the psalm-singing at the siege of York, in 1645, was the most excellent that has been known, far excelling all other, and infinitely beyond all verbal expression or conceiving.

" The abundance of people of all ranks, beside the soldiers, crowded the church, and always before sermon the whole congregation sang a psalm together, with an organ of immense power; and when this vast concording unity of the whole came thundering in, O, how unutterably ravishing, soul-delighting! In the which I was so transported, that there was no room left in my whole man, either body or spirit, for anything below divine and heavenly raptures."

MUSIC AT THE BATTLE OF QUEBEC.

At the battle of Quebec, in 1760, while the British troops were retreating in great disorder, a field-officer, commanding the Highlanders, complained to the general, with great warmth, " You did very wrong in forbidding the pipers to play this morning, — nay, even now it would be of use." " Let them blow away," said the general, " if it will bring them back to order." They played a martial air ; the Highlanders heard, and hastened back to their duty, with alacrity and courage.

AMONG THE ANCIENTS.

The effect of music among the ancients is not altogether fabulous. Their music was simple, merely simple airs, such as steal imperceptibly on the mind. If the son of Jesse could control the ravings of his sovereign by the simple inflections of the harp, why might not Orpheus perform equal wonders in Greece ? Even in our day, many a one will turn from a full choir to hear the simple tones of an itinerant bard.

The reasons of the different effects produced by different species of music, and why one series of sounds should have a peculiar effect on the organ of hearing, and by the auditory nerves on the mind, will be known only by mortals when they shall know why each of the colors of the rainbow has a specific effect upon the eye, some soothing and some dazzling.

PERUVIAN INDIANS.

We read that the character of the Peruvian Indians is uncommonly sombre at the present time, brought about by continuous wrongs, although, if we may believe early writers, it was formerly very different. This gloomy aspect appears in their songs, music and dances. Their favorite instruments are called the *pututa* and the *jaina*. The former is a great conch-shell, producing dismal sounds, to accompany their mourning dances. The jaina, a more modern invention, is made out of a large reed, very simple in its construction. The tone is thrillingly sad, unlike any other instrument, producing a marvellous effect, stilling the wildest horde of Indians in the midst of uproar and debauchery. At its notes they become motionless and mute. A tear will steal into the eye, never before moistened, unless by intoxication, and the sobs of the women are the only sounds that disturb the almost unearthly music. Yet the magic tones are always heard with unabated eagerness. By the different specimens of music, produced under different circumstances, by different instruments, the effect is much the same throughout the world.

LAW-SUITS SETTLED IN GREENLAND.

In Greenland it is said they have no law-suits. If one thinks himself abused, to gain reparation he sets about preparing humorous and sarcastic incidents of his adversary's life and character, setting all to music, and teaching it to his family, with no other object than to ridicule and to use him up. He then gives notice to the neighborhood of the time and place where he will sing *at* his opponent, as they express it. In the same manner his opponent arrays himself. When both parties have sung out, the bystanders decide who has gained the suit, whereupon the parties, having fully vented the spleen of their hearts, shake hands, and are as good friends as ever. This practice is a saving of money, and sometimes blood.

OF NATIONAL MUSIC.

Songs or poetry, connected with the airs or music attached to them, have a wonderful effect on a community. It was the vigorous poetry and music of the Marseilles Hymn, acting on minds already excited by the events of a momentous crisis, that created such an enthusiasm and frenzy. And the music alone, without the poetry associated, has ever since, on exciting occasions, run through the nation. So, in our own country, the simple tune of

" Yankee Doodle " has had, and will have, an effect on all generations associated with the scenes of the American Revolution, and
acting on the feelings of every hearer with an indescribable power,
affecting the whole system.   " God Save the King " and " Rule
Britannia," in England, and the national airs of Switzerland and
Highlands of Scotland, will cause the soldier, when away from his
country, to feel, if not weep, at the sound.

• CASES OF INSANITY CURED.

The unfortunate victims of insanity have frequently been restored to reason by a right use of music, according to reports of
lunatic hospitals.   The victim of sorrow often feels and owns its
magic power in dispelling from the mind and heart gloomy doubts
and fears.   Its power is exercised in its highest perfection in the
service of religion.   Instances are not uncommon, when the sermon
has failed to produce any effect, melting music, like the Saviour's
tender look on wayward Peter, has often pierced the obdurate heart.

Augustine, when entering the church of Milan, heard the Am-
brosian chant.   " The sounds," said he, " flowed in at my ear, —
truth was distilled into my heart; the flame of piety was kindled,
and my tears flowed for joy."   Music is incapable, in itself, of
expressing meanness, or uttering falsehood.

SECULAR MUSIC IN THE DAYS OF OUR FATHERS.

Of secular music in the days of our fathers we know but little ;
and if we knew all, the story would probably be short.   We have
heard songs or narrations sung, that, from the circumstances
related, must have been written more than a hundred years ago.
Through the days of Billings, and long afterwards, nothing of an
instrumental accompaniment, except it might be a few notes on
the bass-viol, was known.   The words were generally an account
of some battle, such as Captain Lovewell's Fight, or General
Wolfe's Death; of Captain Kidd, or, what was still more affecting,
some love-ditty, such as " Cruel Barbara Allen."   At social parties,
songs of this kind, however simple they may seem to the reader,

formed an essential item in the entertainment, and the manner and effect was many times thrilling. The marked attention of all present would be worthy of imitation at the present day. Then, if some one or more were acquainted with a song, and persuaded to sing or unite in singing it, all amusement and conversation was hushed. The melody was sung,— nothing more; except, perhaps, some few notes of bass, thrown in at the close of the verse, by the hearers. Many were the tears that stole down the cheeks of the hearers of these simple ballads. As time rolled on, songs more sentimental made their appearance, such as "Sweet Home." Then patriotic, such as "Adams and Liberty," "Hail Columbia;" and here and there a tinkling second-hand piano was introduced into country villages. The sound of this, however insignificant, compared with the best of the present day, was something new, and truly astonishing. As these instruments were multiplied, new songs, with marches, waltzes, and every description of music, followed; and every performer who could blunder through the notes of the "Battle of Prague," and make the report of cannon on the piano, was considered as having arrived at perfection.

For the last thirty years, songs of every description have been crowded on the public, many of the words too insipid to repeat without music to cover their import.

WANT OF KNOWLEDGE IN MUSIC.

Ignorance and want of taste among hearers of music is sometimes a source of annoyance and provocation to those who are striving to produce effect.

OF A SULTAN AT CONSTANTINOPLE.

A modern traveller informs us that the band of an English ambassador at Constantinople once performed a concert for the entertainment of the sultan and his court. At the conclusion, he was asked which of the pieces he preferred. He replied, the first, which was recommenced, but was soon stopped, as not being the right one. They tried another and another, with as little success.

Almost despairing of finding the favorite air, they stopped, and began tuning their instruments again, when his highness exclaimed, "Ishallah! — Heaven be praised, — that is it."

OSTINELLI'S PERFORMANCE.

We will mention one other instance, among the many similar ones we have known, wherein Ostinelli, who was known through New England as one of the first and best violin-players, twenty years ago, was, with others, making a tour through one of the states, giving musical entertainments on their way. Being invited to visit a certain village, where they were told they would find critics and lovers of music, and be well patronized, they went; found but a small audience. Not disheartened, he determined to win golden applause, if nothing more, by astonishing the few. But nothing seemed to move them. At last, Ostinelli said, " Wait a leetle, I give dem de grand solo." He soon presented himself, with violin in hand, with high expectations of applause, such as he had been wont to receive. He sawed away, getting more and more excited. He flourished his bow, and ran his fingers with astonishing velocity over the instrument, but all to no purpose, — every one looked as though he were *expecting*, not *receiving*. The solo ended with a beautiful finale. He bowed and bowed, and was moving off, when one of his audience bawled out, " Look a here, you; now you have been tuning your darned old fiddle about long enough, can't you give us a good tune, now?"

FALSE NOTIONS OF MUSIC.

After all, in these latter days, while music is heard in almost every house, and it is said to have been advancing with rapid strides the last half-century, we find the grand mass of the people entirely ignorant and unconscious of the grand design of sacred music. They hear, but no effect is produced, because they listen to *noise*, or the *tune*, rather than the *sentiment*, which is mortifying to those who are doing all in their power to make music and words produce the desired effect.

EFFECT LOST MIXED WITH TALKING.

The effect of the best of music is often lost, and worse than lost, when accompanied with the social laugh and conversation of hearers, — or rather those present, — too common, in modern times, in the parlor and concert room; for this inconsistency or jargon, lovers of music have to suffer, while those who have but little soul for music seem to enjoy it; and many times it seems as though some one was urged to sit at the piano and sing to make room for the thoughtless to be heard, for no sooner does the singing begin than the small talk commences. We should think it highly improper to ask one to read to us, and commence conversation as soon as they begin. We should expect the reader to stop instantly, — why not the singer?

Why not stop, I say, instantly, like Corelli, an eminent musician, who, on a certain occasion, when performing a solo, observed Cardinal Ottoborne engaged in talking with another person; he instantly laid down his instrument, and, being asked the reason, replied, that he feared his music interrupted the conversation. One thing is certain, that the finest speech can never be made to harmonize with music; — it says to everything around, " Peace, be still."

EFFECTS OF DIFFERENT INSTRUMENTS.

The sound of the trumpet and the clarion has a powerful effect on the noblest of animals. Used for the battle-field, the sound thereof makes him almost unmanageable, and he rushes on toward the foe. The drum and fife start with agreeable surprise every human being, — even the old decrepit soldier never fails to be innervated and cheered, and caused to move with elastic step. The sailor relieves his gloom with some remembered ditty. The weary peasant is cheered by the charm of melody. The pedestrian relieves his weary steps by the humming of some favorite tune that rushes into his mind. Almost every event of life which is peculiarly interesting is graced with the charms of melody. Above all, religion's holy rites are made far more impressive and exalted, and for this the grand design of music concentrates. But, alas! how often is this heavenly gift perverted and abused, and used for the worst of purposes, to kindle the worst of passions!

VOCAL MUSIC OF DIFFERENT CHARACTER PRODUCES DIFFERENT EFFECTS.

That different music produces different effects no one will doubt. Does any one suppose that a violin would have the same effect to inspire ardor and courage, to rush with fury to the battle-field, as the drum or trumpet? Not so. The sound would have a tendency to calm his feelings of revenge. So the same music, under different circumstances, would have a different effect. What interest would a band of martial music give to a man on a dying bed; although, when in health, the same strains would have animated him? And now, music and words that spoke of a Saviour, which, perhaps, in health, were of little interest, captivate his soul.

IN THE THEATRE.

We shall not enter the walls of the theatre to inquire into the effects of music there. It is undoubtedly very effective; for we presume that one-half of those who attend such performances are enchanted more by the music than the oratory, and the theatre could not be sustained without it. It is ascertained that the money paid to a single violin-player, and also to a single female singer, annually, would support eighty missionaries in a foreign land. We will not attempt to calculate the effects of the thousands and millions of black-faced and cloven-footed notes that have been strung together, and hurried out of sight and mind almost as rapidly as they were performed.

CHURCH-MUSIC OUTLIVES OTHER KINDS.

But we may well contemplate the slower and more solemn strains of music, composed for the church, from time to time, which have lived to affect generation after generation, and will live while time lasts. The authors of such music as " Handel's Oratorio of the Messiah," Haydn's " Creation," and many more, must have had views, and feelings, and powers, not common to man; for even the instruments, in many instances, without the aid of words, seem to place the scene before you. For instance, the introduction to the " Creation," where the curious combination of sound leads the imagination, and almost the eye, into drear and darkness, and while thick darkness broods around, growing more and more dismal every moment, and you can almost feel darkness, when the following words and music occur, " God said let there be light! " what a change! Light flashes upon your imagination, — darkness vanishes, and all around you is changed from despair to joy and astonishment. It is such music as this that affects the better feelings of the soul, and is to be found alone in *sacred* music.

EFFECT OF BAD CONGREGATIONAL SINGING.

The worst of music is that which is *almost* harmonious. An attempt to make music by a promiscuous congregation is sometimes so discordant and irregular, and perfectly horrid, as to lose its effect on the nerves or ear, and to have no more effect than the noise in the streets. A gentleman states that he was once invited to attend a meeting at a church, and was told that the singing was such it was feared he would not be able to remain in the house. The leader, or rather the man appointed to " raise the tune," stood in front of the pulpit. Naming " Shirland," for the first tune, it occurred to him that he was not very judicious to select a tune with a duet for a congregation to sing. He found, however, although he had prepared himself for the worst, that he was not disturbed at all. All appeared to sing, — all seemed satisfied with their own and others' singing. Most of them having neither skill nor judgment, their voices naturally fell into or towards the air of the tune; some an octave above, some an octave below, the pitch; some moved up and down a few notes, when not necessary; some took a surer way to be right occasionally, by keeping on a straight line through the tune, and, like the silent clock, were sure to be right now and then. All this was so far from melody or harmony that it had no more effect on the ear than any other confused noise; it only amused and disgusted.

GOOD CONGREGATIONAL SINGING.

We have mentioned an extreme case of uncultivated congregational singing, void both of melody and harmony. We will now relate another instance of congregational singing, fitted for the church. This was in a German Lutheran church, in a western city, composed principally of those who had probably been educated, in their native country, not only to read, but to sing. The galleries were constructed with long seats, so that the rows of young men and women seemed unbroken in both galleries. We took our seat in the organ loft, or gallery for singers. The organ and choir commenced, and sung a sort of prelude, or introduction to the choral or chorus. Then the whole congregation above and below joined, singing the same part or melody; nothing being added but the harmony of the organ. None had books for either words or tune, — all sung from memory. All was perfect time and tone, not a discordant voice heard. It was a glorious *sound;* — we say sound, for the language was unintelligible to us. When they had closed, and we had time to catch our breath and unfix our eyes, we found ourselves standing some ten feet forward of the place where we took our seat; how we came there we could not tell, for we were not conscious of having moved.

CONVENTION OF SINGERS.

For two or three years past we have attended the rehearsals of musical conventions, particularly the Boston Academy, when four or five hundred performers were present, embracing many of the best singers in New England. All placed in order, they rise, they sing. The effect on the sight and hearing cannot be described, because it probably had a different effect on different minds and constitutions. It was grand, it was sublime, it was animating, — unlike any other earthly entertainment. We could judge somewhat of the feelings of the different hearers by watching their countenances,—some in tears, some animated, some astonished, with every limb and muscle fixed, almost breathless. But, astonishing as it may seem, some few appeared perfectly indifferent to the scene and sound ; and, with an air of levity, with their quizzing-glasses, viewing and making their giddy observations on individuals among the performers. It would seem that none but those possessed of unfeeling hearts, leather ears, and nerves fitted for treason, could have heard without emotion, and being reminded of the employment of saints above, where an innumerable multitude shall sing " Worthy is the Lamb," &c. And when, at the close, the whole audience were requested to join in the doxology, the most giddy were hushed. This was " congregational singing," indeed; and the multitude of teachers and trained singers reminded one of the scene on the steps of Solomon's Temple. The only annoyance was the tremendous crash of the organ, in some instances; when words or voices were overwhelmed with noise, and devotion crushed beneath the sound.

CONVENTION OF CHURCHES.

Who has ever attended a meeting of several churches, or some religious anniversary, where there were a multitude of professors of religion, a great proportion of whom, as we have before said, are always found to be able to join in singing, when they rise and sing a hymn, at the celebration of the Lord's supper, and has not felt the power of sacred music, sung with both the spirit and understanding ? How many, who have been spectators only, at the time, have felt its power, and been led to decide that it was " something to them," who were passing by ; and from that time realized that, unless they repented, they never could join the angelic host, either on earth or in heaven !

ON AN INDIVIDUAL.

In an adjoining town to that where we resided when young, we used to hear it said, as a matter of surprise, at that time, that Deacon S. had singing, morning and evening, at family devotions. We ever had a strong desire to see the man, more especially as he was represented to be a person remarkably fond of music, and as having a powerful voice to sing bass. About the year 1814 he called on us, and, after introducing himself, said his errand was to request the favor of hearing two tunes sung, found in a book called " Lock Hospital," named " Reading " and " Wallingboro'." The tunes, he said, he had never found any one that could sing, being beyond the compass of his voice. He had a strong desire to hear the words and music together, as he so much admired the words set to them. Those to the first air were as follows : —

> " Jesus, my Saviour, in thy face
> The essence lives of every grace;
> All things beside that charm the sight
> Are shadows tipt with glow-worm light.

> " Thy beauty, Lord, th' enraptured eye,
> That fully views it, first must die.
> Then let me die, through death to know
> The joy I seek in vain below ! "

We complied with his request; and, although the performance at the time was very simple, — a single voice, accompanied by a violoncello, — still, those who were present noticed the tears rolling down his cheeks; and I observed it was a long time before he had power to speak. He asked no more, — said no more, but left. As he left, I looked at him for the last time, as I supposed. About ten years afterwards, however, I was surprised to see his face again. It was at a meeting of the New Hampshire Musical Society, at Concord, N. H. Before this, the family, and those voices that used to assist him in singing, had scattered and left him, and at this time he was accompanying a son, a clergyman in a neighboring town. Here we met him under circumstances still more affecting than at our first interview. In the midst of the powerful anthem, " O Lord God of Israel," the door opened into the hall where we were rehearsing, and he made his appearance. We immediately recognized his face as he entered, supported by a friend. At the sudden opening of the door and the burst of sound that met his ear, his whole frame was nearly paralyzed, his whole man trembled, his limbs seemed to refuse to act, and he appeared like a man intoxicated, which created a smile with some. Far otherwise with us, for we were aware of the cause, and never shall we forget the sensation produced at the time. We went to him and gave him a seat; and, when he had power to speak, his first words were, " If I cannot bear the combined voices of a hundred singers here on earth, am I prepared, and can I bear, the sound of an innumerable multitude of voices in heaven, where I soon hope to be ? " He died at Bradford, 1825.

SINGING OF CHILDREN.

What more affecting, at the same time soothing and animating, than the singing of a large company of juvenile performers ? And who ever attended an exhibition of the singing of children, and remained unmoved, where a hundred misses united their voices, perhaps dressed in white, emblem of innocence, when they rise together, and sing of a Saviour's love ? Will not the unsought tear start from every eye, and the hearer be led to exclaim, in his heart, " No wonder that Christ should say, ' Of such is the kingdom of heaven ! ' "

THE CLERGYMAN'S FAMILY.

The effect of music in families, we have said, is many times wonderful. It is a common observation that a singing family is a happy family. An excellent clergyman, possessing much knowledge of human nature, instructed his large family of daughters in the theory and practice of music. They were all observed to be exceedingly amiable and happy. A friend inquired if there was any secret in his mode of education. He replied, " When anything disturbs their temper, I say to them, *sing ;* and if I hear them speaking against any person, I call them to sing to me; until they have sung away all causes of discontent, and every disposition to scandal." Such a use of this accomplishment might serve to fit a family for the company of angels. Young voices around the domestic altar, breathing sacred music at the hour of morning and evening devotion, are a sweet and touching accompaniment.

As a proof that music has a tendency to soften and put to rest discordant feelings, we will mention the following incident : It is well known, by every teacher of common grammar-schools, that it is not unusual for the scholars, as soon as set at liberty, to indulge in some angry, exciting words, and from words sometimes come to blows. But, in the numerous schools where we have attempted to teach singing, we never saw an instance of any contention while in the atmosphere or in sight of the school-room.

ON PREACHERS OF THE GOSPEL.

Notwithstanding the apathy that has prevailed among the clergy in regard to singing, we have reason to believe that discordant music unstrings and unfits them for devotional duties. Many a one has had the same feelings as he, who after hearing a hymn horribly murdered, read another as soon as they had closed it, saying, " Try again ; it is impossible to preach after such singing." " Bad singing," says one, " makes an open window for the preacher's instructions to escape ; and many hearers will escape from the door of a church, where the singing is bad, while good singing will make a cheerful minister, and attract a good congregation."

OF A SINGLE VOICE.

We will mention an instance of the effect of a single voice. A preacher in Vermont, having occasion to officiate in a neighboring town, related the following incident of the day: " When he entered the church, all was dreary and cold. The wind howled, loose clapboards and windows clattered. The pulpit stood high above the first floor; no stove; but here and there an individual in the church, and those few pounding their feet and hands to keep from freezing. He thus soliloquized with himself: ' Can I preach? What use can it be? What shall I do? Can those two or three singers in the gallery sing the words, if I read a hymn?' I concluded to make a trial, and read the hymn, 'Jesus, lover of my soul.' They commenced, and the sound of a single female voice has followed me, with an indescribable pleasing sensation, ever since, and probably will while I live. The voice, intonation, articulation and expression, seemed to me perfect. I was warmed inside and out, and for the time was lost in rapture. I had heard of the individual and voice before; but hearing it in this dreary situation made it doubly grateful. Never did I preach with more satisfaction to myself. And from this incident," says he, " I learned an important lesson : never to be disheartened from seemingly unfavorable appearances, but, where duty calls, go to work cheerfully, without wavering."

THE NOBLEMAN'S DAUGHTER.

A nobleman of great wealth, whose pleasure was drawn from his riches, his honors and friends, had a daughter, who was the idol of his heart. She was highly accomplished, amiable in her disposition, and winning in her manners. At length, Miss —— attended a Methodist meeting, in London, was deeply awakened, and soon happily converted. Afterwards, to her the charms of Christianity were overpowering. The change was marked by her fond father with great solicitude, and was to him occasion of deep grief. He took her on long and frequent journeys, attended her in the most engaging manner, in order to divert her mind from religion; but she still delighted in the Saviour. After failing in all his projects, he introduced her into company under such circumstances that she must either join in the recreation of the party, or give high offence. Hope lighted up the countenance of the infatuated but misguided father, as he saw his snare about to entangle in its meshes the object of his solicitude. It had been arranged among his friends that several young ladies should, on the approaching festive occasion, give a song, accompanied by the pianoforte. The hour arrived, — the party assembled. Several had performed their parts to the great delight of the party, who were in high spirits. Miss —— was now called on for a song, and many hearts beat high, in hope of victory. Should she decline, she was disgraced. Should she comply, their triumph was complete. This was the moment to seal her fate. With perfect self-possession, she took her seat at the pianoforte, ran her fingers over its keys, and commenced playing and singing, in a sweet air, the following words :

> " No room for mirth or trifling here,
> For worldly hope or worldly fear,
>   If life so soon is gone ;
> If now the Judge is at the door,
> And all mankind must stand before
>   The inexorable Judge.
>
> " No matter which my thoughts employ,
> A moment's misery or joy ;
>   But, O, when both shall end,
> Where will I find my destined place ?
> Shall I my everlasting days
>   With fiends or angels spend ?"

She arose from her seat. The whole party was subdued. Not a word was spoken. Her father wept aloud. One by one they left the house. Lord —— never rested till he became a Christian. He lived an example of Christian benevolence, having given to benevolent Christian enterprises, at the time of his death, nearly half a million of dollars.

ON THE BED OF DEATH.

Music retains its place, and soothes and smooths the dying pillow, when every other comfort fails. And we may ask, where have appropriate words, sung in sweet harmony, ever made a more pleasing and lasting effect than in the chamber of the dying ? Ah ! let us go one step further, — who ever erased from his memory the voice of the dying saint, just on the brink of Jordan, seeming to be in full view of heaven ; the voice, as it were, heard here, but the soul so near its rest and joy, that we could imagine but a quaver-rest between the last sound here and its magnetic transfer to mingle with the purer music of the redeemed in heaven !

Where did ever music wake the tender emotions of the soul more effectually than the singing of a hymn at the funeral of a departed saint ?

IMPORTANCE OF MUSIC IN THE WORLD.

We have been attempting to describe music as connected with sacred words, and for sacred purposes. But when we reflect on the import of the word music in its widest extent, we find we have given but a meagre description of the subject. We may well wonder and admire when we contemplate how we are surrounded with music of every kind, to help and cheer us through this world of discord and sorrow. Of this we think but little, because we hear it constantly. It is true there are a few sounds to be heard void of music, grating or unpleasant to the ear, such as the howling of savage beasts, the shriek of fear, or the groans of the distressed. These remain evidently to remind us of the effects of sin. Stop the music of the rustling leaf, the gurgling brook and the singing birds, and how lonely and dismal would be the pathway of those who seek for pleasure in traversing valleys, hills and mountains ! Deprive the ploughman, the mechanic or the housemaid, of the privilege of singing, how would the hours of labor be lengthened and made tedious ! Suffer not the sound of an instrument to lead the way and direct the steps of the civil, political or centennial procession, and how disorderly and ridiculous their movement ! When the word " Forward, march ! " is given to a company, a regiment or an army, of well-trained soldiers, without the sound of music, how soon is animation fled ! Let them be summoned to the battle-field, and no sound of drum or trumpet near, how soon will courage falter and steps grow tardy, unless some hideous yell is substituted ! Take the viol and the song from places of amusement, especially the theatre, and how few would go thither ! At all family and social gatherings, what an important item is music ! The natural propensity of man is to seek and find pleasure in all these situations and changes. Let it be said and known that, from this time, henceforth, music should be no more on earth, what a gloom would spread through the world ! But, when we view music in its noblest light, given by God for the purpose of enkindling devotion in the breasts of those who worship him, and sing the song of redeeming love here on earth, we shudder at the thought of its being hushed ! In a word, blot out music from the face of the earth, and you blot out half that makes life desirable.

Happy would be the result, for all who are engaged in *composing* or in the *performance* of *sacred music*, if they could say, with Haydn, when asked by a friend why his church music was always so cheerful. " I cannot," said he, " make it otherwise ; I write according to the thoughts I feel. When I think on God, my heart is so full of joy, that the notes dance and leap, as it were, from my pen ; and since God has given me a cheerful heart, it will be pardoned me that I serve him with a cheerful and devout spirit."

APPENDIX.

LIST OF BOOKS.

LIST OF COLLECTIONS OF SACRED MUSIC, FOR SCHOOLS AND CHURCHES, IN THE UNITED STATES, SINCE THE YEAR 1810.

In 1764, Josiah Flagg, of Boston, as we have before mentioned, apologized to the public for introducing a *New Book*, there having been, as he said, two or three published, within the last fifty years. Unlike modern times. The numerous sacred music books for the church, to say nothing of books of select music, anthems, secular music, etc., which have been published within the last twenty years, without any *apology*, prove, at least, that an increased attention has been paid to the subject, by the public generally.

Only such works as contain three hundred pages and upwards are referred to in this list.

Ancient Harmony Revived; selected chiefly from American authors; Billings, &c., ... 1840

Aikin, J. B., Church Minstrel, Philadelphia, patent notes, 1847

Billings & Holden Society's Collection, by a committee, D. Copeland chairman, ... 1836

Bridgewater Collection of Church Music, — afterwards assumed the name of Templi Carmina, or Songs of the Temple, — published from year to year, edited occasionally by Brown, Mitchel and Holt, onward from 1812

Belcher, S., Harmony of Maine, ... 1830

Bissell, T., Boston Sacred Harmony, ... 1846

Baker, B. F., and I. B. Woodbury, Boston Musical Education Society's Collection, ... 1842

Baker, B. F., and Southard, Haydn Collection of Church Music, ... 1850

Baker, B. F., A. N. Johnson, and J. Osgood, Melodia Sacra, 1852

Barrett & Coleman, Christian Psalmody, New Hampshire. . 1832

Comer, Boston Musical Institute's Collection of Church Music, ... 1841

Cole, J., The Seraph, Baltimore, ... 1846
Cooper, Wm., Beauties of Music, ... 1800
Carden, Allen D., Missouri Harmony, patent notes, . . 1827
Day, H. W., David's Harp, ... 1842
{ Day & Beals, Numeral Harmony, or Sight Singing, . 1846
{ Day & Beals, One Line Psalmist, — both printed in numer-
{ als, instead of notes, ... 1849
Dyer, S., New York Collection of Church Music, . . . 1828
  "   Philadelphia " " " " . . . 1827
Dutton & Ives, American Psalmody, or Hartford Collection, 1829
Emerson, L. O., and T. M. Dewey, Romberg Collection, . 1852
Fitz, Asa, Congregational Singer, ... 1848
Gould, N. D., Social Harmony, ... 1822
  "   "   National Church Harmony, . . . 1832
  "   "   Sacred Minstrel, ... 1840
Greatorex, H. W., Collection of Church Music, Hartford, . 1851
Hastings, Thomas, Manhattan Collection, New York, . . 1836
Hastings & Bradbury, The Psalmodist, ... 1845
  "   "   New York Choralist, ... 1847
  "   "   Mendelssohn Collection, . . 1849
  "   "   The Psalmista, ... 1851
Hamilton " Songs of Sacred Praise, . . . 1845
Ives, E., Mozart Collection, ... 1846
Jones, Abner, Melodies of the Church, New York, . . 1832
Jones, E., Temple Melodies,   " . . . 1840
Johnson, A. N., Josiah Osgood, and S. Hill, Bay State Collec-
tion, ... 1849
Kingsley, Sacred Choir, ... 1839
Locke and Nourse, School Vocalist, Cincinnati, Ohio, . 1848
Muenscher, Joseph, Church Choir, Columbus, " . . 1840
Mansfield, Rev. D. H., American Vocalist, . . . 1849
Moore, Henry E., New Hampshire Collection of Church
Music, ... 1834
Marshall, Leonard, The Antiquarian, ... 1849
Marshall, L., and H. N. Stone, The Harpsichord, . . 1852
Mason, T. B., Ohio Sacred Harp, patent notes, . . 1834
  "   "   "   "   round " Vol. I., . 1836
Mason, Lowell, Ed. Boston Handel & Haydn Society's Col-
lection of Church Music, ... 1822

Mason, Lowell, The Choir, ... 1833
"   "   Boston Academy's Collection, . . . 1835
"   "   The Modern Psalmist, ... 1829
"   "   Carmina Sacra, or Boston Collection, . . 1841
"   "   The Psaltery, ... 1848
"   "   Cantica Laudis, ... 1850
"   "   New Carmina, ... 1850
Mason & Webb, National Psalmist, ... 1849
Nash, W., Sacred Harmony, Ohio, ... 1836
Paine, David, Editor of the Portland Sacred Music Society's
    Collection of Church Music, Maine, ... 1839
Palmer, James W., Western Harmonia Companion, patent
    notes, Ohio, ... 1832
Paine & Edward Howe, Eastern Lyre, Maine.
Snyder, Wm. B., and W. L. Chapell, Western Lyre, patent
    notes, ... 1831
Standbridge, J. H. C., and W. H. W. Darley, Cantus
    Ecclesiæ, Philadelphia, ... 1844
Stoughton Collection, by Stoughton Musical Society, . . 1828
Sweetser, Benjamin, Jr., Ed. of Cumberland Collection of
    Church Music, Maine, ... 1839
Taylor, V. C.; Sacred Minstrel, Hartford, Conn., . . . 1848
"   "   Golden Lyre, ... 1850
Tuckerman, S. P., S. A. Bancroft, and H. K. Oliver, National
    Lyre, ... 1849
Village Harmony, published at Exeter, N. H., from 1809 to 1819
Webb, G. J., Massachusetts Collection, ... 1840
Whittemore, Rev. Thomas, Songs of Zion, ... 1836
"   "   "   Gospel Harmonist, . . . 1841
Warriner and Hastings, Musica Sacra, Utica, N. Y. . . 1822
Worcester Collection, commenced 1791, published to 1812;
    last editions edited by Oliver Holden.
Willis, R. S., Church Chorals, New York, . . . 1850
White, E. L., and J. E. Gould, Harmonia Sacra, . . . 1851
"   "   Boston Melodeon, ... 1846
Wainwright, Rev. Dr., Music of the Church, New York, . 1828
"   "   Psalmodia Evangelica, . . . 1838
Woodbury, I. B., The Dulcimer, ... 1849
Willis, Robert, Lexington Cabinet, Kentucky, patent notes, 1834
    20*

INTRODUCTION OF JUVENILE SINGING-SCHOOLS.

A very important era in the history of music in America is to be found in the introduction of vocal music in juvenile schools for that purpose, and into the public grammar-schools. Although it is not exactly to be classed with the history of *church music*, yet it is so intimately connected with its rise and progress, that we feel justified in giving a brief account of the manner in which so desirable an object was commenced and accomplished as that of teaching the young the theory and practice of music.

The writer is constrained to say, that if he has any one thing more than another that he can look back upon with satisfaction, during a long life, it is the fact that he was the first to introduce the teaching of children to sing. His first juvenile schools were in Boston, Cambridge and Charlestown, in the year 1824. After teaching three or four years, L. Mason, Esq., came to Boston, commenced teaching on a small scale at first, but soon opened a free school, under the patronage of men of influence, but more especially, after 1833, of the "Boston Academy of Music," where hundreds of children flocked together, with eager steps, to profit by his superior talent for teaching. His instructions and public exhibitions, in addition to what had been done before, satisfied the public that singing was not only a pleasing but profitable exercise for the young. The writer at the same time commenced similar labors in other cities in New England, New York, and New Jersey.

In August, 1836, a memorial was presented, by the "Boston Academy of Music," to the School Committee of the city of Boston, praying that singing might be introduced as an exercise in the public schools, which was submitted to a select committee. The entire report of that committee would be worthy of the perusal of the public, as a document full of instruction in regard to juvenile singing. But we must content ourselves with making a few extracts. The experiment had been tried in the Hawes School, South Boston, in 1837, and the next year in the Hancock, Eliot, Johnson, and Hawes, by Mr. Mason; and not only in these schools, but, by the same gentleman, in the most respectable private schools in Boston. Now appeared to be a favorable time to present the memorial aforesaid. We say favorable, and it was doubly so; for not only were the public satisfied in regard to the utility of such instruction, but the active and energetic Samuel A. Eliot, a man fully appreciating the enterprise, was at the head of the city government, and, at the same time, also of the Boston Academy.

" Music has, in popular language, too generally been regarded as belonging solely to the upper air of poetry and fiction.

" There is a three-fold standard by which education itself may be tried. — Is it intellectual? Is it moral? Is it physical? Among the seven liberal arts which scholastic ages regarded as pertaining to humanity, music had its place. It is not ornamental merely. It may be made, to some extent, an intellectual discipline. Try music morally. There is — who has not felt it? — a mysterious connection, ordained, undoubtedly, for wise purposes, between certain sounds and the moral sentiments of man. The natural scale of musical sound can only produce good, virtuous, and kindly feelings, besides happiness, contentment, and cheerfulness. *Now try music physically.* An American physician says ' that the exercise of the organs of the breast, by singing, contributes very much to defend them from those diseases to which the climate and other causes expose them.' Roger Ascham, the famous schoolmaster and scholar of the Elizabethan age, holds this language : ' All voices, great and small, base and shrill, weak or soft, may be holpen, and brought to a good point, by learning to sing.' ' Recreation,' says Locke, ' is not being idle, but easing the weary part by change of business.' Vocal music seems exactly fitted to afford that alteration. Another consideration : — how naturally and how beautifully vocal music is calculated to mingle with the devotion, at the opening of the school ! It is objected, that we aim at that which is impossible ; that singing depends on a natural ear for music. We doubt not that in this, as in all other branches of education, nature bestows the aptitude to excel in different degrees ; but we are told by a celebrated teacher, that out of four thousand pupils, not an individual had been found who could not be taught to sing. Music is itself a discipline of the highest order, — a subordination of mind, eye and ear, unitedly tending to one object. Melody is concerted action ; and is discipline aught else ? ' Where music is not, the devil enters,' is a familiar German proverb. In answer to those who object on account of its being a newly-fashioned notion, an innovation, etc., they answer, What we propose was old three hundred years before the Christian era. An initiation into the elements of music at school, in the opinion of your committee, seems best fitted to direct the feelings and amusements of the young. 'Music,' says a German writer, 'is the gymnastics of the affections.' Music, and the love of it, may be perverted; who knows it not? Guard it, therefore; guide it; lead it into the right channel. Let all parents understand that every pure and refined pleasure for which a child acquires a relish is, to that extent, a safeguard against a low and abasing one. Once introduce vocal music into the common schools, and you thereby make it what it should be made, the property of the whole people. Music is allied to the highest sentiments of man's moral nature, — love of God, love of country, love of friends. From this place first went out the great principle, that the property of all should be taxed for the education of all. From this place, also, may the example in this country first go forth of that education rendered more complete by the introduction, by public authority, of vocal music into our system of popular instruction."

The result of the action on this memorial was so favorable, that in the fall of 1838 all the public schools of the city were placed under the instruction of Lowell Mason, Esq., he being authorized to employ such assistance as he pleased. This arrangement continued for six or seven years, to the satisfaction of all concerned.

The following named gentlemen were employed as assistant-teachers: B. F. Baker, A. N. Johnson, I. B. Woodbury, George Root, J. Osgood, and Albert Drake.

In 1845, B. F. Baker was appointed to take the place of Mr. Mason. In 1846, 7, 8, and 9, the schools were equally divided between Mr. Mason and Mr. Baker.

In 1850-1, the following persons were employed as teachers, by different committees, to teach such schools as were assigned them, namely, Lowell Mason, B. F. Baker, Albert Drake, L. H. Southard, Eben Bruce, A. N. Johnson, S. Swan, J. C. Johnson, W. Pratt, and John W. Adams.

We have been thus particular in the foregoing history of the introduction of singing into the public schools in Boston, because they were the first in America to try the experiment; and, as Mr. Mason says, in his Address on Church Music in 1851, "The example has been followed far and wide; so that now music is taught in many of the public schools throughout the Union. The result already is, that a multitude of young persons have been raised up who, to say the least, are much better able to appreciate and perform music than were their fathers." About the same time, in like manner, singing was introduced in New York, by T. Hastings, and in Cincinnati, O., by T. B. Mason.

The foregoing committee further say, "Let it mingle with religion, with labor, with the home-bred amusements and enjoyments of life. Let it no longer be regarded merely as the ornament of the rich. Still let it adorn the abodes of wealth, but let it also light up with gladness the honest hearth of poverty."

It may be asked, especially by those who have opposed the movement, What good has resulted from this attempt at universal instruction in music? The general good influences are so obvious that we shall add nothing to what has been already said. But it must be confessed that, in reference to the music in churches, it has not fully answered the sanguine expectations entertained by its friends. A whole generation has now been trained in the public schools, and are probably the regular attendants of some religious society, and we should reasonably expect that by this time whole Sabbath-schools and congregations would be qualified and inclined to unite in the musical service. But not only are we not yet prepared for congregational singing, but we think it will be found that the number of singers attached to the choirs has actually diminished. The long-trained members have withdrawn on account of age, or the plausible excuse that they have done their part, — a most preposterous idea concerning an act of worship, — and their places have not been made good by accessions from the young. We apprehend that a satisfactory reason for this may be found in the almost exclusively juvenile and secular character of the music taught in schools. This is doubtless in a great measure appropriate and necessary; but, at the same time, if a due proportion of the time were spent in the practice of psalmody, a very different result would probably follow.

The desire of all the friends of order and religion is, that the voices of a generation may be so taught to sing, that whole congregations, when met to worship God, may rise and praise God with one heart and one voice.

THE AUTHOR'S SCHOOLS.

At the earnest solicitation of the publisher, the author has concluded to furnish a list of the schools that he has taught. It may savor somewhat of egotism, but he trusts that it will be a gratifying reminiscence to those who have been members of the schools, numbering not less than *fifty thousand*. It will also show that he has not been a mere compiler, but a busy actor in the scenes he has described; and more especially will it show how early and how extensively he was engaged in the establishment and promotion of juvenile singing-schools, since the schools enumerated were, in most instances, the first that were taught in the several places mentioned. In addition to the list of schools, he may be permitted to state that he has presided over nineteen regularly organized Singing Societies.

SCHOOLS.	LOCATION, PARISHES, AND CLERGYMEN.			YEAR.
Adult,	Stoddard, N. H., Rev. Mr. Colton,			1799
"	Mason Village, Centre, N. H., Rev. Mr. Hill,			1800
"	New Ipswich, N. H., Rev. Mr. Farrar,			1804, 7, 10, 12
"	" " " " Hall,			1815, 16, 17
"	" " " " Walker,			1823
" and Juvenile,	Centre, &c.,	"	" Lee,	1838–9
"	Greenfield,	"	" Merrill,	1801, 12
" and Juvenile,		"	" Jones,	1839
Adult,	Peterboro',	"	" Dunbar,	1803
" and Juvenile,				1838, 39
"	Wilton,	Rev. Mr. Beede,		1805, 10
"	Townsend, Mass.,	"	" Palmar,	1806, 12
" and Juvenile,	"	"	" Stowell,	1839
Adult,	Pepperell,	"	" Bullard,	1807
Juvenile,	" "	"	" Howe,	1839
Adult,	Brookline, N. H.,	"	" Wadsworth,	1819
"	Phillipstown, Mass.,	"	" Bascom,	1814
"	Temple, N. H.,	"	" Miles,	1809
" and Juvenile,	"	"	" Jewett,	1839
Adult,	Lyndeboro' N. H.,	"	" Merrill,	1808
"	" "	"	" "	1810
"	Groton, Mass.,	"	Dr. Chaplin,	1814

SCHOOLS.	LOCATION, PARISHES, AND CLERGYMEN.	YEAR.

Juvenile, Groton, Mass., Rev. Mr. Phelps,   1839

Adult,   Boston, private schools,   1820 to 1831

"   "   Park-street Church, Rev. Mr. Dwight, 1819 to '26

"   "   Essex "   "   "   " Greene,   1822

" and Juvenile, Pine "   "   "   " Greenleaf,   1828

"   "   Salem "   "   "   " Edwards,   1829

"   Federal "   "   "   " Malcom,   1832

"   Charles "   "   "   " Sharp,   1826

"   Bromfield-st. "   (Methodist),   1826

"   Franklin "   "   (Catholic),   1827

"   Hanover "   "   Rev. Dr. Beecher,   1826

"   Hollis "   "   " Mr. Pierpont,

"   Juvenile, St. Paul's, "   "   " Potter,   1830

Adult,   Cambridgeport, Mass.,   "   " Gannett,   1819

"   "   "   "   " Jacobs,   1819

"   or Juvenile (private schools),   1819, 1820, 1821, 1824

Juvenile, Cambridge (private schools), Rev. Dr. Holmes,   1825

Adult,   "   College (students),   1821

"   "   "   (resident graduates),   1825

"   West Cambridge, Mass., Rev. Mr. Hedge,   1828

"   Charlestown,   "   "   " Fay,   1819

"   and Juvenile (private schools), 1819, 1820, 1822, 1824, 1825

"   "   Brookline, Mass., Rev. Dr. Pierce,   1819, '24

"   "   Roxbury,   "   "   " Porter,   1822, 1826

"   Waltham,   "   " Mr. Harding,   1821, 24

"   Newton,   "   "   " Homer,   1823

"   Brighton,   "   1823

"   Salem,   "   (private),   1825

"   Dedham,   "   Rev. Mr. Burgess,   1829

"   and Juvenile, Medford,   "   "   " Stetson,   1827

"   Lowell,   "   "   " Edson,   1824

"   "   "   "   " Blanchard,   1832

"   "   "   "   " Freeman,   1832

"   and Juvenile (private schools),   1832–3

"   Woburn, Mass., Rev. Mr. Bennett,   1827

"   Tewksbury, "   "   " Coggin,   1832

"   Bedford,   "   "   " Stearns,   1832

" · and Juvenile, Nashua, N. H. (private),   1832–3

SCHOOLS.	LOCATION, PARISHES, AND CLERGYMEN.	YEAR.
Adult and Juvenile,	New Bedford, Mass. (private schools),	1833
" "	New Bedford, " Rev. Mr. Holmes,	1833
" "	Fair Haven, " " " Gould,	1833
" "	Concord, N. H., " " Bouton,	1834
" "	Hopkinton, " " " Smith,	1834
" "	Boscawen, " " " Bennett,	1834
" "	Dover, " " " Root,	1835
" "	Somersworth, N. H., " " Smith,	1835
" "	S. Berwick, Me., Acad. and Rev. Mr. Keeler,	1835
"	Brooklyn, N. Y., Rev. Mr. Howard,	1835–6
"	" " " " Dwight,	"
" and Juvenile,	" " (private schools),	"
"	New York City,	"
Adult and "	Staten Island, N. Y., Rev. Mr. Moore,	1836
" "	Elizabethtown, N. J. (private schools),	1836–7
" "	" " Rev. Mr. Magee,	"
"	at the Farms, " (private schools),	1836
" "	Newark, " Rev. Mr. Cheever,	1836–7
" "	N. Danvers, Mass., " " Beman,	1837
" "	S. " "	1837
" "	Ashby, " Rev. Mr. Bates,	1837–8
" "	Hillsboro', N. H., " " Atwood,	"
" "	" Centre, N. H.,	"
" "	" at the Bridge, Rev. Mr. Cummings,	"
" "	W. Brookfield, Mass., " " Horton,	1843–4
" "	Warren, " " " Trask,	"
" "	Ware, " (private),	"
" "	Weathersfield, Conn.,	"
" "	Providence, R. I. (private schools),	1842–3
" "	" Munificent Ch., Rev. Dr. Tucker,	"
"	" 2d Bapt. " " Mr. Dowling,	"
"	" Sailor's Home, " " Taylor,	"
"	" Meth. Ch., Rev. Mr. Swinington,	"
"	" New Society,	"
" and Juvenile,	" High-street, Rev. Mr. Parker,	"
" "	Newport, " " " Thayer,	"